Moments of *Grace*

True stories from the lives of the

Carmelite Sisters

of the Most Sacred Heart of Los Angeles

The way of life of the Carmelite Sisters of the Most Sacred Heart of Los Angeles is rooted in the Gospel, the Church, and the spirituality of Carmel as lived out through the charism of our foundress, Venerable Mother Maria Luisa Josefa of the Most Blessed Sacrament. Our vocation is a grace by which contemplation and action are blended to become an apostolic service of the Church as we promote a deeper spiritual life among God's people through education, healthcare, and spiritual retreats.

For more information on our Mother Foundress and the beginnings of our community, see the sections at the end of this book.

920 East Alhambra Road, Alhambra, California 91801
626-576-4910 | contact@carmelitesistersocd.com | www.carmelitesistersocd.com
www.facebook.com/CarmeliteSisters | www.twitter.com/CarmelitesOCD

In our religious family
we know that the accomplishments of this present moment,
the good that our sisters do today in education, healthcare, and retreats,
is only possible because of the tireless dedication, loving service, and sacrifices
of the sisters who have gone before us.
We truly stand on the shoulders of spiritual giants.
With our deepest gratitude and love
we dedicate this book to them.

Contents

Carmel-Light

Encounters

At the Heart of the Church

Our Religious Family

Healing

Wild and Tame

Grace in Action

About Us . . .

Preface

The great Saint Teresa of Avila is said to have remarked, *"From silly devotions and sour-faced saints, good Lord, deliver us."* Indeed, deep reverence and a zestful approach to one's spiritual life are not mutually exclusive. While sad and bittersweet moments are a natural part of life this side of Heaven, the stories contained herein reflect the humor and laughter, joy and love of life that is such an integral part of the life of every one of the Carmelite Sisters – proof positive that in order to be holy or saintly, one does not have to be cranky and sour in disposition. We pray that the following pages will warm your soul and bring a smile to your lips.

Carmel-Light

"From silly devotions and sour-faced saints, good Lord, deliver us."
- Attributed to Saint Teresa of Jesus

Are You a Real Nun?

by Sister Timothy Marie, O.C.D.

O NE DAY THE SISTERS NEEDED SOME SHOPPING DONE, and I volunteered to go to the store. It didn't take long to get there, for the store was only three blocks from our convent. I had been there so many times in the past several years, it was easy to find the few items we needed. As usual, looking for the shortest line, I made my way quickly to the check-out, unaware that a drama –or should I say comedy? -- was about to unfold.

Our purchases were rung up easily enough. I wrote in the amount on our check and gave it to the sales clerk. That's when it all began.

"But we don't accept two-signature checks here," the young woman informed me.

"Ma'am, we've been coming here for many, many years – our convent is only a few blocks away – if you would check with the manager, I'm sure you'd discover our check is good."

"The manger isn't here today." She looked at me long and hard. "How do I know you are a real nun?" she questioned.

"I am a REAL nun," I responded, hoping my Irish temper would remain hidden during this conversation.

"But, I don't know that." The customer line was getting longer and the people were staring at the two of us. That's when the inspiration hit me to show her I was a real nun. For over twenty years I was a Carmelite Sister and for all of those years, we had shopped at this store, and this store had accepted our checks.

"Ma'am, I'm going to show you I am a real nun." I blessed myself, stood straight and tall, and began singing the Solemn Salve Regina in Latin, right there. 'Sal.. ve... Re..gi ... .na.. Mater misericordi.. ae.. Vi..ta du..ce..do..et ... spes ...'

"Sister, stop singing. Everyone is looking at us!"

"Am I a real nun?"

Silence.

'O ... .cle ... ..mens ... ...o ... ...pi ... .a.... ... ..O ... .dulcis Virgo Mar.....i.....a .... .'

"Alright, alright, stop singing."

"Am I a real nun?"

She looked at me and smiled. "Yes, you are a real nun!"

The other customers clapped.

I handed her my check and sang softly ... ..

"Amen ... ..."

Be Careful What You Ask For

by Sister Mary Colombiere, O.C.D.

I HAD AN 8ᵗʰ GRADER – I don't want to give his name because it still embarrasses him – though his now wife delights in telling the story. He was a good boy – clever – and never did anything extraordinarily wrong.... rather something simple like chewing gum. He did, however, have a mischievous streak. Students were not permitted to chew gum on school grounds or in class and if they did, they got a 50 cent fine which was due right at the moment or at latest, the very next day.

Well, this young man would chew gum and I would give him the fine, and, of course, he never had the money so he was supposed to bring it in the next day. Well, the next day would come and he would have an excuse as to why he didn't have the money. He would, however, continue to chew gum and get new additional fines! Finally his fine accumulated to $5.

One day, I went up to him and said, "That's it! Pay now or if you don't have the money right now, you pay tomorrow morning. If you don't have the money, then we are having a conference with you and your parents."

Eyes wide, he exclaimed, "But Sister, I don't have the money!"

I replied, "You knew the consequences, yet you chose to continue chewing gum."

A bit panicky, he asked, "Well, can I work it off?....maybe in the convent yard?"

I firmly replied, "You don't know how to work, so, 'No.' You cannot work it off. The fine is $5 cold, hard cash, that's it," and that was the end of our confrontation.

The next morning I went out the side door of the convent when I saw him coming toward me, flanked on each side by a supporter. In his hands he held one of those metal cake pans covered with wax paper. I could see from a distance and I thought aloud to myself, "Oh no, you got your mother to bake a cake, but it's not going to work!"

I wore a very severe expression as he came up to me, bright smile in place and very proud of himself, and said, "Sister, here it is!" extending the pan toward me.

I asked, "Here's what?"

"What you asked for... cold, hard cash!" he replied with a big grin.

So I peeled back the wax paper and peered into the cake pan. He had frozen 500 pennies in ice... cold hard cash! I couldn't help but laugh. He gave me exactly what I asked for.... I asked for cold, hard cash and that is precisely what I got – cold, hard cash! Be careful what you ask for!!!

Well, my secretary wanted nothing to do with me the rest of the day, since the task fell to her of thawing out and drying every penny separately in order to count it!

So this story remains in its staying power, as even his wife knows – but he really doesn't want his children to know!

What's the Date?

by Sister Imelda Marie, O.C.D.

WHEN WE WOULD TAKE ONE OF OUR ELDERLY SISTERS, who struggled with memory loss, for her visit to the doctor, he would always ask her what the date was.

Interestingly enough, Sister always remembered that he would ask her this specific question, so as we made the drive to the doctor's office, she usually made a point of asking, "What's the date?"

On one occasion, Sister didn't ask the date and that worried me a bit. Upon arriving at the doctor's office and settling down to wait our turn in the reception area, Sister leaned in toward me and said, "I really wish someone would give him a calendar, because he is always asking *me* what the date is!"

The Oreo

by Sister Marie-Aimée, O.C.D.

A SISTER WITH YEARS OF EXPERIENCE in teaching preschool once had a young student who was having a difficult time learning to share. He was an only child and it was a new experience for him to have to allow others to use toys that he wanted to play with. His teachers worked with him daily, helping him travel the hard road from "but its mine," to "do you want to play together?" and beyond to "you can go first." There were tantrums and tears but Sister remained firm and kept reiterating the importance of sharing. One day the little boy trotted up to Sister during recess with a big happy smile and an oreo cookie. Sister greeted him and asked him about his day. He looked up and said, "I brought this oreo for you Sister." At last, a breakthrough! He was sharing something that he treasured and he was doing it willingly without being prompted. Sister was lavish in her praise, telling him what a good and generous boy he was. As he ran back to play with a big smile on his face, she bit into the cookie and realized that he had licked out all the frosting.

A Postulant's Present

by Sister Mary Scholastica, O.C.D.

As a Postulant, I was assigned the care of the Novitiate chapel. Sometime after I undertook my new assignment, our Novitiate Directress stopped me in the corridor. With what I now recognize was an amused sparkle in her eye, she said to me, "Go to the chapel. Jesus has left a present for you."

Being the naïve postulant, I asked, "A present?...for me, Sister?"

"Indeed," Sister replied. "Go to the chapel and you will find it."

Excited, I hastened toward the chapel all the while thinking to myself, "A present! What could it be?"

Looking back on those days, I can't help but laugh at myself. I arrived in the chapel and looked all around fully expecting to find a present...something akin to a cheerfully wrapped package, complete with a pretty bow on top! After a thorough search, I found nothing.

I thought that I perhaps had misheard Sister and decided to seek her out and verify her instructions. When I did find Sister, I reported, "Sister, I did not find a present and I looked all through the chapel. Are you sure that is where you saw it?"

"Oh, yes," Sister replied quite confidently. "The chapel is exactly where you will find the present. Go back and look again."

I returned to the chapel fully intent on finding the present and decided to start looking in one corner and carefully work my way all round and look everywhere. I paused as I looked over the chapel. Suddenly, my eyes fell on something that looked to be a sign propped up in front of the plants and flowers that I hadn't recalled seeing there before. I slowly approached and taking the sign in hand, read aloud, *"I thirst!"*

Lesson learned!

Such a Large Reservoir

by Sister Mary Colombiere, O.C.D.

I HAVE A REPUTATION FOR ALWAYS GETTING LOST. I am simply not wired for direction and never have been. Some time ago, I was going to a meeting and the Sister with me who was driving, was from out-of-state. She was a young sister not that long yet in the community, and she wasn't very familiar with California.

Naturally, we got lost and had to stop to get directions. We finally got ourselves turned around and as we were heading back toward our destination, the Pacific Ocean was on the right-hand side of the car, nearest to me in the passenger seat. Glistening in the morning sun, the Pacific stretched lazily for miles and miles (we were rather far off course having gotten pretty lost!). As we kept driving along, finally the young Sister who was driving turned to me and said, "I didn't know that California had such a large reservoir."

I looked at her and said, "Well, yes….out here they call it the Pacific Ocean."

When You Grow Up

by Sister Juanita, O.C.D.

SISTER DOLOROSA OF JESUS CRUCIFIED celebrated her Golden Jubilee in 2013, which meant that she had faithfully lived as a Carmelite Sister for 50 years! At this time, Sister Dolorosa was assigned to our Little Flower Educational Child Care Center in East Los Angeles, where she worked in the office and also acted as the school nurse whenever the need arose.

Little Flower sometimes will feature guest speakers to come in and talk with the children about various topics, including the job they perform. Guest speakers in the past have included a policeman, a nurse and a veterinarian. An upcoming visit was going to be from a fireman.

On the day of the fireman's visit to Little Flower, Sister Dolorosa attended in order to sit in the midst of the little ones to help them focus and listen just in case some of them became squirmy. The children were brought in and they positioned themselves across the carpeted floor. One little boy sat down right at Sister Dolorosa's feet.

The children eagerly listened to the fireman speak and at one point, he asked the little ones, "What do you want to be when you grow up?"

Several eager hands shot up into the air.

"I want to be a policeman," said one.

"I want to be a teacher," said another.

"I want to be a fireman," said a third.

As more and more of the children volunteered what they wanted to be when they grew up, the little boy sitting at Sister Dolorosa's feet just quietly listened, making no move to raise his hand and share what he might like to be when he grew up. However, sitting as close to her as he was, Sister could see his face and it was obvious he was processing something in his head.

Finally, he turned to look up at Sister Dolorosa and asked in all seriousness, *"Sister, what do you want to be when YOU grow up?"*

"The Television Personality"

by Sister Stephanie, O.C.D.

*I*T IS ALWAYS THOROUGHLY ENJOYABLE talking and catching up with my sisters and brothers during family visits. It was during one such visit that I had an especially engaging experience with a little niece.

The family was gathered around enjoying the time to reconnect. This little girl, about 2½ - 3 years of age at that time, sat a little ways away from me. I felt the close scrutiny of her eyes although she kept her distance. She gave me a serious looking over, up and down. When our eyes met, I would give her a bright smile, hoping to win her over.

Finally, it seemed as if she was ready to warm up, as she came over to me and loudly announced, "I know where I saw you before. You were on my television set!"

The Nun and the Gift Certificate

by Sister Timothy Marie, O.C.D.

W E NEEDED TO BUY SOME CHAIR CUSHIONS for the chairs in our guest rooms and funds were low. On an impulse, I called Sister Janelle and asked her if by chance she had any gift cards left over from Christmas. Yes, it was July and probably no lone gift card had survived the seven months since Christmas, but as my mother always said, "Nothing ventured, nothing gained." So, after asking my question, I held the phone and waited.

"Well, you know, I do have two left," and she named the store in the nearby shopping mall that we like. So, I asked, "May I use them?"

"Sure," she answered. "When do you want them?"

"Now," I replied, "right away. I would like to finish this little project before our new local superior arrives in a few days."

"Great. Come on over and get them."

I walked across our beautiful Plaza del Carmen in our retreat center to her office. She reached into an envelope and pulled them out. Sister Janelle handed them to me. She is always most generous, and I was happy to finish with the project of fixing up the guest rooms.

Did I mention? It was a sizzling hot day. You could have cracked open an egg right there in the plaza and it would fry right away, right there on the ground. So, I got a water bottle, the car keys and got in the car. My, it was hot! If the outside temperature was 105, the inside of that car must have been 115. Or so it seemed to me.

It only took fifteen minutes to reach the shopping mall. I asked at the information desk where the chair cushions could be found and learned they were in the basement. As I traveled down the escalator, I guess I must have looked strange because people stared at me. "Why?" I thought. "Haven't they seen a Catholic nun before?"

Then it hit me. Everyone else in the store was dressed in shorts, tank tops, and even bathing suits. As I said before, it was VERY hot. And right in the midst of them, gliding down the escalator, was a Catholic nun dressed in full religious habit. Well, truth be told, I DID stand out. A woman on a mission, I stepped off and walked to the department I needed, and actually, this is where my story begins.

A young man about twenty-two and a young woman about nineteen were at the desk. One had just finished with the previous customer and the young man was doing some kind of input into the computer. He wiped his brow with a handkerchief and she kept pursing her lips and blowing air upward from her mouth noiselessly toward her eyebrows.

After searching through the aisles, I couldn't find what I was looking for and she was kind enough to go through the catalog with me. A few minutes later, we had found what we were looking for and she was inputting into the computer the information needed to purchase them. I handed her the envelope.

She looked amazed as she retrieved two rectangle-shaped pieces of paper from the envelope. She held them up to the light. Then she looked at me; I mean, she looked at me from my shoes up to my head, taking in the habit I was wearing, the rosary hanging at my side, the scapular, everything. Turning to the young man next to her she said, "Rob *, what in the world are these?" He took them from her, shrugged his shoulders and answered, "Haven't a clue. They look kind of old."

Rob held them up in the air and called out to another sales associate walking by. "Sue, have you ever seen these before?" She walked over. She spent a few seconds looking at them, turned them over once, and answered, "Sure, these are gift certificates." Then she looked over at me and said, "We haven't used gift certificates for over ten years."

Turning again to the young man, Sue explained, "We used to use something called gift certificates before we began using our current gift cards." Curious, I asked him, "May I see these for a minute?" I took a few moments to study these papers more carefully.

Then I saw it. Handwritten in blue ink in the top right hand corner was the date this gift certificate was filled in. 1996. Yes, that's right. Nineteen hundred and ninety-six. Seventeen years ago.

Sue told the young man, "You are going to help this sister. It will cost you, but you will help her. Go over to the main building and get the old paperwork. Bring it back and fill it out. Twice. She has two gift certificates. Each paper will be two-sided and you will need to fill out both sides. When that is finished, take the two gift certificates, plus the paperwork, and exchange them for gift cards."

I guess it wouldn't have been so bad, except that it was so very hot. I wished that I had not walked in at all and was home in our convent going about my daily duties. I wished a lot of things, but they weren't reality. The reality was that here I was in the basement of a large store on a very hot day, bringing two archaic gift certificates to two young adults who had never even heard of the item.

An hour and a half later the transaction was finished. With the paperwork filled out and two shiny new gift cards in hand, our seat cushions were purchased. The young woman who helped me with my purchase was wiping her brow. The young man had already left. The store was about to close.

"Thank you very much," I said.

"You're welcome. Come again." She smiled weakly.

"God bless you."

Twenty minutes later, I was home; mission accomplished. I parked the car. There was still 97 cents on the gift card.

Closing the garage door, I turned and walked toward Sister Janelle's office. I knocked on her door. Silently, I put the sales receipt with the 97 cent gift card on her desk, and looked at her. She asked, "Did you get want you wanted?"

"Yes, I did."

That's when a big smile slowly spread across her face and in the twinkle of an eye, she began to laugh. "Sister Timothy, I knew if anybody could do it, you could. Thanks."

Bells

by Sister Marie-Aimée, O.C.D.

*A*S CONSECRATED RELIGIOUS, we have the tremendous privilege of housing Jesus in the Blessed Sacrament in every single one of our convents. Sometimes it is necessary to move the Blessed Sacrament. For example, if a convent will be empty for more than a few days, we will temporarily transfer the Eucharist to the local parish. Or, in our Motherhouse where there are several smaller tabernacles, we may need to move Jesus from one to the other. Whatever the reason for the move, we always wear our mantle when carrying His Precious Body and if possible ring a small bell as we walk so that others will know that our Lord is passing by. When a sister hears the sound of that bell in the corridor or on the sidewalk, she instinctively looks around for the one carrying the Blessed Sacrament so that she can kneel as He passes.

Many years ago in an inner city portion of Long Beach, one of our sisters was teaching fourth grade. She instilled in them a love and reverence for the Blessed Sacrament, taking them to adoration and teaching them about the Mass. One day she was walking her class across the playground in two neat lines when she heard the bell. The one that meant the Blessed Sacrament was coming. She looked around and didn't see the sister but the bell was getting closer. She turned to her class and told them to kneel. They looked at her confused.

"Kneel," she insisted.

"But sister..."

"The Blessed Sacrament is coming, kneel..."

"Sister, it's the…"

"KNEEL NOW."

So the whole class obediently knelt down just in time to see the ice cream man ride by on his bicycle ringing his bell.

Us Old People

by Sister Imelda Marie, O.C.D.

*L*AST WEEK, WHEN I WAS TAKING THE METRO HOME from USC, a little old lady sat beside me. She looked to be in her late 70s or early 80s. She asked what I did. I explained that I helped take care of the health needs of our older Sisters.

She immediately brightened up and said, "I'm 69. I am so glad you are helping us old people!"

I was quite surprised because I am one year older than she!

The Color of Sister's Eyes

by Sister Marie-Aimée, O.C.D.

ONE OF OUR SISTERS WORKING AT THE DAY CARE with the little ones was having difficulty with one particular little boy who would just not listen to her.

One day, she tried hard to get him to listen, so she said to him, "Look at me." But he simply would not look at her.

Then Sister said slowly, "Look into my eyes." She wanted to make sure he was focusing on what she was going to say. Again, she had to repeat, "Look into my eyes!"

Finally, he looked Sister in the eyes.

She then asked him, "What color are my eyes?"

He looked at her and very precisely replied, "Blue...white … and red!"

The Patriotic Sister

by Sister Mary James, O.C.D.

M ANY YEARS AGO, I RAN A SHOPPING ERRAND for Sister Mary Anastasia, who was our seamstress, back in the 1990s. It was summer, the day before the 4th of July. I was driving down Valley Boulevard (in Alhambra, California) on my way to the store where I needed to make my purchases. I was by myself, as Sister Mary Anastasia did not accompany me.

I was driving along when I came to a red light and stopped, not particularly paying attention to all the rest of the traffic in front of and around me. The next thing I knew, there was a policeman on either side of my car, both waving me forward.

"No, no, keep going, don't stop," said the policeman to my immediate left.

"But it's a red light. I'm not in that much of a hurry," I replied to him.

"Just go, go, go," he said, urging me on.

So I continued on and as I was about to turn into the parking lot of the store, I noticed there was no way to get into the parking lot as a lot of people were sitting in the entrance blocking it. As I looked around, I thought to myself, "What in the world is this?!?"

Then, it dawned on me that I had somehow stumbled into the middle of the 4th of July parade. Suddenly, a large number of kids dressed up in different national costumes were dancing around and passing me in the car. They were quickly followed by yet another policeman shepherding me forward, to keep moving.

"I'm not part of the parade!" I cried to the officer. "I need to turn off into the shopping center two blocks down."

"You can't turn off until the end," the policeman replied.

"I don't believe this!" I exclaimed to myself.

About two car lengths ahead of me was a large truck of some sort and everything seemed to be slowing down. On the truck was a fellow who was acting rather like a carnival barker or perhaps an emcee rousing the crowds to shout, "Happy 4th of July… … Happy 4th of July! Raise your hands and wave, smile!" The crowds are cheering and shouting all around me.

I still couldn't believe how I'd gotten myself into this. It was such a hot summer day and I wasn't interested in the happy, festive goings on around me – not that day! I just wanted to get out of this predicament.

Suddenly, the fellow acting as emcee turns around and spots me in the car. With a big grin he shouts, *"Will the nun in the sedan please smile and wave?!?"* The crowds are cheering in response.

"Dear Lord!" I think somewhat panic stricken. "All this is going to be on TV and how in the world am I going to explain this? I'll never live this down!" At this point, there wasn't much I could do, so I put my hand out the car window and waved to the crowds.

One of the policemen who had been ushering me forward suddenly zipped up next to me on his motorcycle. With a big grin he said, "Thanks, Sister! That was great!"

"Can't you get me out of this?" I pleaded with him, "I'm not part of the parade!"

"Oh, no, you were the best part of the parade. We don't want you out!" he exclaimed. "It's going to end in just 10 more blocks anyway," he added and off he zoomed on his motorcycle.

"Ten blocks?" I said to myself with dismay.

Do you know how long it takes to go 10 blocks in a parade? It takes an excruciatingly long time because everything moves at a snail's pace – one foot every five minutes! Oh my goodness!

Well, I finally got to the end of the parade route and could at last make a right hand turn, where I pulled into a gas station and surveyed the situation. I was now in the aftermath of the parade and trying to circle the block to try getting home was out of the question as the back end of the parade was still going on. So, I headed to the payphone.

With a deep sigh, I called home. "Help! Can someone please rescue me? I'm stuck in the middle of the 4th of July parade!"

Who's That New Saint?

by Sister Marie-Aimée, O.C.D.

OUR SISTER MARY PATRICE GREW UP in a large, close-knit Cuban family in Florida. With plenty of aunts, uncles, cousins nearby, there was always someone around to spend time with, almost always something to celebrate, plenty to share. When Sister professed her Final Vows, a huge contingent flew in from Miami all sporting large buttons that proudly proclaimed "I am here for Sister Mary Patrice," with a photo of Sister on the day of her First Holy Communion.

As may happen with any large extended family, over time various family members end up using the same companies or individuals for certain services. One exterminator in particular was used by a large portion of Sister's family in and around Miami. In any given month, the man was visiting multiple members of the family without realizing that his customers were related in any way.

One day he was making a routine visit and he asked Sister Mary Patrice's aunt, "Who's that new Saint?"

She looked at him blankly, searching her memory for any recent canonizations.

"What new Saint?" she asked.

Pointing to one of the pictures on her credenza, he said, "That one. A lot of my customers have that picture."

Sister's aunt laughed. He was pointing to a picture of Sister Mary Patrice!

His customers, her family members, had all proudly put up the same picture of Sister with one of her nephews and he had assumed it must be a beloved new Saint!

The Chocolates
Didn't Have Time to Melt!

by Sister Gabriela, O.C.D.

O
CCASIONALLY, AS TIME AND OUR WORK
responsibilities permit, we Sisters will arrange an outing. It was during just such an
outing – an afternoon hike – that became the setting for two of us Sisters engaging
in an impromptu re-enactment of a memorable "I Love Lucy" episode!

Sister Mary Colombiere, Sister Lourdes and I set out for our hike with Sister
Mary Colombiere bringing along a two-pound box of See's candy to serve as
a snack. We expected the day to be warm, but we weren't quite prepared for
just how hot the afternoon would become. As we arrived at our trail, Sister
Mary Colombiere had to pause and tie her shoelaces. She handed the box
of chocolates to me, saying "Sister, please hold this while I tie my shoes, and
whatever you do, don't let them melt."

"Don't let them melt?" I thought to myself, "but it's so hot!"

I shot a questioning glance at Sister Lourdes in the hopes that she might have a
suggestion as how to keep the chocolates from melting. Sister looked back at me
with a slight "I-have-no-idea" shrug of her shoulders.

Well, there was only one way I could think of to keep the chocolates from melting.
I opened the box and offered it to Sister Lourdes said, "We'll just have to eat them."

"Eat them?!?" Sister Lourdes gasped with very wide eyes, "The entire two-
pound box?"

"Well you heard what Sister said. In this heat, how else can we keep them from melting?" I asked.

This is where our "I Love Lucy" re-enactment came in. Most people have seen the episode where Lucy and Ethel go to work in a candy factory, where they are assigned to wrap chocolates as the candies glide by on a conveyor belt. Well, as the conveyor belt quickly picks up speed, the chocolates fly by faster and faster forcing Lucy and Ethel to stuff the chocolates in their mouths, pockets and hats just to keep up.

Well....Sister Lourdes and I were doing a fair impression of this, eating the two pounds of chocolate as fast as we possibly could to prevent them from melting. Finally, we were down to one last chocolate! Sister Lourdes and I looked at each other, both of us thinking there was no possible way either of us could eat one more chocolate, when another idea came to me.

"Here, Sister....we'll split it!" I said as I broke the chocolate in two, eating my half and handing the other half to Sister Lourdes.

Just then, Sister Mary Colombiere rejoined us taking the now empty candy box from my hands, immediately noticing how considerably lighter the weight of the box was.

"Where are all the chocolates?" Sister asked in confusion as she peered into the empty candy box.

"We ate them," I volunteered.

"You ate **all** of them?" Sister asked in amazement.

"Well, yes, Sister, we did," I replied, "because you did say that no matter what, we shouldn't let them melt and it is so hot, we couldn't think of any other way to keep them from melting."

"So I did," Sister Mary Colombiere said, still amazed the two of us were able to eat two pounds of chocolate in such record time.

And so it was that we two Carmelite Sisters re-enacted an "I Love Lucy" episode!

"*You want me to gargle with <u>Who</u>?*"

by Sister Miriam Amata, O.C.D.

ONCE UPON A TIME, WHEN I WAS WORKING in the nurse's office at our school in Florida, a little boy came complaining of a sore throat.

I took his temperature, and he did not have a fever, so I said to him "Well, you don't have a temperature. Would you like to gargle with Listerine?"

He was silent, deep in thought for a moment, then asked, "Excuse me, but who is she?"

Honey

by Sister Mary Scholastica, O.C.D.

S ISTER ELIZABETH THERESE AND I attended a vocation event in St. Paul, Minnesota. While there, we had the opportunity to visit with long-time, dear friends of our community – Clare Walters* and her two delightful girls, Lizzie*, age 6, and Amy*, age 4. While Lizzie is quite the little lady, Amy has a personality akin to the Energizer Bunny – running around the room, bouncing up and down non-stop.

We very much enjoyed catching up during our visit, but all too soon, we had to leave, at which time, they presented us with treats for our return trip home. The girls had helped their mom make these wonderful biscuits, which they were now going to present to us, along with all the "trimmings" that go with the biscuits, such as honey, butter and jelly.

"Girls, the Sisters' visit is coming to an end now and they have to start getting ready to leave," Clare said to Lizzie and Amy – at which Amy burst into tears. I can still see her mournful little eyes looking beseechingly at us begging us to stay longer.

"Amy, why don't you give the biscuits to the Sisters," Clare suggested to Amy in an attempt to move things along. "You know we made them especially for the Sisters to take with them to eat on their plane trip home."

As Clare gave us the honey, Amy carried the biscuits to us sobbing all the while.

Then, as she offered us the treats, with a loud wail she cried, "... And they're taking the honey too!"

* = denotes that names have been changed to protect privacy

It All Happened So Fast

by Sister Timothy Marie, O.C.D.

*I*T WAS THE DAY OF THE EIGHTH GRADE TRIP to Disneyland and everyone was looking forward to it. I met the students and the three moms who were going along as chaperones at the school. We all boarded the bus. Traffic wasn't too bad, so we got to Disneyland about 9:45 a.m. As soon as the students dispersed to the various attractions, one of the moms approached me, saying "Sister, we moms would like to take you to lunch at the Pirates of the Caribbean restaurant. Fireflies dance amidst the foliage, there is a waterfall, and we thought it would be a nice way to thank you for your help with our 8th graders this past year."

Not long after, we entered the restaurant and sat down. It was two hours until the students checked in, so we had plenty of time to enjoy ourselves in the picturesque setting.

A lovely waitress approached our table and asked if we would like some coffee, or water, or tea. A little later, she returned with coffee pot in hand – ready to pour. Now, I don't know if she ever saw a Catholic sister dressed in a full habit before, but for whatever reason, she became very nervous as she bent over to pour a cup of coffee. That's when it happened. Somehow or other the coffee landed on me, my headband, the coif surrounding my face and, of course, down it went splashing all over my white collar.

What in the world was I supposed to do? That's when I remembered that in our novitiate we were given the wise advice, "Don't take yourself too seriously."

Well, I had read the story of St. Therese and wanted to also become a simple and humble soul. Here was my chance. I reminded myself, "Not too seriously…." and looked up at the waitress. She wasn't there. She was nowhere to be found. And, she never reappeared. So, I looked up and asked the women, "How bad is it?" and they all replied, "Oh not bad at all, Sister." "Is it on my collar?" "Yes." "Is it on the coif around my face?" "Yes." "Is it on my headband?" "Yes."

That's when I excused myself and headed toward the ladies' room where I could see for myself. It was pretty bad. I sort of looked like a bowl of chocolate rippled ice cream, or a backdrop of rich brown and white marble. Clasping the extra flap over the veil, I pulled it forward and tucked it under the headband. Now I had a Byzantine look. A woman passed by me and clicked her camera. That was the limit! I transitioned back to the regular, though marbled, Carmelite look and returned to the table. I asked the moms, "Well, which one is it? Shall I go through the rides with the Byzantine motif or the marbled ambiance?" I showed them both. They were unanimous in their reply. "Make it the marbled look, Sister."

So that's what I did. I spent from 10:15 a.m. until 8:00 p.m. marbled. With 1/3 of me marbled, I walked straight and tall, looked people right in the eye, and prayed that the wind would blow the coffee aroma back towards me. We had a great time.

The moral of the story is "Don't take yourself too seriously." It works.

By the way, no one even noticed.

"The Church Needs Doctors?"

by Sister Julianna, O.C.D.

In the Roman Catholic Church, the title *"Doctor of the Church"* is an official designation bestowed in recognition of an individual's important contributions toward the understanding of sacred Scripture and development of doctrine. Three requirements must be met in order to merit the title "Doctor": (1) outstanding holiness, even among the saints; (2) depth of doctrinal insight; (3) an extensive body of writings. As of October 2012, there are 35 Doctors of the Church, four of whom are women (Saint Teresa of Avila, Saint Catherine of Siena, Saint Thèrése of Lisieux and Saint Hildegard of Bingen).

So it was one day, while teaching at Loretto School in Arizona, that the lesson for the day in religion class would be about the Doctors of the Church. Before explaining to the children the title "Doctor", I was curious to hear what ideas they might have.

"Today, we are going to learn about the Doctors of the Church," I began. "Does anyone know what a 'Doctor of the Church' is?"

I waited expectantly as the children silently considered my question. After a few moments, a couple of hands ventured into the air.

One little girl enthusiastically offered, "Is it someone who makes the church feel better?"

Another student exclaimed, "It's for when they receive anointing of the sick!"

I smiled to myself at the children's innocence and eagerness for learning about our faith. "Well, those are very good guesses, but not exactly what a doctor of the church really is," I replied.

I then explained to the children what "Doctor of the Church" actually means. Later that evening, upon reflection on the answers the children had come up with in defining what a doctor of the church is, I realized that there was more than just a grain of truth to their innocent guesses. In the wide variety of their writings, they do in fact teach us, inspire us, and yes, "make us feel better" as we make our journey homeward to Heaven!

"I Love L.A."

by Sister Maria Olga, O.C.D.

W E WERE DOING "JESUS TIME", including praise and worship and we were singing different songs. *Alabare* was one of them.

Later in the day, Mrs. Cooper, who is from Ireland, asked "What was the name of the song you sang?"

I asked, "Well which one, we did quite a few."

"You know, "I Love L.A.", she replied.

Surprised at this, I asked, "At Jesus Time?!?"

She replied, "Yes, remember…" and she start singing, *"I love LA, I love LA…."*

"Mrs. Cooper!" I exclaimed, "**¡Alabare!** – in Spanish it means 'I praise'!"

After I shared this with the sisters, it became a fun, little joke, because if it was a bad day, we'd say, **'I love LA'!**

That's Just the Way It Is

by Sister Marie-Aimée, O.C.D.

ONE YEAR AT HOLY INNOCENTS, we had a very precocious child in Kindergarten, who certainly knew her mind from an early age. Both of her older sisters were in the school, so we knew her long before she was old enough to start attending elementary school herself. When Katie* started school, it quickly became apparent that teaching her was going to be a challenge simply because of the strength of her opinions and her insistence on voicing them.

During the first weeks of school, she made several visits to the Principal's office. On the fourth or fifth visit as she stood in front of Sister Margaret Ann's desk, just high enough to see over the edge, Sister began with the usual reminder.

"Katie, you know very well that this is not how we act at this school," Sister began, "this is not what Jesus would do."

At this point, Katie interrupted with a sigh. Placing one hand on her hip and holding the other index finger up to stop Sister, she said, "With you, it's always 'Jesus this,' and 'Jesus that!'

Hiding a smile and swallowing the desire to laugh, Sister Margaret Ann told Katie, "As long as you are at this school, it's always going to be Jesus. That's just the way it is."

Katie, now an alumna of Holy Innocents, is preparing to graduate from high school. When we see her, we sometimes remind her of that day in Sister Margaret Ann's office, when she first heard that "its always going to be Jesus."

* = denotes that names have been changed to protect privacy

The Topic of Age

by Sister Marie-Aimée, O.C.D.

*I*T BEHOOVES THOSE ON THE YOUNGER END of the spectrum to tread very carefully whenever the topic of age comes up. I am in my late thirties and one of our sisters who is seventy often makes me laugh, teasing me if I slip and use the adjective "old" to describe anyone under 100 or make the mistake of admitting that I don't know who Lawrence Welk or Dick Clark are.

One morning I was walking across the parking lot muttering, "take out the trash, get the mail, return the stapler," over and over to myself when I passed her making her way to the office. She smiled and said, "What are you muttering about?" "I have three things I need to do as soon as I get to the office and if I don't keep saying them I will forget them by the time I get there," I replied. Laughing she said, "when I get old that will happen to me too." Which of course made me laugh. To which she said with a straight face, "Why are you laughing?" I laughed again.

She told me that when she was in her late 60's, the sisters were teasing her about getting older despite her protestations that she was still young. One day a volunteer and her eight year old daughter were helping some of the sisters get ready for a function. For some reason the topic of age came up and the young girl was asked for her evaluation of Sister's age. She cocked her head, looked hard at Sister, and shook her head. "She's not old…," the girl began. Sister stood up straighter and was just about to say, "See, I told you so," when the girl finished with, "compared to Moses!"

Burly … and 150 lbs.

by Sister Marisa, OCD

*I*T IS ALWAYS RATHER DISCONCERTING TO BE SUDDENLY JOLTED out of a sound sleep in the middle of the night by the sounds of what could only be an intruder creeping about in the attic overhead. So it was one night in the Sacred Heart Convent.

It was in the wee hours that I was suddenly awakened by an urgent knock on my door. Getting up quickly, I opened the door and found one of the sisters standing there. She was quite frightened.

"Sister, what is wrong?" I asked.

"Sister, I keep hearing a noise overhead," she whispered, "Listen…. do you hear it?"

Just then, another Sister emerged from her room and said, "I hear a noise above us!" her tone urgent and fearful.

So the three of us stood stock still, listening intently, training our ears upwards wondering if the sounds would repeat.

"There! Do you hear that?" the first sister exclaimed, "I think there is someone in the attic!"

Well, sure enough, we all heard a rather loud and heavy thumping noise coming from the attic. Considering the hour, we knew all the sisters were in their rooms, so it couldn't be any of them. We didn't want to go up to investigate ourselves just in case we might actually confront a prowler, so we decided the best course of action would be to call the police.

After telling the police dispatcher our fears of an intruder in our attic, he promised to send out two patrol cars immediately. While we waited for them to arrive, he kept us on the line, trying to not only get more information, but to calm us down as well.

"What did you see, Sister?" he questioned me. "What does this person look like?"

"Well, we haven't seen him, but we certainly can hear him," I replied, as more thumping sounded over our heads.

"From the noise you're hearing, how big do you think this person is?" the policeman asked.

"Oh, the noise sounds quite heavy; he must be big and at the very least 150 pounds judging by the sounds coming from upstairs," I replied.

For the next several minutes, I kept relaying to the policeman on the phone the noises we kept hearing. Then he said, "The officers have just arrived, so I will hang up with you. We hope everything turns out all right."

No sooner had he signed off, than a knock sounded at our front door and we admitted three policemen.

I explained, "We keep hearing noises coming from upstairs in the attic. We know for certain it isn't any of our sisters as they are all in their rooms. We didn't want to go up ourselves in case there is an intruder."

"We'll go up and check it out for you," one of the policemen said. "Can you show us how to get up to the attic?"

We led the officers to the door of the attic on the second floor.

"Please stay down here until we make sure it's all clear," another of the policemen cautioned us.

So we tensely waited in a little huddle by the attic door as we heard the policemen walking across the attic space above us. Our anxiety grew as it seemed to be taking them an awfully long time. Finally, we heard them starting back down and when they emerged from behind the closed attic door, they appeared completely calm.

Although we didn't know exactly what to expect, we felt a little let down when the officers emerged from the attic not with a handcuffed suspect in tow, but with a large black trash bag.

"Why, Officer," I asked with surprise, "whatever did you find?"

"Here's your prowler, Sister – *a rat!*" the officer said with a grin as he held up the trash bag. "Apparently there was a trap up there and the rat sprung it. The thumping sounds you heard was the rat thrashing about trying to escape from the trap."

With considerable dismay, I glanced at the other sisters then back at the policemen.

"This is a bit embarrassing," I said to them, "we are so sorry to have called you for nothing."

"Don't worry about it, Sister, please call us any time," the officer in charge replied with the grin still on his face, as we ushered them back to the first floor and saw them to the door.

Well imagine that! Our burly 150 lb. intruder had in actuality been a four pound rat!

With tremendous sighs of relief we all went back to bed to resume a good night's sleep!

Where's His Car?

by Sister Julianna, O.C.D.

AFTER SCHOOL AT HAYDEN CHILD CARE, we would play outside with the children while waiting for their parents to come pick them up. The children quickly came to recognize which car belonged with which child and as each car approached, they knew who was leaving.

When the brown sedan drove up, as one they happily shouted, "Bye Margaret, bye Margaret!" A blue minivan brought cries of, "Bye Aiden, bye Aiden." And so on throughout the afternoon.

When it was time for holy hour, I told the children, "I need to leave now because I need to go see Jesus."

Looking around excitedly, they said, "Where's His 'thar', where's His 'thar'?

Even with their little lisps, I quickly realized they were looking for Jesus' car and were most curious to see Him picking me up! I clarified, "No, I have to go to the church to see Him."

Slightly disappointed, they said, "Alright Sister, bye."

I walked across the parking lot to the sound of their small voices chanting in unison, "Bye Sister! Bye Sister!"

Things Aren't Always What They Seem . . .

by Sister Vincent Marie, O.C.D.

W HEN I WAS A TEMPORARY PROFESSED SISTER,
a feast day was coming up, and as part of the festivities, two of us (temporary
professed) sisters were going to do a dance. We needed to decide what we were
going to do fairly quickly so that we could begin practicing. We settled on being
hobos and thought it would be fun if we had a couple of exploding cigars in the
middle of the routine. But how and where were we going to get our hands on
exploding cigars? We neither had money nor did we go out. It occurred to me that
perhaps my father would be able to help us in procuring our props.

"I think if I called my father, he would know where to buy some trick exploding
cigars," I said to my partner, Sister Catherine.

"Well then, hurry and go ask permission to call your father from Sister Bertha,"
Sister Catherine urged.

So off I went in search of Sister Bertha, who was in charge of us at the time, and
asked her permission to call my father so he could pick up the props and bring
them to us. Knowing about the upcoming festivities, Sister Bertha granted
permission and I called my father telling him what we needed.

My father then went out and bought some exploding cigars (he bought a few so
that we would have some with which to practice and still have a couple left for
the actual routine) and he also bought one of those long narrow tubes or cans
out of which paper snakes come flying when the lid is removed. He brought the

props to the old Gonzaga wing and the only sister who was there when he called was Sister Maria Dolores, who didn't speak English too well.

My father tried to explain to Sister the purpose of the items he brought. Seeing that Sister did not quite understand, he thought it might help if he illustrated by pulling the lid off the tube. Well, as you can imagine, right on cue the snakes came flying out thoroughly startling Sister Maria Dolores, who promptly began beating my father with her fists thinking he was some wild man who brought these strange objects that pop out of a can! The uproar was finally calmed and Sister Catherine and I at long last had our props in hand.

The first thing we had to do was figure out how the exploding cigars worked, specifically how long from the lighting of the cigars until the exploding of the cigars, so that we would precisely know how to time our routine. Sister Catherine volunteered to do this. The only question was where to do it? She decided to go to the upstairs room that was empty because it was right over Mother Margarita's cell. Sister Catherine made her way upstairs, locked the cell door and got down to the business of figuring out how the trick cigars worked.

Meanwhile, the outside of the convent was being painted and unbeknownst to Sister Catherine, all the windows had to be opened to allow for the painting of the window frames from the outside. Sister Eugenia was at that very moment making her way upstairs to open all the windows on the second floor, including those of the unused cell. Coming to the door of this cell and finding it locked, Sister Eugenia took her master key from her pocket and unlocked the door. Imagine her shock at the sight that greeted her eyes – a temporary professed Sister sitting cross-legged on the floor puffing away on a cigar!

"You will come with me at once!" Sister Eugenia managed to choke out with great indignation and an abject look of horror on her face. She promptly marched off to Mother Margarita Maria's office with Sister Catherine in tow.

Once explanations were made, it was most fortunate that Mother thought the entire story quite funny – what a relief that Mother always liked a good joke!

Encounters

"The Lord does not look upon us all at once, as a mass of people: no, no! He looks at us one by one, in the face, in the eyes, for true love is not something abstract but rather something very concrete. Person to person. The Lord, who is a Person, looking at me, a person. That is why allowing the Lord to come and meet me also means allowing him to love me".

- Pope Francis

The Rose

by Sister Faustina, O.C.D.

*S*EVERAL YEARS AGO, I HAD A FOURTH GRADER who was very shy and withdrawn. Every inch of her demeanor reflected her low self-esteem. She walked hunched over with unkempt hair in her face. Her eyes were most often fixed on the ground and she regularly sat alone seeming quite dejected.

As I got to know her and learned about her family situation, I began to understand the broken heart within her: a recent divorce, a mother who had to work long hours, too much time alone with the television and an older brother. I tried to bring a smile to her face, a little joy into her life, and sometimes I succeeded but it never lasted long.

Early in the year, I had decided to bring the class to the chapel once a week in order to introduce them to personal prayer. On one particular chapel visit I led them in a guided meditation about a garden. They were sitting around me on the floor of the chapel with their eyes closed.

I started by helping them picture the scene. *"Imagine yourself sitting in a beautiful garden. Listen to the birds and feel the gentle breeze blowing through the trees. You are most drawn to the many flowers – all colors, shapes and sizes – surrounding you."*

"Now imagine a very kind and gentle gardener walking through the garden. He lovingly bends down to touch each flower delighting in the uniqueness and beauty of each. As the gardener draws near, you realize that it is Jesus! You are one of the beautiful flowers in His garden and His eyes are full of joy as He sees your unique

beauty. You can see the love in His eyes. He bends down to touch you with His hand. Does He speak to you? Look at Him and speak to Him from your heart. What kind of flower are you in His garden?"

I gave the children some time to listen to Jesus and talk to Him in their hearts. After a few minutes of silence, we ended our time of prayer and returned to the classroom. On the way out of the chapel, I glimpsed the little girl I was so worried about. She held her head high, her shoulders were thrown back, and there was smile on her lips.

Curious about what had caused such a dramatic transformation, I walked next to her and asked, "Did you enjoy our time of prayer today?"

"Yes, Sister!" Her eyes were sparkling!

"Did Jesus have anything special to say to you?"

"Yes, Sister." A radiant joy appeared in her smile.

"Did He tell you what kind of flower you are in His garden?"

"Yes, Sister. He told me I am a rose."

This little girl met Jesus and the encounter transformed her. Her situation did not change but Christ's presence was a powerful beam of light in her darkness. I have since lost track of her but it is my hope that she will always remember the day Jesus told her she was His rose, a moment of deep joy when she knew she was loved.

The Blessing

by Sister Timothy Marie, O.C.D.

*H*IS EYES CAUGHT MINE. THEY SPOKE VOLUMES TO ME. THEY SAID, "HELP ME. OH, PLEASE HELP ME!"

Sister Mary and I drove through the quaint, little town on our way to her doctor's office, serenely praying the rosary as we motored through Monrovia, California. Her appointment was at 10:00 a.m. We would arrive in plenty of time. It was a sunny spring day, beautifully clear. A gentle breeze wafted through the trees and white, puffy clouds, like artsy wisps of angel hair, decorated the skies. The stores lining both sides of the road were waking up. Curtains opened and storefront windows appeared, filled with enticing items coaxing us to stop, to come in, to touch them, desire them and, of course, purchase them.   We passed them all.

For the last three years, ever since I entered our convent, I seldom ventured far from our Motherhouse. I savored the great joy and undeserved privilege of three uninterrupted years of learning how to be a Carmelite Sister of the Most Sacred Heart of Los Angeles. Within the cloistered area of our convent, I basked in the sunlight of prayer and recollection as I grew daily in my love and understanding of a new life in Christ appearing on my life's horizon. I learned about the three vows of poverty, chastity, and obedience. I participated in and became a part of community life in Carmel. I was at first a postulant and then a novice. Weekly retreats provided magnificent opportunities for helping people and serving them as they participated in the events of the retreat weekend. I loved it.

Now, I was a "newly-professed" Carmelite Sister. I had pronounced my vows a short time before, maybe two or three months. Having spent almost three years learning about the vows, the ministries of our community, and other novitiate classes, I moved to Santa Teresita in Duarte, California, to work part-time in our Manor skilled nursing center and attend a nearby college as a part-time student as well. This particular day I had volunteered to accompany Sister Mary to the doctor. Sister Mary had been a Carmelite Sister for many years. She was a seasoned veteran – and I? Well, I was a mere neophyte in the art of being at the service of God's people.

We reached our destination, got out of the car and walked up the path. Golden daffodils greeted us as we turned into the medical building. White, purple and yellow pansies were arranged around the patio in picturesque places, surrounding us with their cheerful faces. Geraniums in window boxes adorned the various doctors' suites.

We quickly found the office of Sister Mary's doctor. As we entered the room, five people were awaiting their turn to be seen by the doctor. I watched Sister Mary sign a patient log-in at the desk, and then we sat down. She immediately opened a book she had brought along. I found a chair near a lovely window overlooking an outside corridor lined with blooming plants of all kinds. Seeing a well-worn copy of Guideposts on the table, I picked it up and began leafing through the pages. We were now seven people in the waiting room, each one of us oblivious of the others, and all of us quite content to await our turn. We all sat there in silence, occupied with our reading material. Maybe five minutes passed when it happened. Someone passed by my window and then passed by the same window a second time – coming from the opposite direction. The front door to the doctor's office opened slowly. A small hand turned the knob and a larger hand pushed the door open. A tall man about 40 years old entered the office, accompanied by a young boy about five years old.

As the man's eyes swept the seven people seated in the waiting room, his eyes met mine. He gave a little nod to the boy. Then he turned and faced me. Taking hold of the youngster's hand, he pointed at me and then said loudly in a deep, resonant voice,

"Son, there is your mama."

I winced. Trying to maintain a cheerful countenance, I looked up – first at the man and then at the child. Within myself I thought, "What? What's this?

What's going on here? They sure didn't teach us about this in the novitiate. Why didn't he go to Sister Mary? She's so much older, so much wiser. She's been a nun for YEARS and would know what to do."

I glanced around the room. Newspapers went down onto laps. Dozers woke up. Readers put their books aside. The receptionist reddened. As I turned to ask for help from Sister Mary, I was appalled to watch her turn to her left and face the corner while keeping her eyes on her spiritual reading book. It became apparent that I would have to "go this one alone." The man spoke again – this time looking directly at his son,

"Son, if anything ever happens to me, I want you to know you can always go to this lady."

Then he looked directly at me. Well, that did it. Anyone who was still reading decided that what was going on in this waiting area was far more exciting than anything in a doctor's office magazine.

You could have heard a pin drop. The little guy wiggled and squirmed away from his dad. It was evident to all present that he would much rather be anywhere else in the world, but his dad was adamant. He then knelt down beside his son and said to him in that deep, resonant voice,

"Son, ask her to bless you."

That was absolutely the very last thing in the world this young man wanted. Vigorously shaking his head from side to side, he let his dad know, in no uncertain terms, that there was no way he would ever kneel down in that office and ask for a blessing from a strange nun. No. Never.

Few things in this world can reduce me to silence. This was one of them. I was taken by surprise: the father, who did have alcohol on his breath; the son, who just wanted out; Sister Mary, with her whole being turned toward the corner, spiritual reading book in hand; and the five gaping onlookers, six if you counted the receptionist. I was speechless. I had never blessed anyone or anything. Never had I even thought of blessing anyone or anything. Besides, the blessing of squirming children was not among my novitiate studies.

A thought came to me – I'm sure as I look back upon it now that it was from the Holy Spirit – to forget myself and my embarrassment and figure out what God would like me to do. As I looked up in the man's eyes, they welled up with unshed tears until there were too many of them and they overflowed onto his cheeks. His eyes caught mine. They spoke volumes to me. They said, "Help me. Please help me." My heart understood his plea. I still did not know who he was, or where he was from, but God had permitted this moment to come to pass right here in this doctor's office and I was part of it. I needed to enter into it. I understood in my deepest soul that I was chosen to be God's instrument, His presence, in this place at this time.

Taking a deep breath I stood up and lightly – oh, so lightly - placed my two hands on the young man's head. Then I leaned over and prayed, "May the Lord bless you and keep you. May the Lord make His face shine upon you and be gracious to you. May the Lord protect you and defend you and give you peace."

The boy became very quiet. His dad's tears stopped. He stood up, took my hand and said, with a voice choked up with emotion, "Thank you, ma'am, oh, thank you, ma'am." He helped his son stand up, and the two of them opened the door and walked hand in hand into the gentle spring sunlight.

Forty-five years have passed since that day. Forty-five years. I never forgot them and often ask God's blessing upon them. I still carry them in my heart.

An Answered Prayer
in the Most Unexpected Place

by Sister Lucia, O.C.D.

A LITTLE WHILE AGO, THREE OF US SISTERS, from the Duarte convent, were up in Wrightwood and one day while taking in some clean mountain air during an afternoon hike, we encountered a troop of cub scouts and their leader along the route. We introduced ourselves, stopped to visit with them and shared a little about our faith. The leader shared that he was a Christian.

"We are from Santa Teresita in Duarte where we provide assisted living and skilled nursing care for elderly people," we said.

The troop leader immediately became very interested. "My wife and I are now in the process of looking for an assisted living place for her aunt. It's been so discouraging and we've started to pray about finding the right place that's also close to us. We live right next to Duarte in Monrovia!" he exclaimed.

We happily shared additional information about all Santa Teresita has to offer.

"We'll be sure to come for a visit," the troop leader promised as we continued on our hike.

The troop leader was true to his word, as a short time later, he and his wife brought the elderly aunt for a visit to Santa Teresita. Better yet, the aunt did indeed come to live at Santa Teresita where to this day she still happily resides.

How amazing to think that even though this couple lived in a neighboring city to Santa Teresita, they never knew about us. But God certainly answered their prayer by having our paths cross many miles away on a mountain hiking trail – definitely a most unexpected place!

"Yes, Jesus Loves Me"

by Sister Timothy Marie, O.C.D.

A HEAVY MARINE LAYER FELL LIKE A PALL over Long Beach, California, bringing colder, damper weather. I had set aside the day to visit my sister and together we were going to visit our mom's grave in **All Souls' Cemetery,** right there on Cherry Avenue, just north of Memorial Hospital. We opened the car doors and began walking slowly to the site. I had not returned since the death of my mom. My sister had come back many, many times. For a long time she had come by daily. This time we went together. The grey morning matched our spirits. We missed our mom.

The two of us walked around the perimeter of her section. We talked very little and we thought a lot. After a while, we ended up at her grave. We both said a prayer and laid some flowers down near her.

Just as we were beginning to leave, we heard some voices. Both of us turned around quickly to see what was happening. We saw an interesting group of people, teenagers, walking to a new grave just up the hill from us. They were dressed in black, complete with piercings, belts that were chains, and a not-so-confident swagger to their walk. They stopped at the new grave on the hill.

Not knowing exactly what to do, I turned to my sister and said, "Wait a minute. I'm going up there." So, I hiked up my habit a couple of inches and began my morning march through the wet grass. Before five minutes was up, I had reached them. To this day, I'm not sure what urged me onward toward them, but I followed my interior nudging and, upon reaching the group, introduced myself and said, "Why are you here - all of you? Have you lost someone?"

One of the girls ventured forward and held out her hand. "I went to Catholic school," she said. "You are a Catholic sister." I nodded. "Our friend Dave* is dead. He was in our gang and the other gang killed him. Both gangs were not allowed to come to the funeral together, nor to the cemetery. We waited until everything was over, and decided to come by later to pay our respects."

I had never heard of anyone being ousted from a funeral. How sad! What a statement of our culture, of our whole society. And at that moment I knew why I felt I should climb the little hill to meet this group of young teens. I could pray with them if they wanted me to. After so many years in religious life, and having participated in so many spiritual retreats and taught in so many classrooms, I knew good and well, that some kind of closure is needed at a time like this. So I stepped in with their permission, and we had a little closure ceremony.

We all formed one large circle. (There must have been thirty or forty gang members including their girl friends who had also shown up after the funeral). My heart embraced them all. I asked the name of the deceased.

His name was Dave*, someone ventured.

"Thank you," I said.

"Will everyone please form a circle here around his grave (we were a large enough group to be able to do that) and then let's all of us hold hands. I couldn't think of a common hymn we could all sing until the words of *"Jesus loves me"* came into my mind. So I began, *"Jesus loves me this I know. 'Cause the Bible tells me so."* They began singing one by one. *"Little ones to Him belong. They are weak but He is strong."* Their voices became stronger. *"Yes, Jesus loves me, Yes, Jesus loves me, Yes, Jesus loves me; the Bible tells me so."* Tears began flowing freely down their young faces.

"Alright, everybody, just continue holding hands and think of one thing, one good thing, you remember about Dave." We'll go around the circle and not finish until everyone has said something. If someone remembers something else, they can add it in at the end."

Then I watched as these supposedly tough gang members, obediently held hands and told their stories and memories of Dave. They laughed. They cried. They shared.

When it was all over, I began the *Lord's Prayer,* and we all said it together.

As I prepared to leave, one of the young men asked me to bless the group. I was dumbfounded. I had never expected anything like that. I was thinking "closure" and the group was thinking "blessings."

So that's the background to the story of how one Carmelite Sister standing on a grassy knoll at **All Souls' Cemetery** in Long Beach reached out to ask God's blessings upon these beautiful children of His. I put my hands on each head and one by one asked their guardian angel to protect them (I was thinking of all those gang wars we have here in the City of the Angels). They formed a line, and silently – oh so silently - you could have heard a pin drop – bowed their heads, one by one, in front of me. As I prayed, I spoke to each one about the beauty of heaven, and the unimaginable love of God, and His magnificent mercy. And I spoke of peace – peace in their hearts, their families, peace in our world.

I was humbled by their true and sincere piety. I was saddened by the circumstances of life which had drawn them into one of the gangs. I was amazed at myself standing in a cemetery on a bleak, wintry day amidst these gang members. After the last one stood in front of me and bowed his head, we all turned toward Dave's grave one last time. Slowly, we wound our way back through the wet grass and down the hill.

I soon found myself at my sister's side once again...

Our loving God can use anybody, anytime, to do anything He wants. And that day, for some reason, according to some divine plan, He used me.

"Wow!" my sister said. That was enough. That was everything.

* = denotes that names have been changed to protect privacy

Prayer ... the Fountain of Youth?

by Sister Imelda Marie, O.C.D.

*L*AST YEAR I TOOK ONE OF OUR OLDER SISTERS to the doctor's office. In the waiting room one of the patients asked what we used on our skin to keep us looking so young.

We replied, "Nothing", at which she seemed somewhat upset, thinking that we would not tell her the name of our "secret" lotion. When I assured her we were telling the truth, she looked quite puzzled.

Then I asked, "Could it be the result of our life of prayer and union with God that you see on our faces?"

She considered this for a moment, then her face lit up!

"Yes," she happily exclaimed, "that is it! It must be the light of your prayer life that I see on your face!"

The Guardian Angel
Who Lends a Helping Hand (Wing?) to the Auto Club

by Sister Gaudencia, O.C.D.

Sister Michelle asked me to go to the Ontario airport to pick-up a seminarian. I took Sister Belen with me. Halfway to the airport, I realized there was very little gas in the car – enough to get us there, but probably not enough to get back. When we arrived at the airport I had a thought: I'd drop Sister Belen off to meet the seminarian while I went to find a gas station, although I did not mention this to Sister Belen.

When we arrived at the terminal, I said to Sister Belen, "Sister, you wait here for the seminarian and I'll go drive around." While driving around, I hoped to find a gas station.

I did find one station near the entrance to the airport. There was a very long line on the side where I drove up, but no line on the other side. So I maneuvered around, pulled up on the other side and filled the car up with gas. Then I returned to the airport terminal to pick-up Sister Belen and the seminarian, who in the meantime had met up with Sister and were waiting together for me.

Once everyone was situated in the car, I headed back toward the freeway entrance, which was in the same direction as the gas station. As we drove up the on-ramp, I noticed the car was slowing down even though I had the gas pedal pressed all the way down to the floor.

"That's strange," I mused aloud, "I just put gas in the car and now it's not only slowing down, it looks like it's going to stop."

The seminarian asked, "What kind of gas did you put in the car, Sister?"

"Well, from the pump that had a green diesel sticker," I replied.

"Sister, you can't put diesel in this car!" the seminarian exclaimed.

"Well," I said, "too late ... I already did!"

So I let the car go down the onramp to get us back on the surface street and thought, "What can we do? Finally, I said to the seminarian, "Why don't you get out and push the car?" So the poor fellow got out and pushed the car.

Then I thought, "This is ridiculous ... he can't push a car with two nuns in it!" and I called to him to get back in the car.

So, we sat there by the side of the road as car after car zoomed past us.

"I don't see a policeman or anyone who might be able to help us," I said to the seminarian.

Out of ideas, I said loudly, "Guardian Angel, do something, push the car, anything, just do something!"

All of a sudden, the car started moving, very, very slowly but at least it started moving.

The seminarian exclaimed, "Sister, don't touch anything!"

"I'm not," I exclaimed back to him.

But I did offer encouragement to my Guardian Angel and said, "Angel, don't stop! You're doing a good job, keep going!" and kept repeating these words, encouraging the Angel! And he came through! He pushed us over the railroad tracks and back to the gasoline station, where I then parked the car.

I approached the attendant and said "I put the wrong gasoline in this car."

He replied, "Sister, you can't drive this car."

"Why?" I asked.

"It's not drivable with diesel fuel. You have to call AAA," he advised.

I had no choice but to call the Auto Club to pick up the car and have the gas tank flushed and cleaned. We set out that day at 9 o'clock in the morning on what was to be a simple, routine errand, but turned into quite the adventure, including finding out that happily, my Guardian Angel occasionally lends a hand, or perhaps wing to assist the Auto Club! Our adventure concluded around 6:00 p.m. that evening when we finally made it home.

The Tough Guy
with the Heart of Gold

by Sister Margaret Ann, O.C.D.

WHEN I WAS TEACHING AT HOLY INNOCENTS, we had an 8th grade student, Kevin*, who projected the air of a tough, macho kid. One day, we were doing "family units" and his attitude clearly showed his lack of enthusiasm for this exercise.

I saw he needed a little bit of prompting. "You've got to take care of your little ones," I told him.

With my urging, Kevin escorted one of the little 1st graders, Annie* toward the stairs to the second floor. With a dubious expression on her little face, she looked up at the somewhat long flight of stairs, which to a six-year-old could easily be intimidating. Annie suddenly reached up and grabbed firm hold of Kevin's pinky finger while looking beseechingly up at him.

Kevin momentarily went slack-jawed as he glanced at me with a look of utter incredulity that said, "You've got to be kidding!"

As Kevin looked down at Annie, holding fast to his little finger, I could just see him melt at the fact that someone – a little girl – needed him. It was such a neat thing to see! Annie was afraid and needed him and counted on him to be her hero. It is precisely what Kevin needed – he needed to be needed. What a joy it was to witness the gift Annie and Kevin gave to one another. It turned out that the tough guy really had a heart of gold!

= denotes that names have been changed to protect privacy

When God Sends Messengers

by Sister Timothy Marie, O.C.D.

WHEN GOD SENDS MESSENGERS, you never know when and where they'll appear… perhaps even in Aisle 3 at Staples.

With a heavy heart, I put down the telephone and sighed. I knew it was right that I, like the other sisters in my Carmelite community, set myself to the task now ahead of us. This was not the first time death had visited us. No, and I knew that it would not be the last. This time, however, death was claiming the one who had worked alongside me for two years. She knew Spanish. It was her native language. Together we were editing the original letters of our Foundress, Venerable Mother Luisita, trying to distinguish the nuances of the expressions and the intricacies of the coded messages written during the dark days of religious persecution in Mexico in the 1920's and 1930's. Sister Piedad not only knew Spanish, but had lived during those historical days and possessed a magnificent historical perspective on the letters. Her input was of inestimable value to our community, both now and in the future. I treasured every moment of my time with her on this holy project.

Toward the end, she could barely read. Yet, she continued, knowing that her input was valuable and most necessary. I can still see her leaning over the manuscript with a humongous magnifying glass reading aloud in Spanish and effortlessly substituting the correct English idioms and, from time to time, adding anecdotes that she remembered.

Soon, I had to read aloud to her and she, in turn, dictated the best phraseology for each passage. As time went on, her trips to the hospital became more frequent, until that final trip, which by some special design of God, took place the day after we finished editing. Not long after, we learned that her condition was not only critical, but that it was also terminal. Death was imminent.

The phone call came to me about mid-morning. I learned that Sister Piedad was dying. Would I begin preparing a bulletin board with photos that would greet people as they came to her Rosary and Funeral Mass, which would be held as soon as possible? Of course, I replied in the affirmative, tidied up the work space I had been using and, after lunch, drove down to Staples to purchase a poster board. Spiritually, I rejoiced that Sister Piedad would actually behold the very Face of God, but on a natural, human level, I was hurting deep inside.

One never knows when God will send us a messenger. On this particular day, God sent a messenger to me in Aisle 3 of Staples on Valley Boulevard in Alhambra, California. I would like to share what happened that day—something that had never happened before and as of today, has never happened since.

To begin with, I couldn't make myself walk down the aisle that had the poster board. I would start out and then hesitate, turn around and look at items in some other aisle. Secondly, I did not realize I was crying big, slow tears that were finding their way, one by one, from my eyes to my chin where they were stopped by the coif that we Carmelite Sisters wear. I wasn't really thinking about anything. I was more or less aimlessly wandering up and down the aisles of the store. I hadn't been long—maybe four or five minutes—when it happened.

I heard a familiar sound, "Sister!" Automatically, I turned around in the direction of the voice.

"What's the matter, 'hon'?" the woman asked.

I looked at her, not comprehending. As far as I was concerned, nothing was the matter. "What do you mean?" I asked.

Her gentle black hands reached over and clasped mine. "Sometimes, I just know. And right now, I know that something's troubling you. I work here part time. I stand in the aisles and help people locate the items they want to buy. What are you looking for? What brings you here today, 'hon'?"

That's when it happened. Great, deep sobs rose from my inmost being and came out as waves of grief, spilling over onto her strong shoulders. She just kept quiet and let me cry until I had no tears left. Looking back, I wonder what the customers thought as they saw this Carmelite sister wailing in the arms of this kind and intuitive woman in aisle 3 of the stationery section of the store. I didn't think of that then. All I could do was ask for a tissue.

She tried again. "So, what's the matter?"

Another surge of tears ran down my face. My coif was wet, indeed. As I looked up into those kind eyes, into that loving face, the words tumbled out of my mouth, "One of my sisters is dying. She is in her final moments right now."

Silence.

"Anything else, 'hon'?"

"I'm looking for a poster board to put photos of her for the people to see at her funeral." My lip quivered.

"Let her go, 'hon', let her go. God's calling her, 'hon'. You believe in God, don't you? And in heaven?"

"Yes, I do." I thought how strange it was that I, who usually was the one comforting people, was standing here in the aisle, sobbing into the arms of a total stranger. Of course, I believe in God. Of course, I believe in heaven. Still, the tears kept coming, falling down my face slowly and surely.

The woman looked at me. "Of course you believe. Will you pray with me? Together we will let Him know that we are letting her go. What's her name?"

"Her name is Sister Piedad of Jesus."

"And what's your name, 'hon'?"

"Sister Timothy Marie."

Still holding my two hands, she closed her eyes and said,

"Father God, here is your dear child, Sister Timothy, meeting with me today in this store. Her sister, Sister Piedad of Jesus, is passing on to You as we speak. We know that You are our Father, and that You are Sister Piedad's Father, and that You are waiting for her with open arms because it is her time to go home to You. I don't want to hold her back. Sister Timothy doesn't want to hold her back. So, here I am, Father, with your daughter, Sister Timothy, and we want to let Sister Piedad go home to you. We don't want to keep her here. She already hears Your voice calling her home. We praise You for calling her home."

Then she looked at me and squeezed my hands and said softly, "OK, Sister Timothy, say after me. 'Father, I want to let Sister Piedad go home to You. I know You are calling her.'"

I repeated the words.

"I don't want to hold her back. I trust You, Father, I trust You enough to let Sister Piedad go home to You."

As I repeated these words, my sobbing stopped as suddenly as it had begun. A deep peace settled into my spirit. I closed my eyes. When I opened my eyes, she was gone.

Did I buy the poster board that day? Yes, and I created a beautiful memory board of our beloved Sister Piedad for her family, friends and all of our sisters to see. Etched into my heart, forever, is that special moment in time when God sent me His messenger to strengthen and comfort me during my loss and grief and to remind me, once again, of His Love.

Change of Heart

by Sister Marie-Aimée, O.C.D.

*T*HE PARTICULAR NEIGHBORHOOD of the city of Long Beach, California, where Holy Innocents School and our convent are located has for many years been a tough area of that city, with frequent police activity being the norm.

In the wee hours one night, many years ago, one of our elderly sisters, who still was firmly in possession of her feisty spirit, awakened to an odd scratching noise. Quickly coming fully awake, she realized that it was not a scratching noise she heard but rather the sound of someone trying to force open her window!

Well, Sister would have none of that! Getting up, fully intending to confront the intruder, Sister strode over to the window, threw up the sash and came face-to-face with a very startled, would-be burglar.

"Just what do you think you're doing?" Sister exclaimed with righteous indignation. "You should be ashamed of yourself! What would your mother say?" She reprimanded the by now thoroughly disconcerted prowler who finally managed to collect himself enough to turn tail and run.

When morning dawned, the Superior called the police. When the patrolmen arrived a few hours later, Sister Superior and the elderly Sister who had confronted the intruder walked around to the outside of the convent to inspect the damage to the window which the hapless burglar attempted to force open.

To their utter astonishment, they found the window completely and neatly repaired!

It appears our dear Sister's feisty spirit inspired a change of heart in this particular intruder.

"God is Coming!"

by Sister Jeannine Marie, O.C.D.

"CLOTHE ME, O MY GOD, WITH THE HOLY HABIT IN ORDER THAT I MAY APPEAR BEFORE YOU IN SUCH MANNER AS MY HOLY HABIT REQUIRES."

An interesting thing happened on a recent trip to visit my sister in Tennessee. My sister and I had planned to visit the Great Smokey Mountains. We decided to go to Cades Cove, an eleven mile loop road for viewing well-groomed valleys, mountain vistas, wildlife, floral, and historic structures. Cades Cove is one of the earliest settlements dating back to the 1850's. It harkens memories of the famed movie, Christy, the story of the one-room schoolhouse teacher of the Appalachian Mountains. We had visited log cabins with authentic cookware still on the tables; blacksmith's shops with harnesses hanging, and several rustic churches. The depth of the people's faith was actually visible in the hundreds of hand prints left behind in the thatched ceiling of the church.

We were just finishing up the tour by visiting the first church built on this early settlement when suddenly something or someone flashed past us, stopped, and whirled around. It was a small girl about eight years old with golden pigtails still vibrating at her side. She stood looking at me with her mouth wide open and her eyes as large as saucers. "God!" she cried. "It's God!" She twirled around quickly, ran up the steps of the church, and disappeared. My sister and I just looked at each other and chuckled that my brown Carmelite habit made such an impression.

When we approached the bottom of the three steps leading up to the front door of the church, the little girl appeared once again at the doorway. At each step I ascended I heard her say, "God is coming! God is coming!" Now, it is difficult to describe the overpowering feeling one has at this type of acclamation. I do not think I have ascended stairs with such grace in all my life! Once inside the church I passed the little girl's father who bent over and whispered, "Bet you never expected that." My sister and I finished our tour and returned to our car all the while wondering at the catechesis the little girl's parents would have to give once they were safely home.

Later in the day, my sister and I decided to stop at a small country store to pick up some groceries. We had traveled down several aisles when suddenly a small boy appeared with his mother following behind with her cart. The little boy took a good long look at me and once he had passed he said to his mother, "What's that?" "She works for God," the mother answered. Once we were safely out of hearing range, my sister looked at me and said, "Well, that's just the way life is, isn't it? One minute you are God, and the next minute you just work for Him."

Some may question whether a religious habit is relevant in today's world. The habit does not make the monk, the saying goes. This incident, however, certainly proved to me that it is a true witness. If a small girl and boy from the Bible Belt, who, I would venture, had never seen a religious Sister, was able to equate "her" with "Him," then witness she is.

Every morning, now, when I am privileged to don the habit and pray, "Clothe me, O my God, with the holy habit in order that I may appear before you in such manner as my holy habit requires," I say a little prayer of gratitude for a small girl in Tennessee.

God's Perfect Timing

by Sister Timothy Marie, O.C.D.

S OMETIMES GOD'S GRACE
REACHES INTO UNEXPECTED PLACES.

Southern California lay under a blanket of heat with triple-digit temperatures rising higher day after day after day. It was mighty hot. The 210 Freeway became a lake of sorts as mirages appeared and then disappeared into the horizon. No, it wasn't hot when I sent in my reservation in April to attend the convention – at that time September weather wasn't even considered. During the first two days of the conference – Friday and Saturday – the heat was bearable. Now, on Sunday, the last day, I was finally on my way together with a sweltering mass of humanity who also wanted to attend the popular workshop that drew me to this convention in the first place.

A huge crowd attended that year, and as a result, some workshops took place at nearby hotels. When I opened the lobby door of the convention center to begin my walk to one of the hotels, I braced myself against the onslaught of a Sahara-desert-wind that blew me onto the sizzling sidewalk. Well, it was worth it. The hotel was less than a five-minute walk, and I was determined.

The Anaheim Convention Center is located in the city of Anaheim, just across the street from California's Disneyland. Visitors, vacationers, businessmen and women, and lots of energetic children wearing Mickey Mouse ears, Tinkerbell shirts, and pirate hats – to name just a few – merged with convention attendees on the outside walkway. Some, dressed in very informal beachwear (ahem), stared at this Carmelite Sister wearing a full, long, brown habit and flowing black veil.

Now, when you are a Catholic consecrated religious and you wear a traditional, beautiful habit, you stand out in any crowd. You become a conversation piece to some, memorabilia to others, and either inspiring or shunned, depending on the religious frame of reference of each person you are with. People often come up to talk awhile. Many ask for prayers or share some personal story. On this particular day, each person walked determinedly to the next workshop, wherever it was held. I was doing the same. It was just too hot to interact.

After a few minutes' walk, I entered the hotel. It was heavenly. With its extraordinarily tasteful décor of deep forest green with just-perfect accents, it was a delight just being there. Green was a cool color and there must have been at least a 30 degree difference between the temperature outside and temperature inside the hotel. I took grateful, deep breaths of cool air and slowly let them in, envisioning my throat, neck, head – all of me – receiving the coolness with gratitude. Smiling, I began humming as I sailed across the marble floor like a ship on the glassy, air-conditioned sea.

For weeks I had been looking forward to this talk on living in God's presence in daily life. My current assignment took such a great amount of my strength and energy that I felt the need to spend quality time in prayer. With the cool air, my head's thinking process came back. Just a few moments before my head had felt more like an egg frying in the sun. I began thinking about the workshop and how to reach the correct room.

I arrived at the marquis listing all of the rooms of the various workshops and saw that mine was located on the second floor. One of the hotel staff walked by and advised me that the room was at the end of a very long corridor. "Great" I thought "it will be wonderful to walk and stretch my legs after all that sitting during the weekend. " I passed by Starbucks and its delicious aroma of carefully-blended coffee. I glided by the boutique and gift items, several clothing shops, and other typical, fashionable areas on the first floor. I was focused on finding the right room and getting to the workshop on time – maybe even a seat in the front row.

Then I saw it – a beautiful escalator winding its way up to the second floor. I had never seen such an elegant escalator, both in design and amidst such exquisite ambiance. It did not go straight up – as from point to point in a straight line; rather, it wound gracefully from one floor to the next. Surrounding it, there was so much greenery, so many fresh floral arrangements, and several lovely potted plants of a variety I had not seen before. I was especially keen on the graceful, potted ferns. Some were like trees, taller than I was, and I am 5'7. No need to think twice. In an instant, I was on that escalator being carried in style to my destination.

About one-fourth of the way up, I heard a voice "Sister, Sister!" Turning around, I saw a man in his early thirties – as I judged him to be – just getting onto the escalator with both arms over his head, waving robustly and calling out, "Sister, Sister! Wait for me. Wait for me." Distracted from my reveries, I finished the ride, got off and waited.

"Are you a Roman Catholic Sister?" he asked.

"Yes, I certainly am."

Then, right there amidst the ferns and orchids and all, he began to cry. I handed him a tissue and he took it gratefully. "Are you alright?" I asked?

"No."

I looked at my watch. My workshop was to begin in only five minutes and I still had that long corridor to walk. Of course, there was only one thing I could do. In the here and now, someone had called out to me and told me they were not alright. So, with a sigh, I thanked God that this burdened man had found me inside the hotel (as opposed to being found on the sweltering sidewalk), so he and I sat down in a in a charming little sitting area near the potted ferns, just off the escalator.

I waited.

He spoke about what had caused him to cry.

Years ago he had been a new student in a Catholic School, beginning the first grade, and he remembered not being happy there. His family had moved to a new town. He had made no friends yet, and it didn't help that there weren't many Catholics in the small southern town. He then shared with me how he had felt while he was in that school and ended by saying how remarkable it was that after all these years, when he saw me that time in his early childhood came back to him. He was embarrassed that tears had fallen and more than a little surprised.

"I spontaneously called out to you," he mused.

His story touched me. It is always amazing to discover how deeply childhood memories can affect each one of us. I began crying also, quiet little tears running in gentle rivulets down my face. I felt truly sorry for this man and for whatever was causing those tears. But what was I to do? I had no part in this. It did not affect my life, only his. I kept on listening while within my heart I continued praying for him.

People on the escalator saw us crying together. One woman after getting off the escalator positioned herself behind one of those lovely potted ferns and continued watching us. It was distracting to me to see, from time to time, a small hand wrap around a fern frond and push it aside, revealing two big eyes anxious to view the next segment of this live drama. That was more than a little disconcerting and it had its elements of humor. When the sobbing stopped, I asked him to tell me about it. That's all. That's exactly what he did.

So I closed my eyes and prayed quietly within myself. I had already given up attending that special workshop I had so very much wanted to attend. As I continued praying, a thought came to me and I decided to act on it.

That's when I stood up – we were sitting on lovely custom-designed chairs – and walked closer to him. Quietly, I knelt down before him. Taking his two hands in mine, I said, "Steven,* what you have just told me about your first grade is very upsetting to me. I see you are surprised that you are crying. Well, here I am crying with you."

The hand wound around the palm frond again. It slowly moved out of the way to show two eyes peering intently at Steven and I. Then, another hand wound around a second frond and slowly moved it away, revealing a woman's head containing those two piercing eyes. It only distracted me for a moment. My heavens!

"Steven, let's pray together here and now. Let's pray that you may find peace. I know it is a somewhat awkward place, here by this escalator, we are not in a church or anything like that; still God told us that whenever two or three are gathered in His name, there He is in the midst of them. We know He is with us now."

Steven answered that yes, he truly wanted to pray. So, that's what we did.

God's moments of special graces can come anywhere, anytime, to any one of us. That sweltering September day, grace rained down upon two of his children – a Catholic sister and a crying man sitting near an escalator during a convention in a hotel.

It was God's perfect timing.

I'm still not sure why I knelt down – it was a spontaneous response. Was it a prompting of the Holy Spirit? Or was it a spur-of-the-moment reaction of one human being who felt compassion for the hurting soul of another human being? Probably, it was both. Whatever the cause, God honored it by giving Steven the grace to heal.

It was a moment of grace.

As St. Therese was fond of saying, "Everything is grace." As the two of us went down the escalator together to the first floor, I turned around and waved good-by to the woman entrenched in palm fronds. Steve and I parted ways at the bottom of the escalator. Retracing my steps, I passed the boutiques, clothing shops, and Starbucks. No, I didn't make it to the workshop on The Presence of God in Daily Life. This time, in His gracious goodness, God showed two of us children His healing presence in our daily lives, right there in the hotel.

I opened the hotel lobby front door and walked into a Sahara-like desert wind back to the convention center. A hot September day in southern California was God's perfect timing to heal a wonderful man named Steven, and one Carmelite Sister experienced, again, God's presence in her daily life firsthand. Praise God!

* = denotes names have been changed to protect privacy

He Will See to It

by Sister Mary Scholastica, O.C.D.

O̲UR FOUNDRESS, MOTHER LUISITA
had unwavering confidence in the loving providence of God, writing: *"How good our God is, always watching over His children! We should rest entirely in His hands, understanding that His eyes are always upon us, that He will see to it that we lack nothing and grant us anything that we need if it is for our own good."* We were recently reminded of the simple truth of Mother's words – that truly the guiding hand of Divine Providence is never far away.

Sister Mary Jeanne was scheduled to have surgery at a time that happened to coincide with an especially busy few months for our community. As a result, the date of her surgery kept getting postponed, and was ultimately scheduled about two-or-three months after the original date. Sister's surgery was successful, after which she had to spend some time recuperating in the hospital. As her recuperation progressed and her release date neared, she was eventually transitioned into the hospital's Transitional Care Unit, which is where Sister Mary Jeanne met Sister Vera.

Sister Vera was given a three-month assignment to work as an intern in the pastoral care program at the Hospital. The chances of Sister Mary Jeanne and Sister Vera meeting were extraordinarily slim, because had Sister Mary Jeanne undergone surgery at the time it was originally scheduled, she would not have been present during the narrow three-month window during which Sister Vera was working there. With the way things worked out, it is quite apparent that Divine Providence decreed the paths of these two religious sisters were meant to cross.

The two sisters got to know each other as Sister Vera often visited Sister Mary Jeanne during her convalescence. Eventually, Sister Vera shared some prayer requests, asking Sister Mary Jeanne's prayers on behalf of the petitioners. As it turned out, one of the prayer requests concerned Sister Vera's own family. Sister Vera asked for prayers on behalf of three of her nephews – Michael, for his upcoming marriage; Luke, who was looking for a job; and for Timothy who had special intentions. For the rest of her hospital stay, Sister Mary Jeanne faithfully remembered in prayer the requests shared by Sister Vera.

The days passed and with her recuperation complete, Sister Mary Jeanne was discharged from the hospital and would not see Sister Vera again.

It was during this same time (and completely unrelated to Sister Mary Jeanne's hospital stay) the Carmelite Sisters' Advancement Office had an open position it was looking to fill. I asked one of our faithful volunteers if she happened to know of anyone with data entry skills who was looking for a job. Within a couple of weeks, our volunteer handed me a list of possible interviewees. We were hoping to find a potential hire who shared in the Carmelite Sisters' vision and mission. In the end, we did in fact hire one of the individuals on the list provided by our volunteer.

In the meantime, a month after her discharge from the hospital, Sister Mary Jeanne received a telephone call.

"Sister Mary Jeanne!" the awe-filled voice on the other end said, "Your prayers are powerful!"

To Sister Mary Jeanne's delight, it was Sister Vera calling, to tell her that Luke, Sister Vera's nephew, for whom Sister Mary Jeanne had been praying, is none other than the very same Luke we hired to work in our Advancement Office!

How wise and right Mother Luisita was! Yes, indeed – if we trust in His Divine Providence, He will see to it that we lack nothing and grant us anything that we need if it is for our own good.

Metro Ministries

by Imelda Marie, O.C.D.

*U*SING THE PUBLIC TRANSPORTATION SYSTEM, I was amazed at how many people come up to me asking for prayers. Why? Is it because they no longer know how to "talk" to God, and feel they need someone dedicated to God to serve as their delivery system from the natural to supernatural?

Once, while waiting for the metro, a teen age boy approached me.

"I know you are busy, but could you please pray for my grandmother?" he asked.

"I am not busy," I told him, "I'm just waiting for the Metro."

After praying for his grandmother, I also prayed for him. His eye welled up with grateful tears.

The Metro arrived just then and we each went our own way.

After getting off the Metro, I had to catch a bus about a block away, which would drop me off near to where my appointment was. As the street light turned green, I started to make a hurried dash to cross the street. Just then, I heard a voice call, "Wait up". With so many people around me, I felt sure no one was calling to me. I took one step onto the street when the voice became an urgent shout: "STOP, WAIT UP!!!"

I stopped in my tracks. My nursing instinct told me to turn around to see if someone was in need of medical assistance. It was then I saw a very large man hurrying toward me indicating he was talking to me. When we met, his loud, demanding voice became very gentle.

"Would you kindly say a prayer with me?" he pleaded, his eyes full of hope that I would agree to do so.

After praying a short prayer, his face became radiant as he quietly said, "Thank you. I am deeply grateful for your prayer."

As I neared my destination for my doctor appointment, I was stopped by one of the attendants in the hallway of the doctor's office and she asked, "Sister would you please pray for me".

I barely had a chance to speak a few words, when the door near us was flung open and several doctors and interns hurriedly passed between us.

"Thank you for the prayer, Sister," the attendant quickly said.

"That really was only a "mini" prayer. I owe you a longer prayer than that!" I told her.

After my appointment, I was retracing my steps back toward the Metro station to return home. Suddenly, another young boy stopped before me sitting on his bicycle.

"Sister, will you please pray for me that I find a girl?" he asked shyly.

"I will pray that the girl you find is the girl you will remain with," I promised him.

The Metro train was crowed on the way home and there were only a few seats available. I sat down next to a middle-aged African-American lady. We began to chat and as our conversation progressed, I felt we were having a "woman at the well experience." Our conversation went from the superficial to the supernatural. I noticed she was reading a Bible.

We would occasionally pause in our conversation to enjoy the passing scenery. As I commented on the beauty of the hills and sky, a thoughtful expression came across her face.

"I feel so sad that there is so much evil in the world. The devil lays so many traps," she said regretfully.

"You know, some of our Sisters call that the "red flannel syndrome." I told her. "When someone is about to receive a big grace, a big problem occurs, and the Sisters will say 'I see red flannels here', meaning the devil is trying to stir up trouble to counter the good," I explained.

"The devil seems particularly skilled in causing plumbing problems!" I added.

My companion had a good laugh. "I certainly never heard it put quite that way," she said, still chuckling.

After a moment's thought, she opened her purse and looked around for something. She pulled out a pamphlet and handed it to me. It was then that I realized she was probably a Jehovah's Witness. The pamphlet was titled *"Who is Jesus?"*

"Well, I think I know the answer to that question," I told her.

"Oh!" she exclaimed. She then rummaged around in her purse again, this time drawing out another pamphlet titled, *"What's after earth"*.

"Well, this is far more promising," I thought to myself.

My companion then explained, "It will be so nice in heaven, where there will be no more wars, no more crime…"

I seized the opportunity. "Heaven and hell really start here on earth," I said to her.

She thought a bit. "Yes, it's true if there were no wars or crime it would be like heaven."

"No," I explained, "Heaven and hell start here on earth, not on the outside, but in our hearts as we make good or bad choices."

The Metro arrived at my destination, but I could see my words had made an impression as she seemed lost in thought pondering this new information.

God's Carmelite Sister Messenger Service completed yet another day of timely message ministries!

Lift High the Cross

by Sister Timothy Marie, O.C.D.

*I*T WAS LATE SUMMER IN CALIFORNIA. The skies were a limpid blue. A balmy ocean breeze blew across the sand. Children were building sandcastles. Windsurfers cut like knives across the Pacific shoreline with windblown hair. And fifteen Carmelite Sisters began walking down the quarter mile-long pier clear to the end. They mingled in two's or three's singing and just enjoying the day before the first day of school. It was a glorious end to summer vacation.

I was one of them. Three different convents were situated within a fifteen mile radius and the sisters decided to join together at the beach before school was back in session. It was a kind of spontaneous thing, which sometimes ends up being the most fun of all.

To say the least, we did stand out at the beach. Amidst the plethora of beach-goers, we appeared as an interesting group indeed – with our veils dancing in the wind gracefully and the echoes of our songs reaching into the horizon. It was fun, peaceful, and, I would say, grace-filled. Anytime we get the opportunity to soak in the beauty of God's creation, listening to the *whish, whish, whish* of the waves washing up on the shore and watching the sea gulls gliding gracefully across the sky, we discover another moment of grace.

As I said, there were fifteen of us, and it took about half an hour to meander our way to the end of the pier and another half hour to walk back.

You know, one can never predict the surprises that come our way in life. Well, this day unwrapped one most unexpected surprise. As we walked back to the shore, a young man, maybe in his twenties or early thirties was walking towards us. He kept getting closer and closer to us and that's when we noticed that something was wrong. We weren't quite sure what, but we could tell there was definitely something.

When he saw that we were Catholic Sisters, he broke out into such intense blasphemy which wrapped him in a darkness, so to speak. We were all so shocked that we didn't know what to do. He seemed out of control and his face contorted in such anger, such hate, such a violent look he had. We were afraid.

Some of the sisters just opened the mouths in shocked disbelief. Others, like me, kept looking around to see if there was anyone who could help us. No one. Absolutely no one. The pier was about a quarter mile long and we were still far from the shore.

All of a sudden one of the Sisters removed the large crucifix she wore as a part of her Carmelite habit. It is about five or six inches in length, silver with an ebony inset. She held that cross as high as she could (she was only about 5 feet tall) and shouted, "In the name of Jesus, STOP!"

The man looked at the crucifix, yelled out in a low anguishing moan, "No......o......o." Then he tried to shout, "Don't hold that up. Put it down." But our steadfast Sister Carol Marie began walking toward him, passing all of us up, and holding her crucifix even higher and in a louder voice yelled out, "In the name of Jesus, STOP!"

We all looked on, gaping at the scene and astonished at our Sister Carol Marie's deep, active, practical faith.

That young man simply quieted down, turned around, and quietly slinked away. With head lowered, and steps faltering, he retraced his steps and returned to the shore.

Sister Carol Marie simply put her crucifix back, looked back at the rest of us, smiled and motioned for us to continue our walk. Which we did.

Well, that is the true story I wanted to share. It really happened. September 14th is the Feast of the Exaltation of the Cross. Each year when it comes around, I remember when Sister Carol Marie lifted high the cross in faith.

Don't underestimate the grace of the moment, or the powerful nudging of the Holy Spirit. Of all the sisters there, only one even thought of holding high the cross of Christ in the face of such utter evil. And she did it.

Why was I surprised? Wasn't I a believer? Wasn't I a Carmelite Sister, a baptized Catholic almost since my birth?

Ours is a living, dynamic faith. If through the trials and vicissitudes of life we have let the light of faith grow weak, or the ardor of our faith diminish, we can as St. Paul once suggests, "fan the flame, stir up the flame, rekindle the gift, keep ablaze the gift of God . . . ." as it comes through in different translations.

A cross, a crucifix, is not an object for ornamentation. Nor is it simply a piece of jewelry. It is a sign of our faith. It encompasses the whole history of salvation and the unparalleled love of Jesus Christ.

Lately, I've been thinking that it is now our moment in history to lift high the cross.

Amen. Alleluia!

"LIFT HIGH THE CROSS"
By George W. Kitchin

Lift high the cross, the love of Christ proclaim,
Till all the world adore His sacred Name.

Led on their way by this triumphant sign,
The hosts of God in conquering ranks combine.

Each newborn servant of the Crucified
Bears on the brow the seal of Him Who died.

O Lord, once lifted on the glorious tree,
As Thou hast promised, draw the world to Thee.

So shall our song of triumph ever be:
Praise to the Crucified for victory.

Not Alone

by Sister Vincent Marie, O.C.D.

*A*S A YOUNGER SISTER WORKING AT SANTA TERESITA, I was on call for the emergency room. In the wee hours one morning, we were all called to the ER because a young man had been brought in with critical injuries. He had been working all night and was exhausted by the time he was on his way home. He fell asleep at the wheel and ended up in a terrible accident. Emergency Room personnel called his wife, who came, carrying a baby in her arms.

The young man was alert and surrounded by the Sisters. We placed the brown scapular on him and he received the sacraments. He never left the ER; he died there shortly after his wife arrived to be at his side. We were able to be there not only for him, but for his wife as she dealt with the hard reality of the sudden loss of her husband. He died in peace, surrounded by prayer, his wife at his side, wearing the scapular of our Blessed Mother, with Jesus Himself present through the sacraments.

He was in his twenties...by the grace of God, he did not die alone.

Faithful Love

by Sister Stephanie, O.C.D.

*T*HERE ARE THOSE SPECIAL PEOPLE, who when faced with life's challenges, rise to the occasion and serve as inspiration to those around them. Pete*, a resident at Avila Gardens, our residence for independent, active seniors, is just such a person. He is a shining example of a faithful and loving husband, and one who does not shy away from sacrifice. Pete and his wife, Helen* were planning to move to Avila Gardens, when illness struck requiring skilled nursing care for Helen. The couple went ahead with their plans for Pete to move into Avila Gardens, while Helen was admitted to Santa Teresita, our professional skilled nursing and rehabilitative facility.

Pete's love and devotion for Helen quickly became apparent. He faithfully drives to Santa Teresita to visit her twice a day, arriving every morning and evening without fail. There are many social activities at Avila Gardens and knowing that the occasional change of scene would do Helen a world of good, Pete drives her over to Avila Gardens so that she can enjoy the activities with him. On these occasions, such as during our "Cruise Week", Pete proudly introduced Helen to the Sisters and to the residents. All of us at Avila Gardens were deeply moved by Pete's generous and loving spirit.

It is always easy to tell if Helen is having a "good" day or a "not-so-good" day. Her condition is mirrored in the expression on Pete's face and by either the concern or the joy shining in his eyes. On Helen's better days, Pete wears a radiant smile and has just a bit of a bounce to his step. When she is not doing well, his expression is pensive, his gait a bit heavier. It does not take a keen observer to see just how much Pete loves Helen.

One of the things Pete is especially grateful for is the fact that he can still drive and thus can continue visiting Helen. His last birthday marked 92 years for him and it was time to renew his driver's license.

His son, Jim* cautioned, "Dad, you're 92…the DMV might not renew your license."

"Well, I don't know whether or not they'll renew my license," Pete declared, "but I'm not about to just sit back and not even try!"

Armed with unshakeable faith and his determination to continue driving to Santa Teresita to visit his beloved wife, Pete drove to the DMV office early one morning and stood in line.

Well, his faith was rewarded! Not only was his license renewed, it was renewed for the maximum five years!

"Sister, that means that I can continue to drive until I'm 97 years old!" Pete beamed at me upon his return from the DMV.

"Congratulations, Pete!" I told him with a big smile. "I'm sure your wife will be very happy, too. Your devotion to her and your faithfulness in visiting her twice a day is truly inspiring," I added.

"Well, Sister," Pete replied, "when you've been married for 70 years, the only thing you really want is to just be together."

Pete's twice-a-day visits to Helen have continued now for a full two years. What a beautiful expression of true love and a faithful commitment to the wedding vows Pete and Helen exchanged over 70 years ago!

May God continue to bless them now and into eternity.

* = *denotes names have been changed to protect privacy*

The Deadline that Changed My Prayer Life

by Sister Timothy Marie, O.C.D.

"WHAT NERVE TO GIVE ST. JOSEPH A DEADLINE! How could I ever give a saint a deadline to "come through" for us? Unheard of! Was that not presumptuous and proud, even arrogant?"

Mornings are God's masterpieces. A new day awakens, filled with potential. The night sky disappears into the heavens, while the sun slowly creeps up out of the distant horizon. Most of the time, I don't see the sun rise. Dawn comes quite early according to any clock and Carmelite Sisters rise even before the sun does.

One day is etched in my memory because God opened my eyes to see what a masterful coordinator He is, and how very much He is into the smallest details of my life. It began like any other day.

The convent rising bell awakened me from a very sound sleep. Opening one eye and then the other, I realized slowly that, indeed, it was time to get up. We Sisters begin each day with a short hymn that we sing while rising, followed by a short prayer. Thirty minutes later we are all in the chapel chanting Morning Prayer of the Liturgy of the Hours, followed by community prayers, a half hour of meditation, and Mass. This particular morning, the sun rose during our breakfast, approximately two hours after rising. During the winter season, it begins to peek out during our Mass.

This eye-opening true story happened to me. Through it, I learned that the saints in heaven are our friends – I mean real friends – and that the communion of saints, which is defined as the "the union which exists between the members of the Church on earth with one another, and with the blessed in heaven and with the suffering souls in purgatory" is not just a theological concept. We are all connected spiritually. I need to eat humble pie in retelling this story, because part of it revolves around my lack of faith and my doubts – yes, even as a Carmelite Sister.

About ten in the morning, Sister Gloria Therese and I began a drive in our convent car from Alhambra to a destination we had never been to before, to meet a person we had never seen before . . . . Well, I'm getting ahead of my story. How about if I just start at the beginning?

The Sacred Heart Retreat House is located in Alhambra, California and this year is its seventieth anniversary. Our retreats were growing in number and in attendance and so we were overjoyed when, not too long ago, the property across the street went up for sale. It was a beautiful piece of land, with a church/ hall, kitchen, meeting rooms, gardens, all a brief one minute's walk from Sacred Heart. We were able to work out the terms for acquiring the property and decided unanimously to name if after St. Joseph. Today, people all around know it as the St. Joseph Campus of Sacred Heart Retreat House.

Over the next few years, our Sisters worked hard to discern its specific niche in the San Gabriel Valley and greater Los Angeles area. It became the perfect location for day and evening retreats, conferences, workshops, youth groups, young adult groups, organizations like the Knights of Columbus and Right to Life and Catholic elementary, and secondary schools, as well as parish religious education programs. We held picnics, and concerts, garden fairs and "spirituali-teas." We also offered bible studies and a spirituality speaker series. Although we were still in "start-up" mode, things were going well.

Just a few years after opening St. Joseph's, Sister Gloria Therese, the director, mentioned at our Friday staff meeting that she thought it was the right time to start a newsletter which would publicize our events and be a means of sharing who we are and what we do. Still in initial start-up, we had very little money. Sister Gloria Therese has great faith in St. Joseph and asked us to pray daily to St. Joseph to ask him to help us find a printing company that would print a newsletter for us free of charge.

Five Sisters were assigned to St. Joseph Campus that year. Now, even though Catholic religious sisters may look alike to the casual observer – we have the same tunic, the same veil, almost the same shoes – each one of us has her own distinct and often interesting personality. Each one of us, in our personal prayer, prays in her own personal prayer style. Some are more devotional, some are more private, and some are more intense. As Sister Josephine would say, "There are many flowers in God's garden."

I was one of the sisters assigned to St. Joseph Campus that year. When Sister Gloria Therese suggested we pray to St. Joseph for a printing company willing to print our first newsletter for free, all of us agreed to pray. She suggested that we could all come together and sing a hymn to St. Joseph, place fresh cut flowers at the base of his statue in the main hall, and pray together asking him to help us find the right printer for our first newsletter. Then the bomb fell. "Today is January 5th," she said, "and we would like to send out the newsletter so it will reach the homes by the feast of St. Joseph, March 19th. So, when we pray, let's give St. Joseph the deadline of 12:00 noon on January 31st to lead us to the printing company he wants us to use."

What nerve to give St. Joseph a deadline! How could I ever give a saint a deadline to "come through" for us? Unheard of! Was that not presumptuous and proud, even arrogant? What on earth was she thinking of? It didn't seem in character for her, usually so sensible. I looked around the table. No one else seemed to mind. They were all nodding their heads in agreement. I kept my thoughts to myself, and for the next three weeks at the conclusion of our Friday staff meetings – sure enough – with freshly-cut flowers arranged in a beautiful vase, we processed up the main aisle of St. Joseph Hall to his statue at the front. Five Carmelite Sisters gathered around St. Joseph's statue in a large hall meant for hundreds of people. Next, we placed the flowers at the base of the statue, said our prayer to St. Joseph asking his help by noon on January 31st, and concluded by singing our hymn. Sister Josephine especially loved it. After all, she had taken St. Joseph's name as a novice. The others prayed and sang loudly and with faith. I was amazed and enthralled at the simple, fervent, expectant prayer of my Carmelite Sisters.

Sadly though, I harbored misgivings about giving St. Joseph a deadline, a little embarrassment at giving him flowers and singing, and a few doubts that he would come through for us. Like I mentioned, even though we Sisters look alike, inside we are our own personality, and our particular understanding of things, just like anyone else.

Time passed.

Then one day, much to my chagrin, I discovered that I had misplaced a photo that was needed for advertising. It was the best, the perfect photo to illustrate the beauty and functionality of our Sacred Heart Room. I had taken it when the early morning sunlight was streaming through the large bay east windows. It depicted young, engaged couples listening to a speaker, very much at ease and with interested looks on their faces. Like I said, it was the perfect photo, and now it was lost. I remember that I looked for that photo for two weeks and couldn't find it. Sister Gloria Therese phoned my office, finally one day, and said we needed the photo that day by noon. Could I please look for it a little harder? That's when I began a systematic, methodical search through every cabinet, drawer and whatever else was in my office. After two hours of searching, I finally came to the last possible place where a photo could be hiding. The bottom left drawer of my desk. It was the only placed I hadn't yet searched.

After removing all the items from the drawer, I thought I saw something. What was that little paper stuck in the back left corner? I tried pulling it out, but it was stuck pretty securely. Avoiding the temptation to just leave it there, I prayed for patience and meticulously and gently pulled at the paper. It finally came out. It was a business card. Turning it over, it was the name of a printing company. It was definitely NOT the longed-for photo of the Sacred Heart Room. I sighed, replaced the items and looked at the clock 11:51 a.m. Time for our midday examination of conscience and the Angelus. I'd better hurry.

On my way to the chapel, I stopped into Sister Gloria Therese's office. "Sister, we will have to go with the other photo of the Sacred Heart Room - our second choice. Sorry, but I just couldn't find the one we liked so much. By the way, do you recognize this old business card? I found it lodged in the back corner of one of the drawers in my desk."

She looked at the card, turned it over and examined the other side. "No," she replied, "I don't think I've ever seen this before. At least, I don't remember it." Then she stopped a moment, looked at it again, and then gave her very unique "Sister Gloria Therese quick step", the running-in-place-dance-step, which automatically occurs when she is absolutely thrilled about something. I remember thinking, what in the world is she so thrilled about? We'd better head over to the chapel; we were late already.

"Sister Timothy, THIS IS A BUSINESS CARD," she proclaimed, her eyes wide with excitement.

"I know it's a business card," I replied. "Remember, I just handed it to you."

"Sister Timothy, THIS IS A BUSINESS CARD FOR A PRINTING COMPANY."

"I noticed that, too," I answered, "but, you can hardly read it anymore."

Again her little quick-step and, "SISTER TIMOTHY, IT IS 11:55 A.M. ON JANUARY 31ST. ST. JOSEPH WANTS US TO USE THIS PRINTER. PLEASE CALL HIM."

Her words hit me like a ton of bricks. Sure enough, it was 11:55 a.m. on January 31st, only five minutes prior to the 12:00 noon deadline we had given St. Joseph. Amazing! Still, how could I ever call a printing company I had never heard of and ask outright if they would donate their printing services for a newsletter for a group of Catholic Sisters.

After our noon prayers, as we were all walking to lunch, I told myself, "I'd better just summon up my courage and my humility and make this call. If I wait, or if I think about it too much, I will lose heart and courage. This will not be an easy call for me to make. So, out came the business card from my pocket and I called.

No one answered and the voice mail activated. Taking a deep breath, I began. "Hello, good afternoon, my name is Sister Timothy Marie, a Catholic nun from Alhambra. I came across your business card stuck in a back corner of my desk." Then I simply told the story. Yes, I included the hymn, the flowers, the prayer, and the faith of my sisters that St. Joseph would answer us by noon of January 31st. Let me tell you, it was one interesting phone call. I ended by saying, "I totally understand if you don't call us back. Please know that I just had to call because we found this card nine minutes before our deadline to St. Joseph. God bless you and thank you for listening."

After lunch was over, I checked my voice mail. A deep, resonant voice spoke, "Hello, Sister Timothy, this is John Hunter from Hunter Printing .* Yes, I remember you. I met Sister Gloria Therese one day in the office of a graphic artist who does some of our graphic design for our business. I remember they were designing a CD album cover for your music CD. I remember the cover of the album had a Sister's photo and a bouquet of red roses. I gave Sister Gloria Therese my business card and said that if she ever needed a printer to give us a call. That was several years ago. Call me back and we'll see what we can do." I took a deep breath, replayed the message and then forwarded it along to Sister Gloria Therese. A few days later, Sister Gloria Therese and I drove to Hunter Printing.

As we walked into the office, John Hunter came out to meet us. He had tears in his eyes. "Good afternoon, Sisters, your phone call meant so much to me. So, you asked St. Joseph to help you find a printer. Well, my wife and I are in the process of reconciliation with the Catholic Church. My wife was away from the Catholic Church and spent ten years in the New Age movement. I'm currently in R.C.I.A. We both listened to your phone message. Your message is a blessing and a confirmation to us. We thank God for bringing us together with the Carmelite Sisters and we want to help you with the printing of your first Saint Joseph Campus Newsletter. We are happy and honored to print the first newsletter for St. Joseph Campus free of charge." Sister Gloria Therese and I were speechless. All of us had tears of joy streaming down our faces.

A few days later, John called and told us that he had called a paper company which agreed to donate the paper, and a mailing company to donate the mailing of the newsletter. Subsequently, his wife gave her testimony as one of our featured speakers at St. Joseph's Campus.

I wish we could see the graces of each day like we see the sunbeams dancing in the sunlight. But we can't. I wish we could see them as they stream forth from God to us. But we can't. We can see them, though, in the goodness of people and in the beauty of solidarity, in the blessing of giving and in the blessing of receiving. That evening as the sun was setting, we marveled at what had happened – the lost photo, the total cleaning of an office, the little business card stuck in a corner of a drawer, a couple reconciling with the Church, a paper company willing to do a good deed, a mailing company going the extra mile and a Catholic Sister who contemplated within her heart a new idea – for St. Joseph actually met the deadline. Friends understand and enjoy each other. I learned that saints can really be our friends and that St. Joseph enjoyed meeting Sister Gloria Therese's deadline.

After all, they are good friends.

* = denotes names have been changed to protect privacy

This story is dedicated to Sister Maria Josefa, O.C.D., who entered eternal life on September 19, 2011 just as this story was being written. Because of the current construction at Santa Teresita in Duarte, California, Sister Maria Josefa had wondered about and worried about the statue of St. Joseph situated in an area marked for demolition. As the statue of St. Joseph was moved to a beautiful new location right in front of St. Joseph Chapel, our Sister Maria Josefa breathed her last and entered into eternal life. This story is dedicated to you, Sister Maria Josefa, for you, too, are a good friend of St. Joseph.

At the Heart
of the Church

"O Jesus, my Love, at last I have found my vocation. My vocation is love!
In the heart of the Church, my Mother, I will be LOVE!"
- Saint Therese of the Child Jesus

"*The Apple of Our Eye*"

by Sister Gloria Therese, O.C.D.

*I*N 1997, I WAS ASSIGNED TO WORK on the World Youth Day planning committee for the Council of Major Superiors of Women Religious (CMSWR). This WYD took place in Rome during the Jubilee year 2000. As the time came closer to the celebration, meetings were planned in the eternal city for April of 1999.

Ten Religious Communities from the United States sent delegates to Rome for a dual purpose: 1. Meet with the CMSWR/WYD committee for WYD preparations and 2. Prepare for the dedication of the CMSWR House of Studies, (the "Domus Sanctae Mariae Guadalupe") the first of its kind for North American women religious who were studying in Rome. During this week in the glorious season of Easter, the Domus shone forth a beautiful array of charisms of consecrated women: Benedictines, Franciscans, Little Sisters of the Poor, Dominicans, and Carmelites. Our week was packed with meetings, cooking and cleaning, dedication preparations, daily pilgrimage tours and contemplative moments. It would take an entire book just to share these experiences!

One of my domestic duties during this preparatory time was to make apple pies for the special dinner following the Dedication Mass at the Domus. Thanks to my Minnesota Grandmother's culinary art of pie-making which she passed on to her grandchildren. It surely came in handy as the many sisters prepared a Thanksgiving banquet for the Cardinals, Bishops and priests attending the Domus dedication dinner.

Of all the special moments in Rome, the most profound encounter for me took place after the Dedication of the Domus on Wednesday, April 28, 1999. One of the Sisters who worked in Rome said to me, "If you make an apple pie for the Holy Father, we'll make sure it gets to him!" Thus, on the Tuesday night before we went to the Holy Father's Wednesday Audience, I went into the kitchen and made him an apple pie with a card that said, "Holy Father, we love you. You are the apple of our eye..." The next morning, at 7:00 a.m. with pie and card in hand, the Sisters walked to St. Peter's Square.

The entire square and streets were packed with people, for it was the week of Padre Pio's Beatification. We passed the Swiss Guards and the Holy Father's attendants as they eyed the pie and told the Sisters who understood Italian, "That's for me, isn't it?!"

We had excellent seating and sat on the main platform just right of the Holy Father. After his arrival and address in five different languages, it was time to depart... except for those who were invited to have their pictures taken or present him with a gift. All those individuals and groups were told to stand in line and wait for their turn. I envisioned this to go rather quickly without a moment to actually greet our Holy Father. The wait passed quickly as we saw young couples in their wedding attire being blessed by the Pope, as well as religious communities and families waiting to pose for a picture. The atmosphere was peaked with excitement and awe as they awaited a sacred moment with the Vicar of Christ.

When it was time for the CMSWR Sisters to have our picture taken, I was standing directly on our Holy Father's right – still holding the pie. One sister was already kneeling at his left side and so seeing an empty space at his right, our Carmelite Mother General, Mother Vincent Marie at the time, gently nudged me saying, "Go..." and so I knelt at the feet of Pope John Paul II with the pie in my hand. I saw his hand resting on the chair so I bent to kiss his ring. When I looked up he was looking directly into my eyes and so taking his hand and he taking mine I said, "Holy Father, we love you." I then proceeded to say, "All the Postulants, Novices and Sisters in America give this little gift to you."

Our Holy Father blessed me by making the sign of the cross on my forehead and the pie was taken by one of his personal secretaries. I experienced that profound blessing as a little girl at the feet of her grandfather. Yet, at the same time, I was profoundly aware that it was the blessing of St. Peter, Christ's Vicar in our day.

Then taking my face in his hands he said, "American sisters, American sisters." I couldn't move, but only looked into his saintly eyes and prayed the American sisters would know his great love for them. Then the moment was over, with a bishop on each side helping me to my feet, which I truly felt unable to do alone.

Lastly, the gift came to full circle on the final day, April 30th. The Holy Father's secretary called the Domus asking if the American sisters could come to the Holy Father's private chapel for Mass! Thus, I came to know the reality that one's own prayer disappears when in Pope John Paul II's presence and you are completely absorbed in his prayer. I tangibly felt I was in the presence of a mystic. After the Mass and time of thanksgiving, we went to greet him. When it was my turn, I greeted Pope John Paul II, bending my knee, kissing his ring. He said to me, "Carmelites." and I said with a smile, "Carmelites." And he replied, "GOOD Carmelites."

This may not seem very significant, but one of my main meditations that Easter season as I prepared for final vows came from St. Augustine's 34th Sermon. The new man sings a new song in the new covenant. St. Augustine stated that "Praise is in the singers themselves. If you desire to praise him, then live what you express." My question then was, "How do you live this praise?" St. Augustine wrote, "Lead GOOD lives and you will BE His Praise." What did Our Holy Father call us? GOOD Carmelites. Thus, we as a Carmelite Community ARE God's Praise. What a grace for all of us to belong completely to God in Carmel and to begin our heaven on earth. May we always lead GOOD lives, so as to BE the Praise of God's Glory and Honor. Amen.

"Be Not Afraid"

by Sister Shawn Pauline, O.C.D.

*T*HE ONE THING IN LIFE THAT I WAS MOST AFRAID OF was having a religious vocation. I remember often at Mass during my teenage years I would cry hearing the song "Be not afraid, I go before you always. Come follow me…" I knew God was calling me, and I was afraid. There was only one voice in the world that kept telling me not to be afraid and it was John Paul II. His words, the very echo of Christ, planted the seeds of my vocation.

This voice continued to urge me onward, gently prodding me to look into religious life. When I went to the Franciscan University of Steubenville in the fall of 1998, I was bombarded with images and quotes of Pope John Paul II. I learned the phrases "Couragio," "JPII we love you," and, "Totus Tuus". It was during this time that I began to understand more the greatness of this man, and the impact he had had on the entire world. Through the example of Pope John Paul II, I grew in my relationship with Mary. I figured that if the pope says he is "Totally Mary's" then I should be too. I committed my whole life to Mary through the Marian Consecration program on campus. The profound simplicity of his motto struck the core of my heart and it was through the consecration that I really began to have a prayer life and follow Christ more closely.

While at college, I also met the Carmelite Sisters of the Most Sacred Heart of Los Angeles. We began a friendship and a deep respect and admiration for them was slowly taking shape in my heart.

A few years went by and while attending a semester in Europe, I had the chance to see Pope John Paul II at a short Wednesday audience. From his balcony window, he prayed the Pater Noster with us. I wept. An overwhelming awe at those words touched my soul. The essence and desire of every person on earth is this; I am a child of the Father who is loved. In that first encounter the three words, father, child, love, adequately express the sense that overwhelmed my soul to the point of tears. I had experienced God the Father in our Pope; I knew I was his child and I was changed forever.

Some more time went by and after I came back to the States, I grew ever closer to God, and the friendship that had started with the sisters blossomed. It wasn't too long before I realized that God was calling me to California, but I was afraid.

Then one day I went to my mail box to find a reply letter from the sister I had met at college, and in it she wrote one sentence that will forever be etched into my memory, "Do you realize that you have been privileged to live during the era of our saintly Holy Father, and now you are heeding his oft repeated call to 'be not afraid....'?" I remember that moment so clearly. I was stunned, shocked, for up until then I had not felt the impact of those words. It was because of him that I had the strength to overcome the fears that plagued my soul. The only thing that was possible for me to do was to become a Carmelite Sister.

After I finished my last semester of college in 2002, I had the great privilege to greet Pope John Paul II with my grandmother at another Wednesday audience. It was finally my chance to see my father face to face. I approached with a great peace, looked for a place to kneel, and landed right in between his red shoes! Then as I knelt there I looked into the eyes of Pope John Paul II.

I was enraptured with his gaze – as if before the Eucharist – I just wanted to look at him. There are moments in life when words are very unnecessary – moments so intimate that words would tarnish them, and this was one of those. He looked at me, his child, smiled, reached out and grabbed my head and kissed me. Total peace flooded my soul, and then something strange went through my mind. I thought, "Why don't I get this excited to receive Jesus in the Eucharist? The pope is just a man, and the Eucharist is God."

I realize now that Pope John Paul II was a person whose humility immediately led you to Jesus. After meeting the Pope, I had a strong sense that he wanted me to know that though meeting the Vicar of Christ is indeed an awesome experience, the encounter with Christ in the Eucharist is infinitely greater. I sensed that he wanted me to know that he was only a man; a man who had responded to grace.

The Holy Father led us all to Jesus, and not himself. That is why we loved him; that is why the whole world flocked to him. By his courageous love he chased away my fears and enabled me to encounter Christ. Blessed indeed is every soul who has lived during the pontificate of Pope John Paul II, for we received his love, wisdom, and guidance and now we reap the benefits of his intercession from Heaven. Forever we remain his beloved sons and daughters.

True Desires

by Sister Mary Scholastica, O.C.D.

W<small>HEN</small> C<small>ARDINAL</small> J<small>OSEPH</small> R<small>ATZINGER EMERGED</small> from behind the curtains on April 19, 2005 as Pope Benedict XVI, his very presence profoundly affected me. There was an instantaneous feeling of love and in my heart grew a desire to see him, to somehow be near him just once in my lifetime. I wasn't sure how this would happen, but I knew with certainty that it would.

Three years passed.

In a very simple fashion, I will chronicle for you the lavish generosity of God in fulfilling this desire of my heart.

To set the stage, I should begin by saying that as I grow older (I was in my 20s then!), I've become more and more a homebody with a dislike for travel. With this said, I can still vividly recall the moment when Sister Joseph Louise caught up with me in our parking lot and told me that I had a letter from Mother Regina Marie in my mailbox. Somehow I knew instinctively that I was going to World Youth Day. I also knew it was related to my desire to see Pope Benedict XVI. Needless to say, I did a little dance in the privacy of my office!

July 4, 2008 – At the airport, Sister Grace Helena and I joined 50 other women religious from the United Stated representing the CMSWR (Council of Major Superiors of Women Religious). Off to Sydney!

July 12, 2008 – Fast forward a couple of days which were full to the brim as we were serving as volunteers for World Youth Day. It just happened that we were at the right place at the right time – God at work. We went to the chancery office for Mass as it was near our assigned place of work.

I remember walking past a Dominican Sister to enter the Chapel. Later I found out she was responsible for the Liturgy for men and women religious in formation. At that time she was looking for one more sister who was in formation, from overseas and from a different community. Yours truly fit the bill. Though I was perpetually professed, I still looked "young" to show that I was in initial formation, am Korean and a Carmelite. She mentioned to me that although I would still need to get security clearance, there was a high probability that I would be one of the 50 receiving Holy Communion from our Holy Father.

How good God is! It is mind-boggling to think that God would literally take me across the globe simply to show me that He is God and that He is near. True desires of our heart do not go unheeded. Years later, as I write this brief reflection, it still amazes me that God would love me so much so as to go to such lengths to tangibly express His love.

July 14, 2008 – We don't usually celebrate our birthdays in Carmel (we celebrate feast days) but wanted to note it here as it was another "special touch" from the good Lord. Sister Grace Helena and I wanted to attend a free concert at the Sydney Opera House that evening. We heard that it was full to capacity, so didn't think much more of it. We attended an early evening Mass and crossed paths with a couple of Dominican sisters who were on their way to the concert. They invited us to attend and we literally careened over in a taxi to the Opera House (it was clear across town) and made it just in time. It was there that the previously mentioned Dominican Sister saw me and presented me with my "official" ticket for receiving Holy Communion from Pope Benedict.

July 17, 2008 – Sister Grace Helena and I were stationed this day to serve at the Cathedral in Sydney. I was assigned to the main body of the Church and Sister to the crypt. Towards early evening after I completed my shift, I went down below to wait for Sister. To get to the crypt, one walks down an alleyway and mid-way to your left is the entrance to the crypt. If one were to continue walking down the alleyway, it would lead you to the next street where the Cardinal resides. It was not possible to get to that side of the block as the alley had a gate that was kept securely locked.

Only two of us were present outside the crypt as most pilgrims had already departed. All of a sudden we heard and saw a swirl of action. There was a sudden influx of security personnel and Sister nonchalantly meandered down to the end of the alley. She gestured for me to join her. I said "No." She gestured more emphatically so I, too, nonchalantly walked over to her. As we looked out through the bars of the gate, we saw our Holy Father exiting out of his vehicle and entering the Cardinal's residence. True, we only saw the back of his head – but you have to understand how close he was to us! Another God-moment. All I can say is "Thank you, Sister Grace Helena!"

July 18, 2008 – The Holy Sacrifice of the Mass at the Cathedral with Pope Benedict XVI. After forging my way through security, I entered the Cathedral and found a seat in the designated section. It was relatively close to the altar and near the middle aisle. As our Holy Father processed in, I could have literally reached out to touch him, that is, if I was open to the idea of running over the two ladies to my right. It is not possible to express the glory of attending Mass where the Vicar of Christ is present. The profound humility of our then Holy Father was tangible and I would presume to say that his sanctity must have been obvious even to those who were hardened of heart. When it came time, I made my way into the communion line. As I got closer and closer, there was a wave of peace that washed over me and I can still hear his voice saying, "Body of Christ." No further words are needed to expound on this experience.

July 20, 2008 – This was the day our Holy Father would be leaving to return home to Rome. Wonderfully, all the volunteers for World Youth Day were invited to attend an open-air gathering at which our Holy Father would make his closing remarks. Just as a side comment – Sister Grace Helena and I left very early to be there on time so that we could get good seats. As was our custom, we headed out in the wrong direction. I was oftentimes the one responsible for this and I have to admit that I've never done so much walking in my life! Needless to say, we got lost but thankfully, another volunteer saw us standing on a corner, pulled up the taxi, and we arrived in enough time to be close to the stage. Just to be in his presence again made everything worthwhile. When he departed, there was an immense feeling of loss as we knew we would no longer see him. I do realize how blessed we were to have had so many close "encounters" with our Holy Father. Most only saw him on a screen. God is truly lavish in His generosity.

For those who have never been to a World Youth Day, it is an opportunity for young people around the world to experience the fatherly presence of the Vicar of Christ, an opportunity for young people to visibly see the Church FULLY alive. To see thousands of young people proclaiming their love for Christ and to see the love and affection they have for the pope, in this case, an elderly man who had wished nothing more than to remain in quiet obscurity, leaves no doubt in one's mind that the Church is alive and that the Holy Spirit is in charge.

What Pope Benedict XVI sacrificed for his love for God and His Church is truly beyond our understanding. I would venture to say that most of us would not have been able to do what he did. Here was a man beyond retirement age, who had experienced poor health in the past, was quiet in nature and delighted in his studies. At this time of his life, he was asked to take on the burden of the Universal Church and in his humility, in his trust in God, said yes and carried the burden well for eight years. It amazes me that the secular press can miss this and focus on things like the color of his shoes. Mind-boggling, really. Enough said on the matter.

Pope Benedict XVI has inspired hundreds of thousands of people around the world, probably millions. One day, we hope he will know that in Alhambra, California, he has deeply touched the lives of a group of Carmelite Sisters who continue to love him and pray for him. To this living saint, we say, "May God reward you, good and faithful servant."

"Windows of the Soul:

The Photo of Pope Pius XII in My Classroom"

by Sister Timothy Marie, O.C.D.

*A*S A SMALL CHILD GROWING UP IN THE 1950s, I attended Catholic school in Long Beach, California. So many impressions of those years remain with me. One still stands out vividly in my mind so many, many years later. It was a photograph of Pope Pius XII hanging on the wall of my classroom.

I was intrigued by his profile. It was to me, even at that young age, a study in his character. I recall a lean face looking straightforward, a firm mouth set in seriousness, large, expressive eyes that appeared even larger through his rounded glasses. It is said that "the eyes are the windows of the soul." Even as a young child in grade school, I had heard that expression, and spent a great deal of time thinking about that as I gazed at the photo when classes seemed boring to the point of pain.

His eyes were clear, open and straightforward. Somehow a feeling of trust emanated from them, a sense of authority, too. They looked to me as if they had seen a lot of suffering. All of us in our class took both the Holy Father and his photo for granted. He was just there in the classroom, along with the crucifix and the statue of Our Lady we crowned with flowers every May and us. His was a comforting presence. We were Catholic, and our church was universal, and Rome was the place where everything was centered.

Every First Friday during those Cold War years, two things happened. We had an air raid drill and when we heard the shrill siren, all of us dove under our desks until the all-clear sounded and we got up and continued our work where we left off.

Another thing happened every First Friday, something that remains crystal clear in my mind today, sixty years later. The 8th grade student body president would say over the intercom before lunch time: "Today is the First Friday of the month. Let us all join together to pray the prayer that Our Holy Father, Pope Pius XII has asked us to pray, The Act of Consecration of the Human Race to the Sacred Heart of Jesus." We would then say the prayer together with him. You don't even need to ask; of course we had it memorized. And as I remember it, we loved to stop our class work to say this all together. It gave us, at least it gave me, a sense of doing something to help our poor, hurting world.

Act of Consecration of the Human Race to the Sacred Heart of Jesus:
"Most sweet Jesus, Redeemer of the human race, look down upon us, humbly prostrate before Thine altar. We are Thine and Thine we wish to be; but to be more surely united with Thee, behold each one of us freely consecrates himself today to Thy Most Sacred Heart.

Many, indeed, have never known Thee; many, too, despising Thy precepts, have rejected Thee. Have mercy on them all, most merciful Jesus, and draw them to Thy Sacred Heart.

Be Thou King, O Lord, not only of the faithful who have never forsaken Thee, but also of the prodigal children who have abandoned Thee. Grant that they may quickly return to their Father's house, lest they die of wretchedness and hunger. Be Thou King of those who are deceived by erroneous opinions, or whom discord keeps aloof and call them back to the harbor of truth and unity of faith, so that soon there may be but one flock and one shepherd.

Grant, O Lord, to Thy Church, assurance of freedom and immunity from harm; give peace and order to all nations, and make the earth resound from pole to pole with one cry: Praise to the Divine Heart that wrought our salvation: to it be glory and honor forever. Amen."

Even as children we already knew that he had written an encyclical called *Mystici Corporis,* Latin for the Mystical Body of Christ. We knew that the Church is the Mystical Body of Christ and we understood that just as the parts of the human body work together, so too do all the members of the Church – that we form one body, one Body in Christ.

During those years, our Catholicism was an everyday natural part of our life. I thank God for my Catholic elementary school and the dear sisters and lay staff who taught us. In our convent, we have a photo of our current pope, Pope Francis. I hope all Catholic homes and schools have one today, that it may be for them the silent testimony that it was for me.

"One picture is worth a thousand words."

Pope Pius XII, pray for us.

A Journey to
the Heart of the Church:
Blogging from Rome

by Sister Mary Scholastica, O.C.D.

*F*IRST IMPRESSIONS OF ROME…
Let's begin with the mundane: the birds, bugs, people and driving. It's quite different in Italy. The birds are louder – pigeons dive bombing sea gulls makes for quite a concert. Mosquito bites don't itch, though it makes me wonder what bit me, and I have yet to differentiate between angry versus loud conversations among the people.

Roman driving needs an entire section for itself. All the way home from the airport, I had to keep pushing my jaw back up. Back in the United States, we have lines that differentiate one side of the street from the other. The lines also clearly separate the direction of the driving. We have traffic lights that indicate whether you go or stop and pedestrians have the right of way. My brief observations of traffic in Italy have led me to the conclusion that passive drivers would never survive. A moment of hesitation could land you in the hospital! On a two lane street, there are usually three lanes of cars and motorcyclists driving in between the cars every which way. Their driving skills are amazing. If you are walking across the street on a green light, you better run fast and look out or you'll be run over.

From the airport to my final destination, my driver got in a mini-accident, though he braked in time for it to be minimal. I still can't tell who was in the wrong as both drivers seemed to be driving erratically and both seemed to be vocal about indicating it wasn't their fault. Amazing. That's all I can say. It's safest on a bus as the bus is so big, it definitely has the right of way.

June 21, 2014

Today is the feast day of St. Aloysius Gonzaga, the patron of our Foundress, Venerable Mother Luisita, who was born on this day in 1866. What a lovely day it was! It began in the best way possible. Our two sisters who live and work here in Rome made it possible for me to attend the private Mass of Cardinal Parolin, Secretary of State for the Vatican. I don't understand a word of Italian but even so, the homily seemed beautiful!

From there, one of our sisters obtained permission to give me a tour of the Apostolic Palace. I can't quite explain what it's like. Rome is quite something in and of itself, but when you are inside Vatican City, you get an even stronger sense of being in the heart of the Church. We walked through the Sistine Chapel, St. Peter's and then made our way to the Angelicum. On the way home, we got off the bus before our actual stop and walked through a couple of churches, the highlight being the Jesu. There is so much beauty everywhere that one needs to step back and just sit with it to more deeply appreciate what the senses are so quickly taking in. The churches here are breathtaking!

June 23, 2014

Shall I give you another entire paragraph or two on Roman driving? I'm hoping that the sisters here aren't getting tired of my ongoing commentary on the driving. It's fascinating. Before I close the topic for now, two drivers did let me cross the street in a most gracious manner so there is hope after all! On a side note – the foot traffic in Rome makes the Los Angeles Airport look boring.

I am blessed to be in Rome to attend a summer study session hosted by the CMSWR (Council of Major Superiors of Women Religious). The study days kick off tomorrow evening and in the meantime I have been trying to get a taste of Rome, acclimate to the time change, etc. Another side note, in case you're ever here and you'd like to know, Romans sleep between 3:30am-7am and between 1pm-3pm. At least this is what the sound level seems to indicate.

Today began bright and early with a morning trip to the Vatican. I learned that within the vicinity of Rome there are 900 churches! There seems to be one on almost every other block.

I had the morning to walk through St. Peter's. Amazing. To think that human hands built St. Peter's! It has the touch of God in every corner, every ceiling, every statue. And it was built without the luxury of electricity and power tools. Goes to show you where there's a will, there's a way.

I had the privilege of praying by St. Pope John Paul II's tomb for a length of time. Because it was so early in the morning there was hardly anyone there and at one point, I was there by myself. It was a most moving experience. In my mind's eye I see him youthful, vibrant, energetic, strong. He epitomized gentle firmness. He was a father to so many of us and I imagine that he is now closer to us then he could ever physically have been in this life. I remembered each of my Sisters by name, and the needs of each of our Carmels as well as all our friends and benefactors. Our Holy Father had the heart of a Carmelite so I figured we were his daughters in a double whammy sort of way.

I spent a good chunk of the morning just walking through St. Peter's and trying to soak it all in. We are Catholic – and proud of it!

From St. Peter's I walked back to our residence, about a 20 minute walk, and visited every Church along the way including the Jesu, where the hand/arm of St. Francis Xavier is on display for veneration. There are so many spiritual treasures, I cannot keep track of it all!

One last interesting note before I sign off for the day, on the way from where we are staying to the bus stop, we pass by the ruins of what used to be some sort of Senate building. It is overcrowded with stray cats. I learned that the city continues to be kind to cats because when the city was facing ruin and the people were threatened with starvation, they lived off the cats. Now to all cat lovers this is probably not what you want to be reading, but at least you can be comforted in knowing that was centuries ago and now the cats enjoy a semi-protected status. When the sisters give me directions, they tell me, "Go past the cats and turn left….or go past the cats and turn right." Forget about the ancient ruins…it's all about the cats!   I'll try to end with a holier thought next time.

June 25, 2014

Today was the first formal day of our summer study session. Father John Cush, our presenter for the first two days, began his first conference by noting that the principal way Rome teaches us is by bringing us out of ourselves. In Rome, we are in the heart of the Church, the heart of an international Church which is composed of people from different cultures, different religious communities, dioceses, etc. We step beyond the borders of what we know and how we do things and turn outwards, growing in knowledge of each other and the world around us.

We attended Mass in the room in which Saint Ignatius died which has been converted into a Chapel. I was surprised to learn that St. Ignatius was very short. I have always unconsciously equated the high caliber of his person, his great sanctity, with physical size. In fact, I pictured him as something of a giant. He was probably only about five feet tall but he had a very large soul! Seeing the mask of his "death face," which was the mold put on his face after his death, the only pair of sandals that he owned and wore, his vest, some of his books and a document with his actual handwriting made him very real to us. It is a gift to walk where the Saints have walked. And by the way, Saint Ignatius had beautiful penmanship.

Father said today that those who come to Rome cannot help but leave Rome a different person than when they first arrived, transformed with a deeper love for the good Lord and His Church. May it be so.

July 5, 2014

As I reflect on these days in Rome, I am realizing how RICHLY blessed we are in our Catholic tradition. So often we only hear what the media presents to us. Journalists and reporters help form our thinking, our opinions. And let's get this straight, if you think the media communicates the complete truth, let me break it to you not so gently – they don't. We had the opportunity of having some media coverage for a project we were working on. Of the five or so different media outlets we worked with, though they all received more or less the same information and the facts were pretty simple, every single one got something wrong, and in some cases skewed the information or misunderstood. This was for a small project. Can you imagine what they are communicating in the way of our Church? Especially since they don't particularly appreciate all that we stand for?

We had the privilege of touring the Congregation of the Doctrine of the Faith (CDF). This is the congregation that Pope Benedict XVI headed as prefect when he was still Cardinal Ratzinger. This tour actually impacted me more than seeing the holy sites because it reminded me that our Church is made up of people. We have our moments – both good and bad – and regardless of the bad, we still have a most beautiful Church. Not the tyrannizing hierarchy that the media portrays, nor a behind the times, old-fashioned institution out of touch with reality and consisting of greedy plotting individuals. Not at all! The Vatican is not separate from you and me – we are one. It's not them and us. It's just US.

Though not minimizing our challenges and faults, we have a rich heritage, a rich history, a rich future. We have the Lord. If you could TRULY understand the richness of our faith, and the holy people who make up the body of Christ, people who love our Catholic faith, you would be inspired, uplifted, renewed. I'll get off my soapbox now. I wish you could see what I'm seeing and understand what I'm trying to say. We Catholics need to learn about our faith, love it. Love the Church, friends. Love her!

July 14, 2014

We've been to many places, seen many beautiful works of art from centuries past, walked in the footsteps of the saints, learned more about the inner workings of our Church and experienced firsthand what it means to be in the "heart of the Church". What I thought I'd do as we wrap up our time in Rome was to share with you some personal highlights.

St. Peter's Basilica … it feels like you're home when you're there. To look upon St. Peter's as you're walking towards it, to see the majesty and to know the history is truly sublime. People from all walks of life and from all around the world are pouring through the doors daily. Priests and religious from so many different communities serving and going to school while living in Rome add a unique flavor all on their own. Most importantly, the presence of the Successor of Peter in residence encompasses it all. The wonderful unity with all the diversity. Pretty amazing, really. What other Church has this? Saint Peter's is definitely holy ground. If you do not know the history of the basilica, look it up. I don't think I would do it justice here. Let me just note that through the centuries, with all who built upon the original tomb, it is only God who could plan it to be so. That the monuments/churches built on top of the original tomb would all line up into one straight line. This happened with people not knowing what was underneath when they were building. Look it up and see for yourself.

Castel Gandolfo … a little town where our Holy Father usually resides during the summer. We were blessed to see the telescope that is housed here and used in the Vatican Observatory. What really blows my mind is all that I am learning about the contributions our Church has made for the betterment of man and for ongoing growth and knowledge. Science is not separated from God, it actually proves there is a God. What was so refreshing here, as well, was the beauty of our surroundings. All the mosaics and paintings in the world, even those done by Michelangelo, Rafael, etc., pale in comparison to God's creation. To just sit and gaze at the beauty of God's creation lifts the soul up and refreshes the spirit. If you have a chance, step away from the busyness of the day to day, the concrete buildings and immerse yourself in the beauty of nature, it makes a difference.

Subiaco... here lies the cave in which St. Benedict lived for three years of his life. When you hear cave, you are probably thinking a hole in the wall near the foot of a hill. Saint Benedict's cave is actually near the top. It was hewn out of the side of a mountain and since then an entire monastery has been built around this cave. The hillside covered with green, green, green trees (did I mention the trees were green!?) is breathtaking. And from their vantage point, you can see way out into the countryside for miles on end. Here in this cave, St. Benedict allowed the good Lord to work in him, to prepare him for what was to come. He then went on to establish at least twelve monasteries and is called the Father of Western Monasticism. St. Benedict is St. Scholastica's twin brother, which is probably why Subiaco was doubly fascinating for me.

All in all, our time here in Rome was richly blessed. The last remembrance I'd like to note is how edifying it was to see and meet so many priests and bishops who not only sincerely love our Church but are striving to be men of God in total service to her. We don't hear about this often – but know it to be true. God bless you and signing off!

Sister Mary Scholastica
Your Roman Correspondent

Our Religious Family

*"Religious profession expresses the gift of self to God and to the Church –
a gift which is lived in the community of a religious family."*
- Fraternal Life In Community, 44

The Wrong Carol

An Interview with Sister Mary Jeanne and Her Parents

from "Spirit of Carmel"

S PIRIT OF CARMEL SPENT AN AFTERNOON amidst the tangible love and faith which abounds in the Coderre home – a time filled with abundant joy and much laughter with the Coderre family. We spoke with Homer and Bertha Coderre, as well as their daughter, Sister Mary Jeanne Coderre, a Carmelite Sister of the Most Sacred Heart of Los Angeles.

SPIRIT OF CARMEL: How did the two of you first meet each other?

HOMER: One day when my Dad returned from deer hunting in New Brunswick, Canada, he told me of a girl who lived on a 150 acre farm there. He said, "That girl can even milk cows." Since I was a country boy, I thought that was great and I decided that I wanted to get to know that girl. My father had asked her if she would like to correspond and be a pen pal with his daughters. I overheard this, and still quite impressed with this girl who could milk cows, got her address from one of my sisters and wrote her a letter asking if she would like to be my pen pal. I sent a photo along with the letter. By return mail, she responded and that was the beginning of a long relationship. Bertha and I recently celebrated our 70th wedding anniversary!

BERTHA: We were pen pals for about a year during 1938. In 1939, there was a big Sportsmen's Show in Boston with a special round trip train fare that would let me travel from my home in New Brunswick, Canada to Boston (about 500 miles) for ten dollars. I arranged to meet Homer in the train station and told him I would be wearing a maroon coat and hat. He found me and met me with a kiss. A year and a half later, we were married and made our home in Auburn, Massachusetts.

SPIRIT OF CARMEL: Your daughter became a Carmelite Sister. Tell us about your family.

HOMER: Religion was always a very important part of our lives. Both Bertha and I were baptized and raised Catholic. I was an altar boy. We were married at Sacred Heart Church in New Brunswick, a little country church. Our son Joseph was born the next year and Sister Mary Jeanne the following year.

BERTHA: We lived out in the country and the priest came only on Sundays. Our little Church was across the river from our house, and we would often cross the river in our little boat to attend Mass. I never saw a Catholic nun until I met Homer's sister, Sister Mary Cyril, RSM.

SISTER MARY JEANNE: I have many memories of visiting my aunt at her convent when I was still very small. To be a Sister was one of the many things on my list of life's choices when I grew up. During my high school years, many other choices took precedence although I don't think that the desire ever left my heart

SPIRIT OF CARMEL: When did your daughter first show signs of a religious vocation?

HOMER: When Sister Mary Jeanne was only five years old she would come home from catechism class and invite all the non-catholic children over to teach them what she had learned in class.

BERTHA: Sister Mary Jeanne learned to love God at a very young age. One day when she was three or four, Homer was composting our trash. He was burying a large stuffed dog that he had removed the wheels from to use for one of his many projects. Sister Mary Jeanne was watching and she asked, "Daddy, will the dog go to heaven?" Homer replied, "No, only people go to heaven." Sister Mary Jeanne thought for a moment and then with a twinkle in her eye responded, "Wouldn't it be a good trick on God if it did!"

SPIRIT OF CARMEL: Tell us about your move from Auburn, Massachusetts to West Covina, California?

HOMER: I liked Auburn very much, but I made a comment that I would like to see California before I died. At the time, work was slow and I thought I might be laid off. My sister and her husband were moving to California, and we decided to do the same. Joe was eleven and Sister Mary Jeanne was ten years old. We arrived in California in December of 1953.

BERTHA: With the two children and our dog we drove to California. Our new home was in West Covina in the San Gabriel Valley. That is where we still live.

SPIRIT OF CARMEL: How did Sister Mary Jeanne let you know about her vocation?

HOMER: One night she asked me if I was in a good mood. She asked if I had any objections to her entering the convent. "Whatever is going to make you the happiest in this life is what will make me the happiest," I remember telling her. After she entered the convent, I can say that I have never, ever, ever had a day when she did not radiate with happiness when we saw her. Some of our good friends didn't understand how we could allow her to go into a convent. All I could think of was, "Well, my daughter is married to Christ, and she will always be happy. When a woman gets married, she sometimes experiences great unhappiness in her marriage. I know that my daughter made a wise choice and she has always been happy."

It was the strangest thing though. Although I had no objection to her entering the convent, the first time I saw her after she had entered, I got the strangest feeling. My stomach did flip flops. It did something to me to see her wearing that postulant uniform. To see her transformed like that, it was then that the realization came to me of what God had called her to.

SISTER MARY JEANNE: In my senior year of high school, the Carmelite Sisters joined the teaching staff, and I remember so well the first time I met Sister Mary Gonzaga, my Spanish teacher. The thought involuntarily crossed my mind that if I ever entered the convent, this is the order I would choose. Some of my classmates and myself signed up to volunteer in the junior auxiliary at Sacred Heart Retreat House, where we met more Carmelite Sisters and the novices and postulants.

After graduating from high school, I attended a local junior college and became friends with a young lady named Carol who was going to enter the Carmelite Sisters. One day, she asked me if I would like to go "along for the ride" when she visited the Vocation Directress of the Carmelite Sisters. I loved being with the Sisters and readily accepted. This time the twinkle was in God's eye! After we arrived, my friend Carol went off with the Vocation Directress, and I was enjoying visiting with the sisters. Suddenly to my surprise, Sister Rosemary came to tell me that the Mother Superior wanted to see me in her office! My name before entering Carmel was Carolyn and at the Retreat House the sisters always called me Carol. When the Superior sent Sister to call Carol (the girl with the vocation), she called me by mistake! I was very shy and told Sister that I was sure that the Mother Superior did not want to see me. Sister answered that she did! I repeated with emphasis that I was sure she didn't want to see me. Sister remained confident that she did! When we arrived at the Superior's office, I told Sister, "Well, even if she wants to see me, I don't want to see her!" Sister gently opened the door and ushered me inside. After speaking with the Mother Superior for a little while the Vocation Directress came in and with an astonished look on her face said, "You have the wrong Carol!" The Superior smiled and calmly responded, "This one is going to enter too!" Carol and I did enter together, and then Carol left six days later.

BERTHA: I wasn't surprised. She would always be helping people, attending church even more frequently than we did, and Homer and I would notice her slipping away to her room to pray for a while. She had a statue of the Blessed Mother, Our Lady of Grace and a picture of Saint Therese, the Little Flower in her room. The statue of Our Lady glowed in the dark. We brought them from Massachusetts.

We know that she is happy, and it seems that anyone who meets her always remarks how fortunate we are to have a daughter like her. Sister Mary Jeanne has done a lot of things over her 50 years as a Carmelite. She worked many years as an X-ray and nuclear medicine technologist, worked in the schools and child care centers where the Carmelite Sisters serve, and was also the archivist of the Community. We are very proud of her.

SISTER MARY JEANNE: When God invites one to the unspeakable joy of being His Spouse, He gently removes all obstacles. My shyness would definitely have been an obstacle to my inquiring about entering Carmel on my own, yet such was His love that He arranged it for me! This has been the story over and over throughout my religious life. God takes our desire to give Him the little that we have, and He returns it one-hundred fold.

I have been blessed beyond recounting. My beloved parents have been supportive of everything that I have done. Their example of love and fidelity has inspired me in my own perseverance in my wonderful religious vocation as a spouse of Jesus

Christ and a Carmelite Sister of the Most Sacred Heart of Los Angeles.

SPIRIT OF CARMEL: On July 14, 2011, Homer and Bertha celebrated their seventieth wedding anniversary and they were present to rejoice with Sister Mary Jeanne on June 29, 2012 as she walked down the aisle once again, celebrating her Golden Jubilee of 50 years as a Carmelite Sister of the Most Sacred Heart of Los Angeles.

(This article is an excerpt taken from Spirit of Carmel magazine, Volume VI, originally printed by the Carmelite Sisters in 2011).

Spirituality Ain't For Sissies

My Reflections on 18 hours
with the Carmelite Sisters

by Jenine Baines

A GLIMPSE INTO CARMEL LIKE "NUN" OTHER...

Recently I received a gift as precious to me as the peridot ring I wear daily, bequeathed to me by my Aunt Edith after her death. This gift, however, is quite different from Aunt Edith's ring. I can't look at it; I can't hand it on to my own daughter or niece; I can't lock it away for safekeeping; I can't clean it or buy earrings to match it. But what I can do is hold the memory of it close, close, close in my heart and do my best to put this gift to great use, as the Carmelite Sisters requested when they welcomed me to spend a day with them – not on retreat, per se, but as one of them.

It's a daunting task, to convey what this once-in-a-lifetime experience – this incredible gift, this wondrous opportunity to "go deeper," to be let into a day in the lives of the Sisters – was like. Usually all it takes is a deadline to bring on a massive attack of Writer's Block. But from the moment I told Sister Mary Scholastica that, yes, I would "shadow the Sisters" then share my thoughts about it, my heart began to race and my brain threatened to shut down in stark terror. "Oh Father God," I prayed more than once. "Please make me worthy of this honor. Please don't let me mess this up."

Aunt Edith's ring sparkles. So does my memory of my day in Alhambra. Now the real work begins. With God's help, may the words I write reflect the peace, joy and wonder that illuminate our lives whenever we encounter the Sisters...

4:23 A.M.

I can't remember when I was last up this early, but I'm due in Alhambra for Morning Prayer at 5:25 a.m., and I don't want to be late. When my alarm went off at 4 a.m., I thought of how the Sisters awaken – with song. I love that about the Sisters, how one Sister begins singing when it's time to get out of bed (does SHE use an alarm clock?) then the others join in.

It's dark, and I'm hesitant to turn on a light because I don't want to disturb my husband, but in the end, it's just too scary-hard to see. So, I relent and flip the switch on a small lamp near the doorway. I note that there are some sheaves of white paper on the floor and stoop to pick them up. It's the program from the day before, when Sister Margaret Mary and Sister Catherine Marie made their Perpetual Profession of Vows at Santa Teresita in Duarte, California. Instantly, my heart lifts. I know it's going to be an extraordinary day. Because what line do my eyes fall right on? "With joyful hearts let us sing."

5:25 A.M.

I'm not feeling quite so joyful right now. And I'm certainly not feeling like singing. I'm ticked off, to put it mildly. OF COURSE I got behind; barring a miracle, I'm going to be late for my Big Day. Yet another light turns red just as I approach it… And it hits me: a line that I know I'm going to have to use somewhere in the article. A re-working of Bette Davis' famous lament about old age.

"Spirituality ain't for sissies."

Truly, this early morning start to a day is tough. Yet, the Sisters do this EVERY morning, year after year, and somehow I doubt they're ever late. How do they do it!?

As I throw a smile at Sister Mary Scholastica and catch my breath in the back pew, the Answer is sent. I recall the words of Mother Regina Marie, when I asked her how to find time for prayer in a busy day: "In your living daily life look for truth, goodness, beauty and love. These are four names of God and when you encounter Him you will desire more. You can't help it. Love impels. And then it is easy to find times and ways to be with someone you love. It takes the spiritual life out of the arena of compulsion or obligatory burden. Love impels. Love is creative."

6:15 A.M. AT MASS

It comes to me that the Sisters are called "Sisters" for good reason. They are indeed a Family. Their shared faith and love of God binds them at least as much, if not more tightly than shared genes and chromosomes.

"The Sisters have a genuine love for one another," Father Anthony, the Sisters' Chaplain, tells me later in the day. I am a member of the family, too, I discover. Mass has become a teaching moment: "Good morning, my dear Sisters…and Jenine," Father Anthony greets us.

6:45 A.M. WAITING FOR BREAKFAST

I'm waiting in the chapel for Sister Timothy Marie to fetch me to breakfast. The quiet brings an irresistible deliverance. I make a vow to start my own day everyday like this. Quiet first. Coffee, feeding the cats, answering email – all can wait. As the Carmelites have written: "And if we need to purify, empty, purge, clean (the human heart) out so God can fill it with Himself, then so be it. This is Carmelite spirituality."

Sister Mary Scholastica has loaned me a prayer book. I open it at random and begin reading. One set of responses strikes me hard:

V. Seat of Wisdom
R. Pray for us

At some point before breakfast, Sister Timothy Marie gives me a brief tutorial on the history of the Carmelites. We tour a series of exhibits tucked off in a couple of rooms in a corner of the convent. I find myself especially intrigued by the photos of the Carmelites' founder, Mother Luisita. What courage she had and what faith! (To learn more about her story and the religious persecution she and the early Sisters fled from in Mexico, visit the Sisters' website, www.carmelitesistersocd.com/foundress/writings.asp.)

A weird but thoroughly reverent thought comes to mind: there are such things as super heroes. The Venerable Mother Maria Luisa Josefa of the Most Blessed Sacrament is a true Super Hero…a crusader in a habit, not a cape or tights. Mother Luisita comes to life not on celluloid or in a comic book but in our hearts. "For greater things you were born," she exhorts us.

And what are those greater things? As Mother's daughters now tell us, "This means that we must make a decision, with God's grace, to no longer fill our minds with rubbish, spend our money on unimportant trivial trinkets that in the end only rot away, or set our hearts on worldly, inconsequential entities that do not nourish but only weaken the human spirit."

Amen.

BREAKFAST

Breakfast is heaven. For one thing, I'm hungry. (You don't know fear until you're at Morning Prayer, when the silence shouts, and your stomach persists in growling at rock music decibels.) For another, I didn't have to prepare it.

I am in the capable hands of Jessica. Jessica is not a Sister – not yet – but already she's got the Loving Thing down. I feel very blessed, very well cared for, and very welcomed.

I pull out my iphone to snap a photo because I am tickled chartreuse when I discover the teabags. Scripture verses are printed on them – scripture verses!

And mine blows me away. It's Proverbs 3:5-6, the first verse I memorized after a 15 year long 'dark night' as a reluctant, angry atheist. It's a verse I hold dear and recite to myself often. "Trust in the Lord with all your heart and lean not on your own understanding; in all your ways acknowledge Him, and He will make your paths straight."

10:00 A.M.

The Lord – and Sister Mary Scholastica – have set me on a path I certainly didn't expect. I am going to take a break from making devotions and make scones instead. Sister Meredith, a novice, and Sister Maria Goretti, (who, I learn to my delight, once shared my love of high-heeled shoes,) will guide me.

The scones are for guests attending the coming weekend's retreat. As the two Sisters whip up batter, my job is to take each heaping mound of dough, flatten it into a pancake-sized mound, set each circle on a baking sheet, then cut it into eighths.

I'm hesitant because I am no Paula Dean. But, after a brief, panicked prayer that I won't thoroughly humiliate myself, I give it a try. This is to be a day not only of discovery but transformation, after all. I only wish the transformation hadn't included wearing this really ugly black hairnet but it's chocolate chips, lemon or coffee the Sisters want in the batter, not a long unruly hair, so I comply and thank God that the Carmelites aren't into mirrors.

(Amazing factoid learned: the Sisters have no mirrors in their rooms. They act as one another's mirrors, if a veil needs to be straightened or a sleeve adjusted.)

We're having a grand time, the girls and I. We laugh a lot. These girls are REAL, a discovery I have long sensed but have this morning confirmed about all the Sisters. Nevertheless, my heart nearly breaks and a lump comes to my throat when I hear how Sister Meredith makes a request of Sister Maria Goretti; it's almost too beautiful to be borne.

"In your charity, will you please…," Sister asks.

Duly, Sister Maria Goretti passes the sugar or whatever and what does Sister reply? "God reward you."

The Sisters have made a request of me… and, oh, how I am already being rewarded.

MID MORNING CLASS

The weather is absolutely perfect so we meet outdoors, all the postulants and novices and I. They're taking a break from classes, which include but are not limited to human formation/development, Christian courtesy (oh, how the rest of us could benefit from courses in this!), Catholic doctrine, Scripture study, and Carmelite spirituality. Course work also delves into the Carmelite order's Constitutions, Vows and Liturgy.

The route to 'graduation' – to receiving a ring as a sign of total consecration to God and becoming a Perpetually Professed Sister – takes far longer than I expected.

The process begins with one to two years in Candidacy program. "It's a time of serious discernment to our community by living an approved lifestyle," the Candidate Directress, Sister Mary Patrice, explains. "The young woman continues to grow in her spiritual life through a deeper living of a sacramental life and develops an authentic prayer life. It's also a time where both the candidate and the community begin to determine whether she can live a vowed life in our community."

Candidates live together in the Carmelites' candidacy house but, while they work with the Sisters and pray with the Sisters, they receive payment as a staff member and retain their own goods such as a car, cell phone and iPods.

For Postulants, the going gets a bit more rigorous. These are the young women you see wearing blue uniforms but no veils. They live now in the cloister and, for six to twelve months, deepen their commitment to prayer, doctrinal study and community living. "The postulant gradually and calmly accustoms herself to the detachment spoken of in the Gospel which is indispensable for prayer and service," Sister Mary Patrice tells me.

I might twitch at that word "detachment," but any young woman wearing a white veil has made her peace with the concept. She is a novice, now, and officially part of the Carmelite order. As such, she takes on a new name, "Sister (fill in the blank)." The novitiate lasts for two years. "Six months prior to the end of the two year period, if the novice has grown stronger in her conviction that God is calling her to our community, she requests in writing to make a profession of the vows," says Sister Mary Patrice.

After making her vows, the novice becomes a Temporary Professed Sister. The vow lasts for a period of one year. Then, for the next six years, the Sister continues to renew her vows. Only at the end of this cycle does the Sister make her Perpetual Vows.

Total commitment in time: ten years.

So, as we chat, I study the girls intently. I don't quite get them: how on earth do they find the inner grit to make the sacrifices a life of chastity, poverty and obedience requires? What can their decision teach me, a flawed, too frequently materialistic and vain creature of the secular world?

What I ultimately figure out is this: New to the process as they are, these young women are head over heels in love. It's no accident that, when they make their vows, readings from Song of Songs make up part of the liturgy. Christ is indeed a Sister's bridegroom and her children, the rest of us. Besides that, the silly stuff I focus on – not being able to shop in the mall for an outfit or a pair of high heels or to eat a large popcorn at the movies – is just that, silly and, well, kind of embarrassing.

A vocation is not a sacrifice. It's the best gift possible. It's a foretaste – sheltered and nurtured within the cloister's walls and the order's daily rituals – of Heaven.

THE EXAMEN
This is where the pedal meets the metal, so to speak. Every day, in their private

chapel, a bit before noon, the Sisters practice the Jesuit Examen of Conscience. An ancient practice developed by St. Ignatius in his Spiritual Exercises, the Examen asks us to reflect on the events of the day and ask God's guidance in discerning His presence and direction for us.

Alas, I find myself distracted. Here, there are no pews, as you and I would expect to find them, but individual prayer 'cubbies,' (choir stalls), one for each Sister. Sister Timothy Marie shows me to mine and, following the Sisters' example, I kneel.

Within moments, the expression "spirituality ain't for sissies" has enhanced meaning for me. Try kneeling with no support but your own body, no pew to relax against, and you'll soon understand what I mean. My knees ache, my back feels every one of its 55 years, and I suddenly am very aware that I awoke at 4 a.m.

I don't pray per se. But, as I focus on breathing God in and, then, breathing the dark 'stuff' of life out; in and out, in and out – advice garnered from my great friend and advisor Sister Carmelina – I reflect on the Evangelical term 'prayer warriors'. Here, in this chapel, are God's five star generals.

And I am awed. While my knees and back still fuss and groan, my heart sings a small soft song of gratitude.

LUNCH
Lunch is a treat and a blast with Sister Mary Scholastica ... and Mother Regina Marie! She has hurried back from a meeting in San Pedro to keep our 'date', I learn. This is where I also learn how humility really feels. That Mother has taken time to meet with me when she is so incredibly busy is such an honor: it scares me stiff. I am haunted with the hideous certainty that, when it's time to face that blank screen on my computer, no words will come. I can't do this. There is no way I will rise to this challenge if Christ isn't sitting there beside me and the Holy Spirit working away within me.

(Interesting factoid: The Sisters usually eat breakfast and dinner in silence. At lunch, talk is allowed. On a Sister's feast day, the celebration includes the opportunity to talk at all three meals.)

QUIET TIME
After lunch, I have a few hours to myself while the Sisters go about their duties.

Sister Timothy Marie arranges for me to meet with the order's "CFO", Sister Janelle. Sister is also a trained engineer who now uses her skills to function as the convent's resident IT specialist as well as financial wizard.

This reminds me of how Sister Meredith was a successful businesswoman prior to entering the convent and Sister Maria Goretti a public relations graduate. Through the Sisters' example, I begin to grasp – really get it in my gut – how Christ could have been fully human as well as divine. How He could have been a carpenter and pal to the disciples as well as a mentor, Master, and Son of God.

EVENING PRAYER
A lovely quiet time of prayer, personal examination, and the Rosary. I highly recommend it.

DINNER
Tonight the Sisters are celebrating Sister Mary Scholastica's feast day. When I first returned to my faith, I used to half-joke that I became a believer because I loved how Christ was such a great guest at a party. How I loved it that His first public miracle was to make sure that His family and friends didn't run out of wine.

We don't have wine at Sister Scholastica's party, but we do have fun. I also find myself in tears as I watch each Sister present Sister Scholastica with a rose and a hug. Then they sing:

"We are bringing you this flower as a symbol of our love, asking God to ever shower richest blessings from above."

AFTER DINNER
I'm not sure who has a better sense of humor: God or the Sisters. As dinner ends, I turn to Sister Mary Scholastica and quip, "Who's doing the dishes?"

"You are," she replies with a smile.

She's not kidding. I'm on kitchen duty. Sister Timothy Marie loans me her apron. I'll be helping with the drying.

Here as always the Sisters work as a team. Some take up their positions at the sink, rinsing and placing plates in the giant industrial dishwasher; others, like me, take places at the other end of the assembly line. I am instantly smitten with what the

Sisters call their "Mickey Mouse gloves" – the thick terry cloth gloves they don to dry dishes with their hands. It's hugely efficient and makes dish drying a heck of a lot more fun than I'd expected.

(Note to self: suggest to the Sisters that they sell these gloves at their next boutique. They'd be a huge bestseller.)

RECREATION TIME

Before Night Prayers, the Sisters have an hour or so to meet up and chat with one another. I'm not sure where they usually gather – throughout the day, I never saw the actual cloister; that area was kept strictly off limits – but, for my stay, we met in the Library.

Here, again, it strikes me how the Sisters are truly friends with one another. They're like any group of gals getting together except they dress differently: they swap stories, discuss what's going on in the lives of those they love, make plans, ask advice, reminisce....(Sister Timothy Marie shares a great story about her early years as a nun teaching at a high school.) But, as you'd expect, talk is quiet...and never catty or gossipy like it might degenerate to among the secular rest of us.

The shopper in me is also struck breathless when Sister Maureen enters the library, her arms brimming over with the folds of the beautiful, handmade, intricately smocked dress she had mentioned to me over dinner. The Sisters are expert craftsmen. For instance, Mother Regina Marie tats and both Sister Jeannine Marie and Sister Grace Helena knit.

Considering the schedule they keep – and how bone-tired I am beginning to feel as the day draws to a close – I wonder how on earth the Sisters find the time and THE ENERGY to make lace, sew and smock dresses, knit, make cards and femo dolls, bead rosaries, and embroider on top of everything else. But then I recall words I once read somewhere: "The Holy Spirit is God in action." And I have a feeling I know what – or Who – helps propel the Sisters.

NIGHT PRAYERS

That feeling – that it is the Holy Spirit who acts as the Sisters' Vitamin B 12 –solidifies during the last prayers of the day. Here, as the Sisters gather on and around the Chapel altar to ask Jesus' blessing for the night, the presence of the Holy Spirit in our midst is so palpable that it could almost be bottled like Holy Water.

Oh, if only it could! I crave gallon jugs of It, to set in the trunk of my car as I step into the moonlit parking lot with Sister Mary Scholastica. Then, perhaps leaving wouldn't be so hard. I would have the Sisters' Essence on hand, to pour over my thirsty world-racked soul, whenever necessary.

I'm beyond tired, and so glad the Sisters have entered into Grand Silence, because, now, the experience heightens further. Before me, as the Sisters lift their arms in prayer, almost as if embracing Christ, is a tableau so moving, so exhilarating, so extraordinarily intimate that I vow never to speak of it to anyone. No words, Holy Spirit inspired or not, can adequately relate what the Sisters and I are experiencing.

But I made another vow. To the Sisters. To try to convey their lives with others. So, here I am, breaking my silence. I sort of speak.

A Suitable Sign

by Sister Marie-Aimée, O.C.D.

W HEN I WAS FIRST INTRODUCED TO SAINT THERESE as a young adult, I did not like her. She seemed to be enshrined in such a cloud of saccharine sweetness, scattering roses of every shade with each step, that I was positive that she and I would never be friends. I didn't mind if others wanted to pray her novenas and I rejoiced with friends who received a rose from her but none of that for me, thank you very much. As it turned out, Saint Therese had her own ideas about this relationship that I was so opposed to.

During college I took a year off to serve for a year as a missionary to the youth of the United States. Part of a team of young adults that would travel to parishes throughout the country, I got sick a few weeks into our ministry. Not just a cold or a flu, but a virus that promised to knock me flat for months. I continued to travel with the team for awhile but wasn't able to do much more than pray and offer it up for my teammates and for the young people. During those weeks of helplessness and "uselessness," our Lord convinced me that the teens we were serving needed so much more than a few hours of talks and fellowship. They needed our prayers and our sacrifices, they needed us to offer up our suffering for them. So that is what I did.

Next thing I knew, my supervisor wrote asking, "Have you ever heard of Saint Therese?" She proceeded to share a quote from "Story of a Soul" that spoke directly to my situation. Then another friend wrote to me about Saint Therese and someone we met in the parish brought her up. Wherever I turned, people were telling me about her. To tell the truth, I felt like she was stalking me! I couldn't avoid her. Finally, I capitulated and sat down to read "Story of a Soul."

I must admit, my main intention was to marshal all the reasons she and I would not be friends. Well, long story short, I was ambushed by grace and found one of my truest friends through the pages of her manuscripts. But friendship was only the first step in her relationship with me, she wanted more.

During my senior year of college, I began to seriously discern my vocation. Sometime in November, I told Jesus, "Look, in six months, I am going to graduate and I will need to start making some big decisions. I need to know what you want me to do with my life. If you want me to be a religious, you've got six months."

No joke, I gave God a deadline. Now, I am not the type who asks for signs, so I proceeded to discern this question in very practical, concrete, rational ways. I visited several communities, I joined a discernment group at school, I talked to a spiritual director, and I prayed. Over Easter break, I was invited to visit a community of women religious in the Midwest. Pretty sure that I did not have a vocation to their community, I visited anyways thinking that a "no" there might make a "yes" somewhere else clearer.

It took the better part of a day to drive to their Motherhouse and as we drew nearer, it became clear we were not going to arrive in time to pray evening prayer with the community. Sitting in the front seat of that packed mini-van, watching the minutes on the dashboard clock tick by, wishing I could make the sister behind the wheel drive a little faster, I realized the one desire of my heart was to be in that Chapel praying the Divine Office in community. It was a moment of grace, a moment when I recognized that being a sister resonated deep in my heart.

During the week I stayed with the sisters, I spent some time talking with their Novice Directress. I now felt sure I was called to religious life, but I was equally certain that it was not to their community. However, I could not explain how I knew, and Sister pressed me to identify which spirituality I felt called to, if not to theirs. "Are you Dominican? Franciscan? Carmelite?" Miserable, all I could say was "I don't know. I just don't know."

That evening in the Chapel, I wailed to Jesus in prayer, "I don't even know what spirituality I am!" As we started the Divine Office, I told Him, "Look, I have never asked you for a sign and I am not asking for one now. I am not even asking you to show me what Community you want me to join. But can you at least tell me what spirituality I am?" The sisters chanted evening prayer around me and all the psalms seemed to echo my confusion and distress.

During a few moments of silence there was a loud noise over in the corner of the chapel, and at that moment it was like a wind blew through my soul, sweeping all the turmoil away. Steeped in a sudden deep peace, I knew I was a Carmelite. Later, I went to the Novice Sacristan and asked her about the loud noise in the corner that preceded the huge grace I had just received. She laughed and pointed to a large picture of Saint Therese perched on a little shelf. "The candle in front of Saint Therese exploded. Someone must have been praying for a sign."

Saint Therese got her way. More than friends, now we are sisters in Carmel forever. Some people get roses, me, well, I got an exploding candle. Which, if you know me, is a pretty suitable sign.

The Rising Bell

by Sister Margaret Mary, O.C.D.

*E*ACH MORNING THE SISTERS ARE AWAKENED by a Sister ringing the morning bell and singing:

> *"Praised be Jesus Christ and His Virgin Mother,*
> *come to prayer, Sisters, come to praise the Lord."*

Because of this "automatic alarm clock", most of us don't set our individual clock. This is true especially in the Novitiate, as the only person who has an alarm clock is the Novitiate Sister in charge of ringing the bell. We simply rely on the bell, although we do all have watches.

When I entered, there were two Sisters in the Novitiate and two of us newly entered, who were still being trained into our duties. One morning, early in my postulancy, the bell rang. We all quickly got out of bed, knelt down and said our prayers, hurried to the showers and then got dressed. The duty I was being trained into was the Novitiate laundry. The first thing we did was gather the laundry, fill the washing machine with water and start loading in the clothes. Suddenly, as the two of us are going about our tasks, the novice who was training me and I heard a knock on the laundry room door.

The Sister novice who had rung the bell stuck her head around the door and said, "Go back to bed."

"Go back to bed?!? Why go back to bed, what are you talking about?" we exclaimed with great surprise.

"I rang the bell at 3:55 instead of 4:55. Go back to bed!" she said sleepily.

Later, after breakfast, the novice directress asked us, "Did anyone look at their clocks this morning?"

"No, the bell rang and we got up!" we replied.

Then she explained that she herself, heard the bell, got up, and as she went into her restroom, she happened to look at the thermostat on the wall, which happens to have a clock on it. She noticed the clock and the time, but it didn't quite register as she kept going about starting her day. Suddenly, what she saw dawned on her and she hurried back to the thermostat/clock and this time took a careful look. Then she turned to look at her alarm clock to verify and that's when she realized the actual time – it was an hour early! Then she called the novice who rang the bell to go and inform the rest of us that we could go back to bed for another hour. Needless to say, we had a very early jump start to our day, but on the plus side, we got to go back to bed!

Our Habit Is A Language

by Sister Imelda Marie, O.C.D.

*A*FTER 48 YEARS OF WEARING THE HABIT, I often forget the silent language and witness the habit gives until I am reminded by the reaction of people I meet at the most unexpected times and the most unusual places. The following are a few of my own stories as well as the stories shared with me by some of our sisters about the impact of the habit on those we meet. Sometimes funny, sometimes profound, people rarely fail to respond to the sight of a sister wearing the habit.

For 10 years, I worked the night shift in the Intensive Care Unit of Santa Teresita Hospital with another Carmelite Sister, Sister Virginia Therese. There were so many times when a patient would wake up from a major automobile accident or major surgery and seeing two sisters dressed in the white habit at their bedside would ask, "Am I in heaven?" One man took one look and said, with a huge sigh of relief, "I made it!" He sure was disappointed that he was in the hospital and not in heaven.

As a Mobile Intensive Care Nurse, I would accompany the paramedics on their emergency calls. One time, we were called to a park where a young man had overdosed on heroin. I was beside him in the ambulance en route to the hospital when he regained consciousness. He had the most puzzled look on his face when he, too, asked "Am I in heaven?" The paramedics never forgot this young man's question.

Once as I was standing in line to register for classes at a nearby college, a young boy pulled away from his mother in front of us and asked about the rosary he saw hanging from our cinctures (belts). We explained that when we pray the rosary, we talk to God. The young boy immediately grabbed the large medal we have on our rosary, put it to his mouth as he said: "God, do you hear me?" He then put the medal to his ear and waited for the answer! We gave him a one-minute catechesis on how we talk to God in prayer, and how we have to be very quiet on the inside to be able to hear His answer. He was very interested but he also seemed a little disappointed that the medal wasn't going to work like a telephone.

We cannot help but smile when a child in a stroller or shopping cart or holding onto his mother points in our direction and cries out, "Mary!" referring to Our Lady. There was even an occasion when a little one shouted, "It's God's wife!" at the sight of one of our sisters. Another little boy, less than three years old, called out "Jesus, Jesus, Señora de Jesus!" from his seat in the shopping cart as his mother passed us in the store.

One sister was waiting in line at the store and noticed that the mother standing in front of her seemed tired. A little girl clung to her hand and leaned against her. As the line moved forward, the child noticed sister standing behind them. Her eyes got big as she tugged on her mom's hand. "Mom, mom, is that an angel?" The mom turned to look, and the effort to explain just seemed to require too much energy, so she looked down at her little girl, smiled, and said, "Yes."

Yes, our habit is a language.

It speaks of who we are, our consecration to God and how we should act as a chosen people on a journey through this land of exile to the kingdom of God.

It speaks to others, reminding them of the importance of spiritual values, calling them to join us on this journey to God, who is very close to each one of us, if we only take the time and make the effort to hear His quiet voice speaking to us in our hearts.

Lost in Translation

by Sister Vincent Marie, O.C.D.

*E*ACH MORNING, EVENING, AND NIGHT, WE GATHER together in the Chapel to pray the Divine Office, also called the Liturgy of the Hours. Made up of psalms, other readings from the Old and New Testaments, intercessions, and prayers, it is prayed by priests and religious around the world, extending the liturgy of the Mass to all the hours of the day and night.

One of the psalms used in the Office is Psalm 115, which reads in part:

> *Their idols are silver and gold*
> *the work of human hands.*
> *They have mouths but do not speak,*
> *eyes but do not see.*
>
> *They have ears but do not hear,*
> *noses but do not smell.*
> *They have hands but do not feel,*
> *feet but do not walk;*
> *they produce no sound from their throats.*
>
> *Their makers will be like them,*
> *and anyone who trusts in them.*

Some years ago in a house with just a few sisters, we were praying Vespers together, when all of a sudden in the midst of Pslam 115, one of the sisters started laughing uncontrollably. We certainly couldn't figure out why. Finally, she managed to contain her laughter and we continued with the evening prayers. Suddenly, she lost it a second time.

Finally, upon finishing our prayers, we asked her as we left the Chapel, "What in the name of Heaven was so funny?"

She replied with a smile playing about her lips, "As we were chanting the Psalm, Sister chanted: '...I have eyes, but do not see, ears that do not hear and *feet that do not smell'*." Granted, that is a rather *unique* translation of Psalm 115:6!

The second time she lost it, was because the rest of us didn't even blink an eye, we just kept chanting. We knew what the sister had meant and we just ignored that which was lost in translation!

The April Fools Flood

by Sister Mary Joanne, O.C.D.

*E*ARLY IN THE MORNING ON APRIL 1, 2014, at 4:44, I got up to get ready to ring the bell. When I came out of my room, I heard the sound of water rushing and I thought "It must be raining terribly hard."

As I got closer to the closet where the bell was, the sound increased in volume. This couldn't be rain. I looked all over but couldn't see any sign of water. I rang the bell and another sister came out of her room and said, "That sound has been going on since 2 a.m."

Well, when we started down the stairs, we found the source of the rushing water. It was coming from the broken pipe in the closet! The water was gushing from the ceiling downstairs and there was practically ankle-deep water down in the lobby flowing almost into the chapel. There was water everywhere, as well as big bubbles in the paint where the water was trying to get out. We searched and searched to find a way to turn the water off. So instead of going to morning prayer and meditation like we usually do, we were trying to swim through the waves to dry out our convent!

Finally, Sister Caridad was able to get hold of the custodian who had arrived at 5:30 a.m. over at the school. He came and was able to locate the source of the water and turn it off.

We then went to Mass over at the Church. The entrance antiphon for Mass this day was:

"All who are thirsty, come to the waters," says the Lord,
"though you have no money come and drink with joy."

Then came the first reading:

"The angel brought me, Ezekiel, back to the entrance of the temple of
the Lord and I saw water flowing from beneath the threshold of the temple
toward the east for the façade of the temple was toward the east.
The water flowed down from the right side of the temple south of the altar.
He led me outside by the north gate and around to the outer façade
facing the east where I saw water trickling from the right side.
Then when he had walked off to the east with a measuring cord
in his hand he measured off a thousand cubits and had me wade
through the water which was now ankle deep."

Well, needless to say, we were all trying to hold back the laughter during Mass!
God played His little April Fools' joke and He got up early to do it!

Raffle Tickets!

by Sister Margaret Mary, O.C.D.

*S*ISTER BELEN USED TO GO over to Hayden Child Care Center and just sit in the background and knit. As a result, all the children were quite familiar with her as were many of the parents. As Sister Belen got older and different health issues cropped up, she was no longer able to go to Hayden on a regular basis.

On occasion, Sister Belen would pick some fruit from Casa convent gardens and happily take it to share with the Hayden teachers. This particular time, it happened to be Hayden's open house and she had the opportunity to help. Sister was assigned to sell raffle tickets. Well, Sister Belen manuevered a spot right in the middle of the high traffic main doorway, which is the door all the parents and visitors use.

Sister Belen was in her 90's, under 5 feet tall, her face creased with wrinkles as she greeted each guest with a grin and twinkle in her eye. Situated in the doorway, she earnestly showed the tickets to every single person who wanted to pass through the door. Needless to say, everyone complied with the "entry fee," obediently buying their raffle ticket. Sister Belen is probably the only one who could have pulled this off!

Sisters Pray Everywhere

by Sister Imelda Marie, O.C.D.

I MADE A TRIP TO WALMART TO PICK UP COLD MEDICINE for one of our Sisters, but I had trouble finding it among the vast selection. The pharmacist apparently noticed that I was spending quite a bit of time peering over all the shelves because he came over and asked if I required assistance.

"Can I help you find something in particular?" he asked.

"Yes, I am trying to find this cold medicine," I replied showing him the paper with the name of the medication written on it.

"You'll find that right there," he said indicating a bottom shelf a few feet up the aisle from where we were standing.

So in order to see better, I got down on my knees hunting for this particular brand of cold medication.

Just as I find what I am looking for, a man in his late 30s came walking down the aisle and with a big grin threw up his hands and cried out, "A nun praying at Walmart!"

Matching his grin I replied, "Indeed! We pray everywhere, every place, every time – even at Walmart!"

The Multiplication of the ... Fudge?!

by Sister Gaudencia, O.C.D.

EVERYONE IS FAMILIAR WITH JESUS' MIRACLE of the multiplication of the loaves and fish. Aside from the Resurrection, this is the only miracle performed by Our Lord that is recorded in all four Gospels. Well, a couple of years ago, during the preparatory time leading up to our Fantasia Family Festival, we experienced a sort of a variation on the theme of the original Biblical miracle.

Fantasia is our annual fall family festival, held each November, and features something for every member of the family: a holiday boutique, lots of great food, children's activities including meeting and taking photos with Santa and Mrs. Claus, music and entertainment and even a classic car show. Fantasia takes place at Santa Teresita, our assisted and skilled nursing and rehabilitative facility in Duarte, California.

One of the most popular items featured in our Carmel Kitchen are our homemade baked goodies, especially our fudge, all of which we make here on the premises in our own kitchen. Because it takes at least two weeks for all the necessary ingredients to arrive, advanced preparation for fudge making is definitely required. This particular year, I worked with Sister Noella on this baking project and we ordered five cases of all the ingredients we needed to make our big batch of fudge. The cases arrived and the fudge was duly baked and ready for the festival.

On the big day, sales were brisk. In fact, one customer bought such a large quantity of fudge that he realized he would have to come back the next day in order to take his purchase home. His purchase actually filled four boxes, which we set aside to keep for him.

After a few busy hours in the Carmel Kitchen Booth, it was time for us to take a break and two sisters came to relieve us. We returned about 15 minutes later and found our "relief" sisters in a very happy state.

"The fudge is completely sold out," one of the sisters reported with a big smile on her face.

Sister Noella and I were about to offer congratulations, when suddenly, we turned to look at each other as the same sinking feeling struck both of us at the same time.

I hurriedly looked behind the counter where we had left the boxes of fudge our customer had purchased earlier in the day. The boxes were gone! The fudge had been sold. Sister Noella and I looked at each other in dismay.

"I wonder if we check down in the basement if we might find more fudge," Sister Noella wondered out loud.

"No, Sister, there're none," I replied, "all the supplies are gone."

"Well, just go and look," Sister Noella urged me, "perhaps you will find one."

"Very well," I said, none too hopefully, "I'll try."

So I went down to the basement and looked everywhere about the room. Nothing. Returning to Sister Noella, I shook my head and reported, "No, Sister, I found nothing."

"Well, go back down and look again," Sister Noella said, "and be sure to look carefully in every single corner, nook and cranny."

So again, down to the basement I went being careful to look really hard in every single corner, nook and cranny as Sister Noella had instructed. Again, the same results – nothing!

I went back up to Sister Noella and reported, "Nothing, Sister."

By this time, we were both close to desperation. Suddenly, an inexplicable feeling urged me to go back down to the basement for a third time in the hopes that I'd uncover at least one box of fudge hidden away in a cabinet that I had somehow managed to overlook in my two previous searches.

As I made my way back to the basement, I sent a glance heavenward and said out loud, "Lord, please! You multiplied the loaves and fish, surely you can multiply the fudge!"

By then I was back in the basement, shaking my head and wondering where to look where I hadn't already, when suddenly, I noticed something out of the corner of my eye. I turned toward the object and lo and behold! A box, a case really, was sitting there waiting for me – just like that, out of the blue! I opened the box and found that it contained exactly the amount of fudge we needed, no more, no less!

"Oh my goodness, it's fudge! Well, Lord, You did say, 'Ask and you shall receive!' Thank you!" I offered up very gratefully as I hurried back to the Carmel Kitchen Booth to let Sister Noella know our problem had been solved.

Jesus listens to our prayers, even when we ask for fudge!

His Power

by Sister Marie-Aimée, O.C.D.

*P*OSTULANCY IS THE FIRST STAGE OF RELIGIOUS LIFE and no matter how old one is, or how much life experience one has, this initial introduction to life in the convent has a way of dismantling any existing illusions of self-sufficiency. Religious life is a supernatural life of faith that is expressed in the very real, very concrete details of daily life. Learning all the customs and procedures, the hows and whens of accomplishing even the simplest tasks in a new way, can feel daunting.

Of course, you are not alone. The novices, veterans of one year or maybe even two, are eager to share the riches of their "vast" experience. Sometimes, depending on how many novices there are and on the intensity of their eagerness, this can make you wish for a moment that you were alone. I remember approaching our Directress one morning overwhelmed by the number of things I was discovering I didn't know how to do the convent way and wailing, "I don't even know how to clean the shower!" She just smiled and said something about it being a little early to get discouraged since I had only been a Postulant for four days.

She was right. And although my first weeks and months of religious life were at times bewildering and humbling, they were also a powerful experience of His grace working in my weakness and a deepening of the realization that this One who was calling me to be His spouse could be relied on in all the ways that counted. During the months I spent as a postulant, a man whom I greatly loved and admired, gave the world a moving witness to this very same truth on a much greater scale. Pope John Paul II's testimony to the power of God at work in every human life no matter how weak or filled with suffering seemed to resound with ever greater strength and clarity as he grew physically weaker. Finally he stood at the balcony for the last time and the words would no longer come. We watched the footage in the refectory and knew that our time under his care and guidance here on earth was drawing to a close.

Just so you know, we don't watch TV in the convent except for the occasional Catholic news show or the secular news when something of great significance is occurring in the world. As you can imagine, the last days of our beloved Holy Father were of the greatest significance to us and so that week found us watching and mourning with the world the death of Pope John Paul II. We accompanied the casket as it processed through the Vatican. We attended the Mass, watching the wind whip through the pages of the open book of the Gospels sitting on the wooden coffin holding his remains. I wondered through my tears if I could love our next Holy Father this much.

In college, my friends and I, all Pope John Paul II fans, had a joke about his election. We said the Cardinals must have gotten together and said "One, two, three, NOT IT." And Cardinal Wojtyla, off in a corner praying, missed it and was elected. In the quiet days after the funeral, I began to learn about the real procedure for electing the pope. Since I was three at the time of Pope John Paul I and Pope John Paul II's elections, this was a whole new experience for me. I quickly picked up the professed sisters' excitement and began to wonder who God was going to choose for us. I watched with fascination as the doors of the Sistine Chapel closed and hoped we would get to see them open again.

CNN had a camera trained on the chimney that would show the smoke when the ballots were burned and the live image was in the corner of the screen even while the regular news and other shows were occurring. The excitement heightened when Mother Regina Marie announced that we could leave the TV on during the day with the volume muted and the professed sisters could "tune in" online. The first person to see white smoke was to ring the large outside bell and everyone would congregate in the refectory to see our new Holy Father. I was in the back kitchen quietly cutting vegetables for the priests' lunch surrounded by industrial equipment humming and buzzing so I didn't hear the bell. Someone told me later that our bell, usually rung with a sedate and solemn, "dong, dong, dong" to call us to prayer, was pealed with wild abandon. All I knew was that I looked up just in time to see a novice run through the front kitchen. Now, sisters, as a general rule, don't run. Postulants forget this, but novices usually remember. So the sight of her veil flying could only mean one thing…white smoke! I abandoned the bell peppers and tomatoes and joined the sprint for the refectory.

A group of professed sisters was already there with more streaming in every moment. I have never before or since seen so much excitement in the convent. Everyone was talking at once and no one could stand still. As we were waiting, I glanced at the clock and realized that the priest who gave us our Tuesday classes would be arriving soon. I knew that I should offer to go and meet Father so he wouldn't arrive to an empty classroom but the classroom was on the other side of the building. What if the Pope came out? I wrestled interiorly for a few seconds and finally went to our Directress to make what felt like the ultimate sacrifice. Before I could open my mouth, she said, "Can you please go into the classroom and set up the TV to see if it gets this channel over there?"

"Sure, Sister!" Relieved that I wouldn't miss the event after all, I took one last long look at the empty balcony and calmly walked out of the refectory. I held the swinging door to make sure it closed quietly, turned away, and sprinted through the kitchen, through the dish room, past the priest's dining room, down the hallway to the classroom. With trembling hands, I yanked the TV cart over to the outlet, plugged it in, said a prayer, and turned it on. Victory! The empty balcony came into view and I knew I had not missed anything. I returned to the refectory door in record time, pulled up short, and walked calmly to our Directress letting her know that the TV did indeed work. "Good," she said, "now we can go over there and watch while we wait for Father to arrive."

This time we all trooped over to the classroom in the company of our Directress. Father arrived and joined us in our vigil around the TV. We stood in a semicircle chatting, coming to attention every time the curtain on the balcony stirred. Finally, the curtains were really parting and a small group processed to the edge of the balcony. By this time some of us were on our knees. The novice next to me had grabbed my hand and in her excitement was alternating between squeezing it and pumping it up and down. "Habemus Papem." Cheers from the movices and then more words in Latin until the clearly spoken "Joseph" and we were all on our feet laughing and crying and hugging because we didn't have to hear the name "Ratzinger" to know that our new Holy Father was someone we already knew and loved dearly.

St. Teresa identified herself as a daughter of the Church and St. Therese found the fulfillment of her Carmelite vocation in the realization that her mission was to be love in the heart of the Church. The day of Pope Benedict XVI's election, I experienced the intense joy of life at the Heart of the Church and rejoiced that I was following Jesus in the company of these Carmelites, daughters of the Church. The election of the Pope marked our postulancy in more ways than one. As our entrance to the Novitiate was drawing near, the sisters began to speculate about what names Mother would choose for the two of us postulants. The novices gleefully tormented us with suggestions like Sister Bede of the Holy Rosary but the names which won the acclaim of all were suggested by a professed sister one day at lunch. Mother called us over to her table to hear our new "names," *Sister Habemus* and *Sister Papem*.

Eight years later, I am now perpetually professed and I see my newest sisters in their blue uniforms and postulant hair cuts from the other side of the refectory. Now I know that even though postulancy ends, the learning is a life-long process. My first superior in my first assignment after professing first vows and leaving the Novitiate, moved into her assignment the same day I moved into mine. She looked at me, smiled, and said, "We'll be postulants together." And she was right. Every new opportunity brings the same glorious mixture of grace and humor and humbling experience as one navigates the process of learning new people, new places, new duties. Pope John Paul II's witness to the power of God radiantly visible in and through our greatest weaknesses continues to resound, growing louder in the moments when I find myself a "postulant" again, learning in ever deeper ways how to rely more fully on the strength of the Lord.

The Best Christmas Memories

by Sister Margaret Mary, O.C.D.

SOMETIMES THE MOST PRECIOUS CHRISTMAS MEMORIES are simple moments of grace that touch our hearts.

My very first Christmas as a professed Sister, I was assigned to Casa Convent at Santa Teresita in Duarte. After midnight Mass at Saint Joseph Chapel, the main chapel on campus, the Sisters from Casa started trickling across the parking lot to Casa Convent. While some of the Sisters went straight to the recreation room for our traditional Christmas greeting, some of us stopped first in the convent chapel.

Earlier that day, the sister in charge of the chapel had decorated for Christmas, replacing the dark purple of Advent with the whites and golds of the Solemnity of Our Lord's Birth. The small crib under the altar, surrounded by gentle white light, was still empty. As we gathered around the crib, Sister Marina, the superior at the time, retrieved the baby Jesus from the sacristy. It was time to put Him in the manger. I was kneeling across from one of our older sisters, Sister Maria Belen. A very small sister, bent with age, her arthritic hands were clasped and her face was alight with joy.

Sister Marina was approaching the altar to place baby Jesus in the crib, when she happened to glance at Sister Maria Belen's radiant face. Sister Marina turned and handed Sister the infant. A smile of delight spread across Sister Maria Belen's face. She looked like a small child receiving the most precious gift in the world as she held the infant Jesus in her hands. Although her hands were bent from arthritis, she held the tiny infant with such care and such love. The infant was really small, so she held Him with her two hands cupped together as she carried Him carefully up to the altar.

Once she laid Him down in the manger, she remained kneeling before Him, oblivious of the arthritis and the pain kneeling must have caused. For the longest time she stayed there praying in a low voice. Although I do not speak Spanish, the reverence of her voice and the love clearly written in her gaze on the Infant in the crib, spoke volumes to me. She had been a religious for 67 years, I was newly professed, yet we were united by our love for the One lying in the manger.

Sometimes the best Christmas memories are simple moments of grace, when the sound of someone's voice, the look in their eye, the love they express remind us why we celebrate Christmas.

Bubble Trouble

by Sister Faustina, O.C.D.

*D*URING MY SECOND YEAR IN THE NOVITIATE, I was assigned to be the kitchen assistant. The duties of the kitchen assistant included helping with food preparation for the retreatants on the weekend and the sisters during the week. One of the things we did daily was cook breakfast for the sisters while they were in a brief morning meeting. Each of the novices also had specific duties such as turning on ovens, opening certain windows, unlocking gates, doors and cabinets…a whole check list of certain tasks that were done as part our normal morning routine to whatever duty area we were assigned.

As kitchen assistant, each morning I opened some windows, unlocked some doors and prepped the deep sink where we washed pots and pans. We helped the cooks get started on the dishes by making sure the sinks were ready to be used. There were three large metal sinks; one we filled with about two inches of water and concentrated soap; the third sink we filled with two inches of water and turned the heater on to warm the water.

Each morning when the rising bell rang at 4:55 a.m., I would climb out of bed, pray, get dressed, and make my way down to the kitchen. The routine I established for myself began at the sinks where I turned on the water. I let them fill as I circled the kitchen completing other tasks until I ended back at the sinks to turn the water and soap off before heading to the Chapel where prayers would begin at 5:25 a.m.

This particular day seemed just like an ordinary day until we returned to the kitchen after Mass.

I hurried to the stove and went straight to work on breakfast. I was cracking eggs in the skillet when I realized that the other Novices were not moving and working around me. Turning to find out why, I saw them standing near the coffee machine, transfixed by something in the pots and pans area which was blocked from my view by a wall. In a flash, it dawned on me that I had turned on the water and soap earlier, but I had no recollection of turning them off before I went to prayers. With great trepidation and a strong desire to run and hide, I went back to the eggs knowing that the sisters would be coming shortly for breakfast.

Eventually, one of the Novices came to take over for me at the skillet and I rushed to the pots and pans area picturing all sorts of disaster. I reached the area at the same time as the first professed sisters coming into the kitchen for breakfast. Nothing I had imagined prepared me for what I saw.

The high concentrate soap dispenser had been running with the water for an hour and a half. The result? A wall of bubbles. From the floor to the ceiling. From wall to wall. Bubbles. One of the novices had mercifully ducked into the bubble glacier and turned off the water and soap so it was no longer growing. I heard a noise and realized I was not alone. Mother was standing next to me trying unsuccessfully not to laugh. Sisters crowded behind her, someone giggled which set off uncontrollable laughter down the line. Mother capitulated and opened recreation.

We had guests in the dining room, visiting superiors, priests in the priests' dining room that day and one and all made a little field trip to the pots and pans to see the bubble glacier. The sisters discovered that the soap was light and could be "picked up" in handfuls that could be wafted into the air for a game of "catch" or a bubble fight. The guests took pictures. Our chaplain got a lot of mileage out of the whole incident, even making some spiritual connections to it in his homily the next day.

Like a scene worthy of an "I Love Lucy" episode, the bubbles just seemed to expand and advance through the door into the refectory of their own accord. I spent a long time that morning cleaning up bubbles. As far as I was concerned, the best news was that the community didn't see the wall of bubbles as an obstacle to me professing our First Vows! We all make mistakes, some are just a little more memorable than others.

The Tiny Spark

Excerpts taken from <u>To Love Me In Truth</u> and the Early Chronicles

F ATHER LEROY CALLAHAN KNEW OF MOTHER LUISITA'S HOPE for a retreat house, and like Mother Margarita Maria, he never forgot it. Once the congregation became established in the diocese and after the passing of Mother Luisita into eternal life, Father Callahan continued to urge Mother Margarita Maria to give serious thought to a retreat house. He wanted the Carmelite Sisters to have a novitiate and retreat house in California.

In 1939, just one year before his death, he again quietly turned to Mother Margarita Maria and urged, "When are you going to be brave and try to buy some property for a novitiate and a retreat house? Look for some property, look for it. You know it was Mother Luisita's wish."

Never had Mother Margarita Maria forgotten it, but neither the time nor the circumstances seemed right as yet. Two more years passed and it was then the spring of 1941.

Mother Margarita Maria, now Regional Superior, thought the congregation should consider the acquisition of additional real property. She had in mind a large enough parcel for a retreat house and a future novitiate. First, of course, the approval of Superiors had to be obtained. Mother Mary of the Eucharist and her Council were in full accord. Mother Margarita Maria next consulted the Archbishop. He, too, gave his approval and his blessing on this undertaking.

There was no retreat house for women east of Los Angeles; thus the San Gabriel Valley was chosen as the general area in which to search for possible properties.

Thirty-two different properties were examined, but either they were not suitable or they were too costly. Some of the Sisters were becoming discouraged, but Mother Margarita Maria reminded them that the Sacred Heart would provide when He wanted the work to commence. For their part, they would continue to pray and keep looking.

On Holy Thursday morning, Mother Margarita Maria received a telephone call from Monsignor Thomas J. O'Dwyer, who wished to inform her of a property in Alhambra which was for sale and which he thought would be of interest to her. Later that same morning, she received a telephone call from Mr. Francis T. Moore of Altadena. The Moores were personal friends of Archbishop Orozco y Jiménez of Guadalajara and it was through him they became interested in the Carmelite Sisters. The Moores knew the Sisters were looking for property for a retreat house.

He began, "Mrs. Moore and I have found the ideal property for you in Alhambra, Mother. It is spacious with many trees, a 26-room house which, however, is badly in need of repair. It has a triple garage with living quarters above."

It turned out to be the same property about which Monsignor O'Dwyer had phoned earlier!

Mr. Moore had not seen the inside of the house, but he told Mother Margarita Maria that it was being sold to close the estate of Judge Walter Haas. The judge's brother, John B. Haas, an attorney, was the Executor.

Mr. Moore continued, "If you think you are interested, Mother, Mrs. Moore and I will drive you over to see it next Monday." This was most agreeable to Mother Margarita Maria.

Afterwards, she admitted that the minute she had her first glimpse of the property, even before they got out of the car, she thought, "It is going to be ours."

The Moores, Mother Margarita Maria and her companion walked through the entire house. Its rundown condition had certainly not been exaggerated. As they proceeded from room to room, Mother Margarita Maria was very quiet, thinking of how the house could be converted for their purposes. She concluded that cleaned up and with a minimum of remodeling, twenty-eight retreatants could be comfortably accommodated, and there would also be space for the Sisters. The grounds, too, had been badly neglected, but were planted with beautiful trees, many of which had been imported from remote parts of the world by Judge Haas. It was an ideally secluded property in the midst of a lovely residential section of Alhambra. Yes, Mother Margarita Maria appreciated the potential and could envision the possibilities. She was also looking to the future as she surveyed the spacious grounds realizing that if the need arose, there was plenty of space to put up additional buildings. There remained just one possible hurdle – the selling price.

There was little conversation on their return trip to Duarte. Mother Margarita Maria was unusually quiet and reflective, but inwardly, she admitted afterwards, she was very excited. She telephoned Mr. Haas, the Executor, immediately, telling him she had seen the property in Alhambra and that she was interested in it. He replied that he and his family would be delighted to have a religious community purchase it. It had been on the market for over a year and it was holding up the closing of his brother's estate.

Mother Margarita Maria then asked the price.

"We are asking $26,000 and that is without the furniture in the house," Mr. Haas said.

This was more than double what the Sisters could afford!

"Oh, that is too much for us," Mother Margarita Maria replied.

Mr. Haas asked her to make an offer, but she was embarrassed to do so and did not want to offend him.

"I am afraid you will be provoked."

"No, not at all," he answered her. "What is your offer?"

"Ten thousand dollars – that is all we can afford to pay," she replied.

For a few moments, there was silence. Mr. Haas could not believe what he heard. Then he asked if she realized how far apart they were. To her quiet, "Yes", Mr. Haas terminated the conversation by saying very politely, "We are not going to waste time. If you change your mind, call me." Mother Margarita Maria asked him to do likewise if he changed his mind.

She knew it was the ideal place, the kind of place she had been looking for, but the price was way beyond what they could afford. Upon Mr. Moore's advice, they did not call Mr. Haas, but the Sisters and the patients at Santa Teresita began a novena of prayers to the Most Sacred Heart of Jesus.

Four days later, Mr. Haas telephoned to see if Mother Margarita Maria had changed her mind.

"Yes," she replied, "I have changed my mind."

"And what is your offer now?" He inquired of her.

"Ten thousand-one hundred dollars."

In the brief conversation which followed, Mr. Haas came down to $21,000 – $5,000 less than his original price. But Mother Margarita Maria's offer remained. At this point he invited her to come to his office where they could discuss the matter further.

Negotiations continued. There were thirteen heirs to be satisfied. Finally, they agreed on $13,500, wherein each of the heirs would receive $1,000 and the additional $500 would cover escrow costs. However, since it was an asset of an estate, final approval of the Probate Court was necessary to consummate the sale. This meant it had to be offered at public auction.

The real problems were about to begin. First, there was the question of zoning and to use the property for a retreat house necessitated a public hearing and the approval of the neighbors living nearby.

Mr. Haas initiated the proceedings for the variance; however, the neighbors were furious when they learned that the Sisters wanted to purchase the property. They were bitterly opposed to a religious community or a retreat house in their neighborhood as they felt it would depreciate their own properties. So they united, even the Catholics, against granting the variance. Joining in this opposition was the pastor of the Catholic church, a short block away from the Haas property. He telephoned Mother Margarita Maria and reprimanded her for considering the purchase of a house in the parish without first obtaining his permission.

During the 14 years Mother Margarita Maria had lived in the United States, she had more than once experienced prejudice. It always hurt, but never like this.

She decided to set the example. She would forgive; she would seek peace; she would try to win over these people. She and a companion started out, going from house to house of the neighbors close by, but it was to no avail. In each instance they were not even received with politeness. The response was open hostility and animosity. Quite simply, they were not wanted, even by those of their own faith.

Mother Margarita Maria needed both advice and encouragement, so she requested an appointment with Archbishop Cantwell. She told him in some detail of events as they had occurred. He was appalled, but he remained firm that she proceed with the purchase of the property and keep him apprised of developments. He also telephoned the pastor in Alhambra to inform him that Mother Margarita Maria had selected the Alhambra property with the approval of the Chancery Office; that he, the Archbishop, wanted a retreat house for women in the area, and he asked the pastor to help and not oppose the Sisters, reminding him that this foundation would be of great benefit to the parish. The Sisters left the Archbishop with his blessing and full approval.

Throughout these trying weeks, Mr. and Mrs. Moore staunchly supported and encouraged the Sisters. They were always ready to accompany Mother Margarita Maria to various business appointments and Mr. Moore, who was a successful businessman, gave them valuable advice.

The public hearing on the zoning variance was set for July 2, 1941, before the Planning Commission at Alhambra City Hall. It happened to be the first Friday of the month, the day especially dedicated to the Sacred Heart of Jesus.

Mr. and Mrs. Moore arrived with Mother Margarita and her companion shortly before the appointed time. The Council Chamber was filled to capacity – standing room only – with the neighbors who came to oppose the granting of the variance.

The Sisters looked about; the only other friends they saw were Mr. Haas and Mr. Adams, their architect. As they moved up the aisle to the front row, Mr. Moore whispered to Mother Margarita Maria, "Don't worry, Mother, and don't say a word. Let me talk for you."

As soon as they were seated, the meeting was called to order. Many questions were asked and insulting accusations, some very personal, were made. It seemed that everyone had something to say against the Sisters and their purchase of the property.

All the while, Mother Margarita Maria and her companions sat quietly listening, never making any attempt to answer nor defend themselves. It was as if they were criminals being criminally charged before a court. Finally, the President of the Council, turning his attention to Mother Margarita Maria, addressed her directly, "Do you wish to make a statement of any kind?"

Mother Margarita Maria stood up and faced the assembly. Within, she was shaking, but outwardly she appeared very calm.   Quietly and firmly she answered, "Yes, I have plenty to say. We will abide by the law, but we will be free in our own house, as you are all free in your own homes."

There was much talking going on, and Mother Margarita Maria tried to continue, but she was actually shouted down. The session had become very emotional and was completely out of control.

To avoid any further commotion, the President announced that the public hearing was terminated and asked the people to leave. He said the Commission would adjourn to a closed meeting. One of the members of the Commission approached Mother Margarita Maria and suggested that they not go too far away. He said the closed meeting would be brief.

After about ten minutes, Mr. Haas thought they should return. The room was empty except for the Council members who had resumed their seats. They had come to a unanimous decision. The variance was granted.

This was indeed a great victory for the Sisters. The many prayers offered to God by the Sisters and their friends had been answered. Without the zoning variance the property would have been of no use to them.

Mr. Haas was delighted for now the sale might be consummated very shortly and the estate closed. However, even though this first hurdle was passed, there was no absolute assurance that the property would go to the Sisters. There was still the possibility that someone might outbid them at the auction. Yet, for the present, it was still a victory.

As they were leaving city hall, Mr. Moore, who was as jubilant as the Sisters, said, "This certainly is the occasion for some special celebration, Sisters, and I have a little treat in mind for you."

Knowing that their Rule did not permit the Sisters to partake of food in a private home or in a public restaurant, he drove to an ice cream parlor on the way back to Duarte and ordered ice cream sodas for everyone which they could enjoy in the car. It was, indeed, a most unusual treat for the Sisters.

News of the granting of the variance was all over the neighborhood by that afternoon and it only fueled the animosity of the residents, who were more determined than ever to block the sale of the Haas property to the Sisters.

Mr. Haas proceeded with arrangements for the auction to be held on August 1, 1941 – again the First Friday of the month – and was set to begin at eight o'clock in the morning. As required, notices were mailed so that all interested parties might attend and bid.

Once again, Mr. Moore advised the Sisters, "Let us plan to be there one hour early."

He feared, and with good reason, that the neighbors had not given up. He really wanted the Sisters to have the property, but the neighbors were equally determined that they were not going to have the Sisters or a retreat house in their neighborhood. They planned to outbid them at the auction and prevent them from obtaining the property.

Promptly at seven o'clock in the morning, the Sisters arrived with Mr. and Mrs. Moore at the location where the auction was to be held. The auctioneer was already there, but no one else.

Mother Margarita Maria approached him and said, "You know, we would like this property very much, but I have two requests."

Surprised, he asked, "And what are your requests?"

"First, that the auction commence at eight o'clock sharp."

Before she could continue, he interrupted, "Well, that is simple enough. It is my job to start on time. Yes, it will begin at eight o'clock sharp. And what is the second request?"

Mother Margarita Maria, happy she had won the "simple" request, continued, "When you auction the furniture, please offer the dining room as one unit and offer all the benches in the basement as a unit, and likewise all the bookcases." She watched the auctioneer's face closely and saw the furrows in his brow.

He was listening, wondering at this request, but by this time he was impressed by the sincerity and enthusiasm of this Sister. He didn't know why she was making this request concerning the furniture, but it did not matter to him. He was there to sell it.

"Yes, I will do it for you," he replied.

Mother Margarita Maria anxiously kept looking at her watch and then at the door. No one else had arrived. It was as if time had slowed down to a virtual standstill, as the hands of the clock crept ever so slowly toward the hour. Then only three minutes remained … two minutes … .one minute – finally, eight o'clock! Still no one else had arrived.

The formalities of the auction began. The property was offered. Mr. Moore bid for the Sisters - $13,500, the price agreed upon with Mr. Haas.

Three times, the auctioneer repeated the bid, and then said, "The property goes to the Carmelite Sisters." No sooner had the auctioneer finished speaking those words, a man came running through the doorway breathlessly, followed by a woman, obviously, intending to bid – but it was too late. The property was sold.

Next was the auction of the furniture. The auctioneer wasted no time. Mr. Moore continued to bid for the Sisters. Other people were arriving and began to join in the bidding. There was the 16-piece dining room set of beautifully carved Australian wood. Another bidder asked that the table and chairs and extra pieces be sold separately, but the auctioneer said it was to be offered as one unit only. It went to the Sisters for $29.

True to his word, the auctioneer announced the benches as one unit. The winning bid came from the Sisters. In the same way, they acquired the bookcases, and were also able to purchase a few other odd pieces, including a large leather chair in which, they learned later, Judge Haas, the owner of the property, had died while reading his Bible.

A few weeks later, the legal formalities were concluded and the transfer of money and property took place.

Days of cleaning and scrubbing followed, which the Sisters did themselves. They were overjoyed with the thought of the new retreat house and the great benefit to souls who would come to spend "a few days apart with the Lord."

The property restrictions in the area did not permit a sign of any kind, but the Sisters had selected the name by which this new foundation would be known – "Retreat House of the Sacred Heart."

The basement of this residence was to be occupied by the Sisters; the second and third floors were furnished for retreatants. The large parlor on the first floor was remodeled as a chapel. Also on the first floor: conference rooms, the retreatants' dining room and a large kitchen and Mother Margarita Maria's office, which doubled as her cell at night.

On September 29, 1941, the first Mass was celebrated by Monsignor Thomas J. O'Dwyer for the Sisters and a few friends. Their Foundress, Mother Maria Luisa Josefa of the Blessed Sacrament seemed especially near that day as another apostolate of her daughters commenced. Her desire for a retreat house for women was to be fulfilled at last.

In November, four ladies from San Diego arrived for the first weekend retreat. Initially, the groups were necessarily small as retreats for lay-women had not yet become commonplace at the time. However, the Sisters found many ways to stimulate interest. The tiny spark had enkindled a slow, but steady fire which would soon begin to burn brightly.

*   *   *   *   *   *   *   *   *   *   *

A MOST Unlikely Benefactor...

Excerpts taken from To Love Me In Truth and the Early Chronicles

WITH THE PURCHASE OF THE PROPERTY at 920 East Alhambra Road, the Sisters assumed a $22,500 debt. Additionally, there were expenses for some remodeling, cleaning, painting, and putting the house in a usable, habitable condition. Also, furniture had to be purchased for the retreatants' rooms.

As to how they would be able to pay off this large debt, Mother Margarita simply said, "Pray, pray, pray. We are doing the Lord's work. The Sacred Heart will provide."

At this time, they were short of trained personnel and Mother Margarita Maria divided her time between Duarte and Alhambra. Upon returning to Alhambra after several days' absence, she was met at the door by one of the Sisters who was breathless with excitement, "Mother, Mother, a lady has left a message for you. She wants you to go visit her. I think she is going to pay the entire debt for the retreat house."

Upon learning the identity of the lady, Mother Margarita Maria said with much disbelief, "Marie Felton? Marie Felton has money? I don't believe it."

No one would have questioned Mother Margarita Maria's disbelief as this woman was always shabbily dressed, looking much like a beggar when she came to the retreat house. However, she had asked that Mother Margarita Maria come to see her at Queen of the Angels Hospital the next day as she was soon to have surgery for cancer. Mother Margarita Maria was happy to perform this act of charity.

Mrs. Felton always spoke in a brusque manner and tone and scarcely had the Sisters entered her room when she said, "You don't believe I have money, do you?"

Mother Margarita Maria replied, "Maybe you do."

She continued, "I love the Sacred Heart and I have great devotion to the Sacred Heart. Because of this I want to pay off your debt on the Sacred Heart Retreat House and the balance of the money will be for a new chapel. The one you have is too small."

After a brief pause she continued, "I will send you the money tonight. I am tired now. Please go."

The Sisters waited that evening wondering if it could possibly be true. Could Marie Felton really have money? About eight o'clock the door bell rang. A Mrs. Felton lookalike – an elderly lady, shabbily dressed, with a shopping bag in each hand – stood on the doorstep.

"Are you Mother Margarita Maria?" she inquired when Sister opened the door and without waiting for a reply she continued, "Well, then you know what these contain. Take them," she then turned around without another word and walked down the walkway headed for the street.

The Sisters could not imagine what the bags contained, but they were heavy. When they looked inside, to their amazement, all they saw were old cleanser cans. They spread some papers on the floor and Mother Margarita Maria took the lid off the first can. Yes, there was money inside. Can after can was emptied onto the floor in a pile – thousand dollar bills, five hundred dollar bills and other large denominations. It was incredible.

"Mother," one of the Sisters said, overcome at the sight and knowing what it meant to them, "look how good God is to us," and she began to cry.

Two very heavy cans, which obviously contained coins, had been put aside to be opened last. No one was prepared for what they saw when the lid was taken from the first of the cans. Coins! Gold coins – in fifty and one hundred dollar pieces. The currency and gold coins amounted to $46,000! To even keep such a large sum of cash in the convent over night seemed hazardous, but what to do?

Mother Margarita Maria resolved the problem quickly. "We will take it to the bank."

It was then past nine o'clock at night and the banks had been closed several hours. However, the manager of a branch of Bank of America in Monrovia was a personal friend of the community and when Mother Margarita Maria telephoned him and asked him to open the bank so they could deposit a large amount of money just received in a safe deposit box for overnight, he agreed to do so.

The next morning, as soon as the bank opened, Mother Margarita Maria promptly paid off the debt on the retreat house. It was indeed a happy day for the Sisters! They had been struggling to meet the interest on their loan and to also pay off a little on the principal to reduce their indebtedness. It had meant very real sacrifice, and the Sisters often went without.

While Mrs. Felton was hospitalized in Los Angeles after her surgery, the Sisters went to visit her several times. However, she never made any mention of the money at any time. Two weeks went by and she was then able to be up and around. She telephoned Mother Margarita Maria and her first words were, "Mother, I have changed my mind. I want my money back. I am getting well. I am not going to die and I will need it."

The Carmelite Sisters of the Sacred Heart was a diocesan community and so was required to report all financial transactions to the local ordinary. When Mother Margarita Maria explained to Bishop McGucken what had happened, how they had been given money and that Mrs. Felton now was demanding its return, he said, "How do you feel about it?"

Mother Margarita Maria replied, "The same, Your Excellency. We will return what is left. Surely, you must know that we paid off the debt on the retreat house at once, the very next morning after receiving the money. That was Mrs. Felton's request. Now we will return what is left."

Bishop McGucken also felt that was a proper decision.

Mother Margarita Maria obtained a cashier's check for the balance of the money and took it to Mrs. Felton explaining that she had paid off the debt as requested.

"Where are my gold coins, and where are my large bills?" Mrs. Felton asked, as she looked at the check.

"We turned all the money into the bank and they gave us credit for it. Now I am returning the balance to you."

Marie Felton lived for several more years. She continued to visit the Retreat House and was always graciously received.

Then one day she telephoned to tell Mother Margarita Maria that the cancer had returned and asked if she would come to her home the next morning at eleven o'clock to see her. Mother Margarita Maria assured her she would be there. However, early the following morning a call came that Mrs. Felton had been taken to the hospital by ambulance and was in a coma.

She lingered for several weeks, never regaining consciousness. During that time, even though she was not conscious, the Sisters went regularly to visit her and three Sisters were with her when she died. It was Friday and the feast day of St. Margaret Mary Alacoque, the saint chosen by our Lord to spread devotion to His Sacred Heart throughout the world; the saint to whom He revealed His twelve promises to those faithful to this devotion.

A large chapel was constructed on the grounds of the Retreat House several years later. The Sisters never received any further money from Marie Felton nor her estate and they never knew what happened to the balance of the money they returned to her at her request. The Sisters placed a plaque in the new chapel in their own choir adjoining the sanctuary in gratitude and as a memorial to Mrs. Marie Felton – a most unlikely benefactor – for her generosity.

The Baths at Lourdes

by Sister Imelda Marie, O.C.D.

W<small>HEN IT WAS ANNOUNCED THAT</small> I <small>WAS GOING TO</small> L<small>OURDES</small>, the first question put to me was: *"Are you going to the baths?"* In 1996, I had the privilege of going to Lourdes. Most of the Sisters went to the baths, but I chose not to, as at the time I was healthy, and saw no reason to subject myself to cold water immersion. This time, however, because of my heart problems there was no doubt in my mind that I would go to the baths. I knew that if I started to have health problems after the Pilgrimage, everyone would point out it was because I had neglected to visit the baths. So, for selfish, personal reasons I decided to go.

Before continuing with my story, it might be helpful at this point to provide some background information about the Lourdes Baths for those who might not know its history and significance. In 1858, the Virgin Mary appeared to a local girl, Bernadette Soubirous, 18 times. During the ninth apparition on February 25, our Blessed Mother instructed Bernadette to dig in the ground and drink from the spring she found there. When Bernadette started to go toward the River Gave, our Blessed Mother called her back and pointed to the ground in the grotto. Bernadette started digging a hole in the dry earth with her hands and after a little while the hole started to fill with a small amount of muddy water. Bernadette brought a handful of the muddy water to her face, took a few sips and "washed" by smearing the mud on her face. Everyone present started to laugh at the sight.

After Bernadette left the grotto, the hole slowly filled, then overflowed with a small trickle that became a stream of water and the muddy water became increasingly clear. A blind man washed his eyes in the water and was healed.

A sick child was immersed in the water and became well. Since then, a steady procession of pilgrims, many with a host of different illnesses and maladies, have gone to Lourdes and followed the instructions of Our Lady to "drink at the spring and wash (bathe) in it." Although there have been only 69 confirmed physical cures, there have been countless spiritual and emotional healings.

One of the Knights of Malta explained to me that the spring at Lourdes is an "artesian well", which usually lasts for only a short while, and the water pressure varies. The water at Lourdes has been flowing at a constant pressure for over 150 years – most unusual for this type of spring. The water itself has been examined by many different scientists and has been subjected to many scientific tests. It is "virgin water", very pure containing no bacteria – a symbol of the Immaculate Conception, (no stain of original sin on Mary's soul); the name by which Our Lady referred to herself when Bernadette asked her who she was.

It is said that no one goes to Lourdes without being changed in some way. Upon arriving home, when asked, *"Did you go to the baths?"*, I realized just how true this is. The first few times I told the story of my experience, I was overcome with such a tidal wave of emotion that I had a hard time articulating myself. I felt quite overwhelmed with emotion, and it was only through my tears that I could express the impact this experience had on me.

Returning to the story… our first day in Lourdes was cold and rainy – in the low 50s – quite the contrast to the dry, over 90-degree weather back home in southern California of the day before. It was on this day that we were scheduled to visit the baths. Several Sisters advised me to "dress lightly" on the day I would go. The helpers were instructed not to go to the baths on the day which is reserved only for "the malades" *(Term used by members of the Order of Malta when referring to the sick they are caring for)* – who make a pilgrimage to Lourdes to drink at the spring and bathe in it, seeking healing from their illness. Keeping this in mind, I felt free to dress very, very warmly.

My experience at the baths can be summed up as such: God threw me, a reluctant pilgrim, into the waters, not once, but twice!

On this first day, the malades went into the baths while the helpers remained outside. This particular day the process apparently moved faster than expected, because the helpers were invited to go to the baths. At first, I declined the offer because I was "over-dressed" for the occasion and I remembered we were told not to go to the baths on the first day.

Mary Rogers*, the Malta Dame on my team, took my bag and coat and emphatically said "GO!!!" She explained that this was a very rare opportunity and I should take advantage of it, so off I went.

After a few minutes' wait to go into the "undressing" area, I spent the time trying to recollect myself. I felt inspired to offer the experience for all the prayer intentions I brought to Lourdes: for all the Sisters in our Community, those discerning a vocation to the religious life, our friends, relatives, benefactors and all in need of prayer.

When I was called into the undressing area, I became very nervous about the process. I felt rushed because I did not want the sick to have to wait for me. A volunteer held a heavy blue drape around and above me as I undressed. I started to put my clothing on the chair in front of me. Wrong!

"No, no, no," the volunteer said in a heavy French accent as she waved her finger at me.

She then pointed to a small hook above my head. I felt it was a miracle of Lourdes that I was able to fit so much clothing onto such a small hook! At this point I realized that the night cap I had so wisely brought with me for this occasion was in the bag that Mary was holding outside for me. The same "privacy" drape that was held in front of me as I undressed was now wrapped tightly around me like a tamale wrap, or more like a shroud. Then I realized I had forgotten to take off my new watch! There was no way I could get my hands free to remove the watch, so I tried to explain to the helpers that I needed to take off the watch. Wrong. I was told to keep it on!

As I waited my turn, the lady who went into the water before me screamed, "It's cold! It's so very cold!"

I closed my eyes tightly and tried to recollect myself again praying, "Lord, do not let the cold distract me from the graces of this moment."

When it was my turn to go into the inner draped area of the baths, I was instructed to pray before the procedure and when I was ready, to make the Sign of the Cross. I again repeated my prayer intentions with a plea that the coldness would not distract me from the graces of this special moment.

I must have taken too long, because they asked me if I was ready. I nodded yes and I was guided down two steps into the deep tub-like area. I waded toward the statue at the end of the tub, kissed the statue and started to turn around. Wrong! I was asked to semi-sit down, then, I was rapidly lowered into the water and back up. As I started to exit the tub, I realized I forgot to make the Sign of the Cross! So I made it rapidly and thought with a bit of dismay, "That's not the way Our Blessed Mother would have taught Bernadette to make the Sign of the Cross!" What amazed me most was that even though the water was "exteriorly" very cold, I felt deep peace and spiritual warmth. I was also amazed to notice that I was dry! Another of the unique and unusual features of the baths is that no towels are needed to dry afterward. As soon as one emerges from the water, one is dry!

After arriving back at the hotel, one of the other Dames of Malta who always wears a smile on her face, asked me to tell her about my experience at the baths. I told her how nervous I was with the mechanics of the event: worry over where to put all my clothing, worry that I would ruin my new watch, sorry that I forgot to make the Sign of the Cross at the right time.

The Dame suddenly became very serious and said to me, "Promise me that you will go back to the baths a second time before you leave Lourdes. Now you know the mechanics of the procedure. When you go back again, I promise you that the second experience will be completely different."

I assured her that the experience was a once-in-a-lifetime adventure that I had no desire to repeat. Once was more than enough for me.

She put her hands on my shoulders, looked me in the eye and said very solemnly: "Promise me you will go to the baths a second time. I promise you the experience will be completely different."

I reluctantly promised that if there was an opportunity to go to the baths a second time, I would do so, but I quickly sent an "SOS" prayer Heavenward that there would be no opportunity to repeat the experience. There were so many events to attend, one after another that there was never time to even think of going back to the baths.

The last day of our Pilgrimage, Mary Rogers and John Stevens*, my team companions, had to leave Lourdes a day early, so I was assigned to a new Dame of Malta for the last day. She came up to me with "marching orders" to meet her at 8:15 a.m. because our new malades wanted to return to the baths!!!

As it turned out, Mr. Stevens had invited us to go with him to make the Stations of the Cross at the same time we were to return to the baths – a perfect excuse for not going back! I asked Mother Judith what I should do. She wisely reminded me that we were here at Lourdes to help with the sick, so I should go where my team was planning to go.

Just as the Dame had promised, the second trip to the baths was indeed a totally different experience – and one that I did not expect.

The mechanics of preparation went very smoothly this time. I was dressed lightly for the occasion, I did not worry about my watch, and no one was screaming about the coldness of the water. Since the weather was warmer, I thought the waters might be warmer, too. As I waited my turn, I again closed my eyes and tried to recollect myself. This time, I felt drawn to go into the waters praying for sinners just as our Blessed Mother had requested Bernadette to pray for sinners.

How can I describe my experience? Everyone who knows me knows of my love for the *"Epiclesis"* of the Mass, (the part of the Eucharistic Prayer by which the priest invokes the power of the Holy Spirit's blessing upon the Eucharistic bread and wine) and how much that small word had opened for me the hidden treasures of the Mass. In trying to find the word or words to describe the experience during my second Lourdes bath, the best and only word that I can use is *"Anamnesis"* (the part of the Eucharistic Prayer following the Words of Institution spoken by Jesus ending with "Do this in memory of me.")

The last few years I have been drawn to this word – "Anamnesis," which means "remembrance". As I grow older, "remembering" daily things becomes more of a challenge. The term Anamnesis, referring to the time immediately after the consecration when we remember the events of Christ's Passion, Death and Resurrection, is not a recalling of a past event that occurred 2000 years ago, but is rather a remembrance that makes these past events present on our altar and in our lives **now**. Pope John Paul II, Pope Benedict XVI and even Pope Francis have often spoken about this.

What does this word Anamnesis, used for the liturgy, have to do with my second experience at the baths at Lourdes? As I approached the water, I looked down at it and felt as if I was looking at the water with the eyes of Jesus as He looked at the waters of the Jordan River at His baptism. I felt so closely united with Him as He, though sinless, entered those waters to take upon himself our sins and wash away the sins of the world.

But the beauty of this experience was abruptly changed with my first step into the water, which was so very cold! At each step, I felt a bitter, biting coldness. I quickly repeated my prayer, "Do not let the coldness distract me from this moment", but the more I prayed, the colder I felt and the more pain I felt! The thought came to me that maybe I would be the first pilgrim to leave Lourdes with frostbite!

As I reached the steps to exit the bath, I was angry at myself for being so distracted by the cold. I asked God why He allowed me to be so distracted and in a split second the answer came. At the first bath, I took with me the prayers of all those who are close to me and to our Carmelite Community. Even though the water was cold, I felt the warmth of their love. At the second bath I took with me prayers of all sinners, of all time. God allowed me the special grace to feel the coldness that Jesus felt as He came to give us the warmth of this love, but only received the cold indifference of hearts not open to His love.

This time, I made the Sign of the Cross as I exited the bath, but it had such a powerful meaning to me. In some small way, I felt I had just experienced the privilege of "making up" in my body what was "lacking" in the sufferings of Christ.

As promised, I did have a totally different experience the two times I went into the baths. Later I realized that I had completely forgotten to pray for my health, which was the primary reason I went to the baths to begin with! It is so true that in giving we receive. In forgetting myself, I felt so enriched in praying for others.

Later that morning I met Susan*, the Dame of Malta who had insisted that I promise to revisit the baths. She asked how my second experience went. As I described it to her, her eyes started to fill with tears.

She asked, "Why?"

Only then did I realize that this different experience was not the "different experience" she had expected me to have. I told her about Epiclesis – the insight I received regarding sharing in the sufferings of Christ for the sinners and the salvation of the world. I then gave her a copy of my 50ᵗʰ Jubilee card. On it is a picture of a Carmelite Sister kneeling at the foot of the crucifix holding up a chalice in one hand to collect the Precious Blood, as her other hand is extended over the world in an Epiclesis prayer for sinners and the salvation of the world.

The quotes I chose for the card were really brought to life at Lourdes:

- *"Oh, I won't let this Precious Blood be wasted! I will spend my life collecting it for souls."*
  – St. Therese of Lisieux

- *"Being always at the foot of the cross, the Carmelite receives the Blood of Jesus and pours it out through her prayers on the whole world."*
  – St. Teresa of the Andes

- *"By her prayer, the religious says an epiclesis over the whole world, and it will be heard, for it is a sharing in the prayer of Christ Himself."*
  – Saint Pope John Paul II

* = *denotes names have been changed to protect privacy*

How Does She Do That?!?

by Sister Mary James, O.C.D.

Y EARS AGO, WHEN I WAS IN THE NOVITIATE, we were told that the first one who cleared away and washed the Superior's dishes received a plenary indulgence. Now, I don't know how accurate this is, but it is what we were told. Needless to say, there was always a healthy competition amongst us to be the first one to gather the Superior's dishes. As a footnote, I'll explain here what an indulgence is. According to the Catechism of the Catholic Church, an indulgence "is a remission before God of the temporal punishment due to sins whose guilt has already been forgiven … An indulgence is partial or plenary according as it removes either part or all of the temporal punishment due to sin." Now, returning to the story.....

In our refectory, there are long tables and we sit on each side across from one another. The novices and postulants were sitting on one side and I made sure to sit opposite them in order to have a clear line of vision to the Superior's table. I even took pains to move the silver coffee pot (placed at intervals on the table so we could serve ourselves) to ensure it did not block my view of Mother. Sister Michelle usually sat directly opposite me with some of the novices on either side of her. Sister Michelle could not see the Superior's table as she was sitting with her back to her. As it turned out, much to my chagrin, at each and every meal, Sister Michelle would beat me in gathering up the Superior's dishes. Having something of a competitive streak, I was getting tired of Sister Michelle beating me in racking up plenary indulgences and resolved to reach the dishes first at least once.

At every meal from that point forward, I kept an eagle's eye watch on the Superior, hardly eating, so intent was I to be the first to see her stand so I could dash over to her table to collect her dishes. Alas, all to no avail. Despite my watchfulness, suddenly before I even realized what was happening, Sister Michelle sprung up from her seat and collected the dishes! *How does she do that?!?*

When Sister Michelle returned to our table, I just had to ask. "I can't stand it any longer!" I exclaimed. "How do you get over to Mother's table when you can't even see when she is standing up and you're with your back to her and I'm sitting here watching her every move?"

"Oh, I see her reflection in the coffee pot," Sister Michelle nonchalantly replied, "I keep an eye on the coffee pot so I see when Mother starts to stand and I can go collect her dishes."

Well! Who would have thought!

"Let me try that," I said, turning the coffee pot around.

It didn't seem to work for me – I couldn't see Mother's table. It was then I realized, I had to be sitting on the opposite side of the table from where I was sitting with my back to her in order to see her reflection!

Right Out of Ghostbusters!

by Sister Mary Scholastica, O.C.D.

S AFETY DRILLS are something we practice regularly at our Motherhouse/Retreat House and one recent safety drill focused on what to do in case of a fire. During the fire drill, we were instructed that if a "code red" is announced via the intercom, we are to gather in the back parking lot for a headcount to ensure everyone is accounted for. We were also told that if we have a fire extinguisher near us, we should grab the extinguisher and go directly to the location of the fire to help fight it. Unbeknownst to us, the timing of this drill was providential.

Shortly after this drill took place, a code red was called and it was the real deal, not a drill. Confident in our recent training, I got up from my desk and in one fluid motion quickly grabbed a fire extinguisher that I saw on my way out of the office. I was on my way to help fight the fire.

I made a dash for the basement of the convent where the fire was located. En route, I encountered Sister Gloria Therese rushing in the same direction lugging an impressively hefty-sized fire extinguisher. As my eyes fixed on the extinguisher in her hands, I glanced downward to take a better look at the extinguisher in my own hands. Much to my chagrin, there in my hand was a tiny, little bitty fire extinguisher that was at the most eight or nine inches in length! Oh my goodness! When I grabbed it, I was so focused on getting to where the fire was, it didn't occur to me to look at how big my extinguisher was! Well, I'd just have to make the best of it!

When Sister Gloria Therese and I arrived at the basement door, what followed was a scene reminiscent of the film Ghostbusters. Sister threw open the door and flew down the stairs brandishing her fire extinguisher. I was right on her heels. Sister Janelle stood at the bottom of the stairs and was somewhat surprised to see us flying down the steps. We hurried toward the large laundry room which had ominous black smoke billowing out its doors.

Sister Gloria Therese planted her feet, pulled the pin and started spraying foam everywhere. Suddenly, out of the smoke and foam, a rather ominous-looking figure loomed, staggering toward us. What looked like a specter out of Ghostbusters turned out to be one of our staff members! Sister Gloria Therese in bravely wielding her fire extinguisher in an attempt to fight the fire, was actually spraying our staff member covering him in foam. There I was right behind her with my miniature fire extinguisher ready to spring into action and help fight the flames if necessary.

Well, it certainly seemed like a comedy of errors: two Sisters flying down the stairs, one with a defunct little, bitty fire extinguisher and the other with a huge unwieldy extinguisher, that by virtue of its ungainly size sprayed foam with such force that the foam was getting on everything and everyone except the fire! Eventually, Ross, our staff member, managed to navigate his way through the flying foam and said, "Sister, Sister, give me that fire extinguisher. I'll take care of it!"

Later, upon closer inspection, we discovered that my mini fire extinguisher didn't even work!

Needless to say, we still laugh about our adventure in fire fighting.

Faithful Until Death

by Sister Imelda Marie, O.C.D.

*A*T THE END OF SISTER GEMA ALICIA'S LIFE, she was very sick with pulmonary problems. We knew she was dying, but she remained alert almost until the very end. On that last day she was fully responsive and as we Sisters turned her over to change her position, her blood pressure suddenly dropped and her breathing became very slow and labored.

We summoned all the Sisters and began the prayers for the dying. We sang the Salve Regina and then started to recite the renewal of vows.

Just as we got to the very last line, *"May Your grace fortify my weakness in order to be faithful until death in this consecration to You, my God"*, Sister Gema took her last breath, yielding her soul into the Hands of the Creator, having indeed been faithful until death.

Healing

*"We can never have too much confidence in the good God who is so powerful
and so merciful. We obtain from him as much as we hope for."*
- Saint Therese of the Child Jesus

I Witnessed a Miracle

by Sister Timothy Marie, O.C.D.

BEFORE THE MIRACLE, I BELIEVED. NOW I KNOW. The following story is true. It happened to me. I will never, ever forget it.

I had been a Carmelite Sister for many years when this story occurred. It changed my life forever, and I came away from the experience with an explosion of faith bursting within my soul.   To cut to the quick and bring forth the significance of the experience right away, let me just say that two other teachers and myself found ourselves teaching an eighth grade class with a special problem, or should I say burden? Whatever you want to call it, these students carried an unseen burden that permeated them and their classroom as well. It was some kind of oppressive sadness. Honestly, it's true. The atmosphere was palpably, distressingly – there's no other way to describe it – sad. You could cut the atmosphere with a knife. We asked each other what happened to bring about this deep sadness.

The students were so young – only in eighth grade. What could have caused it? The only thing we were able to discover was that they had some tough years together as a class, and quarrels and factions that started out in the younger grades snowballed as the years went by. You mean that children can have that much sadness? So young? Yes, that's exactly what I mean.

So, what did we do? We three teachers prayed briefly one late March afternoon, asking the Holy Spirit for direction and guidance. These young teenagers would graduate from eighth grade in just a few months and it seemed such a shame to have them go forth from our school carrying that big load. By the way, we never spoke to them about what we noticed, thinking that some things are better left unsaid.

Enter the Holy Spirit.

Shortly after our prayer for guidance, one of us received an idea, taking form slowly at first and then turning into the concept of having a customized retreat of sorts for the members of this class. The principal agreed we could hold it on the school premises, because we did not have a budget for an off-campus retreat.

This is where I need to tell you about the rocks.

There were some rocks of various sizes left at a construction site near the school. I went one afternoon and loaded several into the back of our van. The first day of our on-campus retreat, the class walked into our parish multi-purpose room to begin the retreat. Beautiful praise music was playing in the background as they entered. Before them, in the center of the room was a pile of rocks – yes, the same rocks from the construction site. Those rocks are essential to the story.

Well, we sat down in a circle with the rocks in the middle. Now, I'm not one for gimmicks. I've been through the sixties and the seventies and I've seen more gimmicks used in retreats than I care to remember. They are just plain goofy. The rocks were definitely not a gimmick. They were the concretization of the heaviness, the symbol of the "burden" that each one of these dear children seemed to be carrying. So, that's what we told them. We asked them to see if they could find a rock that would match the heaviness of any burden they carried within their hearts. It was amazing. They took it so seriously. As the students' names were called, they all chose their rock and put it in their backpacks. They continued carrying their "burdens" for three consecutive days. This had an unforeseen, electrifying effect throughout all grade levels.

There were so many other components of the retreat, the "Sorry's" whereby every single member of the class was urged to write their "Sorry's" to anyone in the class they had slighted, made fun of, or hurt during their years together as a class. Paper bags were taped to the sides of the desks and, yes, they kept filling up just like on Valentine's Day; the excerpts from films which had forgiveness themes which we watched and discussed; the art class where each one received a template of a human person – with a large heart in the center – to be transformed into his or her image, and added to the others on the bulletin board, all holding hands.

It was an amazing thing to see how often the students' eyes turned toward that bulletin board to watch their figures during the day.

One girl colored on top of her heart so it couldn't be seen.

Another student broke her heart in two.

We teachers said nothing. We prayed and watched.

Now, back to the rocks. Ten copies of the class list were made. Every hour or hour and a half during the school day, which continued with its regular lessons, a bell was rung. The box was brought out containing a complete list of class names cut up, with each name folded in half. The first student came up and took a name. Let's say he picked Mary's name. He would walk over to her and say, "Mary, may I help you carry your burden?" Then Mary, after giving him her rock, would pick a name from the box and go to that person and ask to carry that student's burden. This went on until there were no more names.

Wonder of wonders, we heard a knock on the classroom door and a child from a younger class gave me a note. It was from the Art and Science teacher. It read, "I would like to be a part of this retreat, too. Can I get a rock, too? I also have a big burden on my heart right now." For some reason, this was a turning point for the class. They insisted on getting a rock and a back pack and presenting it to this Carmelite Sister who had requested it. Well, that did it. The teachers got rocks also. All our names were put in the box. We carried students' burdens and they carried ours.

One student's comment impressed me. "Hey, why is Susan's * rock so big? Look at it. It hardly fits in her backpack. She has everything! What kind of burden could she possibly have?" After that comment, the class became noticeably reflective and, thereafter, when someone picked Susan's name and asked to carry her burden, that student was noticeably subdued, thinking, ruminating on that huge rock from the girl "who had everything."

We had chosen Holy Week for our on-campus retreat. Our Easter vacation would begin on Holy Thursday at 12:30 p.m. We decided to end the retreat before then. How? We ended with the Sacrament of Reconciliation, followed the next day, by a profound moment in the convent chapel when each student laid their burden at the foot of a large cross in the sanctuary. We invited students who wanted, to kneel on a predieu, alone in the center aisle, and we prayed for each one who chose to kneel there for a few moments.

That's when it happened.

If you would ask me, "What happened?" I couldn't say it in words. All I could do would be to say that something sweet and profound, an anointing, descended upon our chapel.

As the concluding Mass of our retreat began, the oppressive sadness just lifted. Poof! Gone.

After Mass, with my own eyes, I saw these beautiful children of God, run, skip, and yes, dance out of the chapel and into our school playground. But, where are they going, I asked myself, as they entered the school building?

A few moments later, they emerged from the music room – they had borrowed some of the musical instruments from the teacher. There they were with tambourines and maracas, triangles and bongos. One had an auto harp. Another played a xylophone – and we teachers?

We watched as these precious children of God formed a conga line of sorts, right there in the school playground. We had no camera. No need, really, for a camera as the moment was embedded indelibly into our souls.

The same God Who healed with a word, a touch, a thought, the same God Who raised from the dead, gave speech and hearing and restored healthy limbs, the same God who set prisoners free, in one sovereign almighty act, restored the joy and innocence of childhood to these children.

We teachers just stood there and wept, transfixed in the moment, eyes glued to our students, listening to the happy laughter and the unrehearsed music coming from their souls through those school instruments. We simply soaked in the moment in silence.

This, then, is the story of the miracle I witnessed.

Before the miracle, I believed. Now I know.

God can and He will, and He does hear our prayers.

* = *denotes names have been changed to protect privacy*

'Finding God's Healing Grace

by Sister Maria Kolbe, O.C.D.

*T*HERE ARE TIMES GOD GENTLY NUDGES US out of our comfort zone, especially when He chooses us to be the vehicle by which He pours out His salvific and healing grace to the soul most in need of it. I must admit, however, that I never imagined I would find myself in just such a role.

I had always been a classroom teacher, but one year, Our Lord decided He needed me to serve as the Campus Minister at one of our high schools and it was precisely into this position I was assigned. In the weeks leading up to the opening of the new school year, I found myself frequently lamenting to the Lord my lack of qualification to be a campus minister.

"Lord, what are you doing?" I asked a bit frantically in prayer. "I'm a classroom teacher, not a campus minister! But I suppose you have your reason for asking me to do this, so I will do my best to make your love known to the students in my new role, but please help me." Deep down, I knew this was His work, His apostolate and that He indeed would qualify the unqualified, namely me! I took comfort in the words of Saint Paul: "Therefore, I am well content with weaknesses … difficulties, for Christ's sake; for when I am weak, then I am strong" (2 Cor 12:10).

Over the course of my years working in our education apostolates, one thing I quickly realized is that Adoration of the Most Blessed Sacrament is deeply enriching spiritually for all our students regardless of age. Adoration and quiet contemplative prayer before our Eucharistic Lord is something we introduce early on to our youngest charges in our child care centers and continue to expose students to Adoration into the elementary years and continuing throughout high school.

At this young age, it is so beautiful to see that the students are able to experience God's love openly and without self-consciousness; they have the capacity to deeply open their heart and soul to the Lord. For His part, God never appeared to tire of displaying His majestic loving power and tender mercy to the students and to me over and over again.

One of the "perks" of being the Campus Minister allowed me to stay with Jesus in the Blessed Sacrament during the entire course of the day. The religion teachers would bring in their students period by period. Adoration was led a bit differently for each class period, in whatever way the Holy Spirit would inspire. It sometimes consisted of silent prayer, other times we recited the Rosary together aloud and at other times contemporary Christian music softly playing in the background motivated and inspired us to praise God. The chaplain was always available to hear confessions. Adoration always concluded with Benediction.

The profound effect of Adoration on the students was apparent. Most of the juniors and seniors, accustomed to coming to Adoration since freshman year, loved the peace they found in front of the Blessed Sacrament. Remarkably, even those students who appeared to be "less religious" found great solace in the Lord's presence. It was beautiful to see these young people praying in rapt attention. Occasionally though, we would have a class, usually the younger, lower classmen, who squirmed restlessly or had difficulty focusing in the silence. As the students would contemplate our Eucharistic Lord, our chaplain faithfully sat in the makeshift confessional, (the sacristy), ready to hear confessions. Because it was not uncommon for someone's confession to overlap into the next class period, I had at the ready "excuse" passes to sign, time and date for students returning to their next class.

One particular morning around 9:30 a.m., shortly after the start of the school year, there were about 95 students in the chapel for Adoration. This particular group of juniors and seniors became readily immersed in God's presence. Christian praise and worship music played softly in the background as students went to Confession.

I was spontaneously moved to remind the students, "Tell Jesus whatever is in your heart. He already knows what it is, simply hand it over to Him."

Suddenly, one of the seniors, David*, began to cry out softly to the Lord. I was kneeling in fairly close proximity to this young man and I could tell his cries were from an inner anguish that welled up from deep down inside.

I moved over beside him and put my hand on his shoulder softly said, "David, Jesus is with you. We are with you. I am with you. Let Jesus have it because He can handle it all."

Not a single one of the other students in the chapel stared at David. I noted two very evident things: they all knew inner pain and they were all praying with and for David.

In due time, the ringing bell announced the change in classes.

I quickly moved next to David and quietly told him, "You don't have to go; stay as long as you want. He will do all for you." David neither moved nor verbally acknowledged that he heard me; only his sobs grew louder.

The next class, a mixture of seniors and freshmen, came into the chapel. Realizing what was going on, the seniors quickly knelt in prayer, their solidarity with David palpable. Unfortunately, the younger students, the freshmen, didn't quite know what to make of David's tears and cries, as they awkwardly kept glancing about and staring at David.

In order to focus the freshmen's attention on God and draw it away from David, I led them in a short Biblical meditation about God's love and how He wants to reach out to each one of us. David's unrelenting cries and groans only became louder. I knew he was releasing this inner pain and turning it over to Jesus. While most of David's words were inaudible, every once in a while a word of pleading could be understood.

I returned to David's side and again placed my hand on his shoulder only this time, I didn't speak to David, but rather silently, fervently addressed my Eternal Spouse, "I beg you, my Jesus, heal this young man and give him what he needs."

I must add a little footnote here. I have never liked "lookie-loos" – you know, those who don't mind their own business but stare, better, gawk, at everything. Well, as it turns out, this group of seniors didn't like it either, as several of them shot "it's not cool to stare" looks at those freshmen who still were taken aback at the sight of David crying in Adoration. This was a great help to me, for in previous Adoration times, I had to continually remind this freshmen class to sit up straight and focus. Well, they were certainly sitting up ramrod straight now with eyes locked on the Lord!

In the meantime, I was busy trying to choose the most meaningful music to play. While each song played, I quickly scanned the playlist of each CD for additional songs. I'd whisper, "Lord, show me the right song to choose that will help David."

This second class period passed and David's tears still ran and his muffled yet continuous words flowed to the Lord. Every once in a while, I'd approach David and assure him that God wanted very much to heal him.

The third period bell rang. David glanced in my direction, his eyes beseeching me to permit him stay. I gently nodded my approval as I had absolutely no doubt that this young man needed to be in God's presence.

The next group of students entered the chapel. David's heartfelt prayer was clear to all of us, especially when he lifted his bowed head to look up at the Blessed Sacrament as he continued to pour out his heart in supplication.

About half-way through this third period, the tension that had been so tightly coiled in David's body began to relax and his tears began to dry. Some minutes later, David stood and came over to me.

"I'm ready to go back to class now, Sister," he said to me.

I regarded him without speaking. The tension indeed was all gone and I knew God had spoken to David's heart. "It's now fourth period," I said quietly, "You'll need a pass."

"Yes, Sister, I know," he replied with the hint of a contented smile playing at the corners of his mouth that told me the burden had been lifted.

As I continued with Adoration for the subsequent classes that day, I spent most of that time with one prayer on my lips: "Thank you, Lord Jesus, for the wonderful healing graces you bestowed on David and on all the rest of us!"

The days turned into weeks, which turned into months. I would see David in the hallways almost on a daily basis and he'd greet me with that great infectious smile of his. He never mentioned that day during Adoration nor did it ever occur to me to ask him.

Several months later, it was time for the senior young men's overnight retreat. It was an exceptional retreat filled with graces for all participants, myself included. The last session of the retreat consisted of a simple sharing of experiences by those who wished to reveal the graces God had given them. Many of the young men, David included, went up to the microphone to share and it was deeply touching to hear them speak about all that God had done for them. Finally, it was David's turn.

"What I'd like to share began months ago at the beginning of the school year during Adoration," he started, his voice firm with conviction. "But for you to understand what happened during Adoration, you first have to know a little about my background," he continued.

"My biological father left my mom at the hospital the day I was born to raise me by herself. My mom eventually married another man, but I didn't find a father figure in her new husband. All those years growing up, being fatherless made me feel abandoned and very alone....until that day during Adoration.

"That morning, Sister told me that I can tell God anything. I felt secure there in the chapel and suddenly, I couldn't hold it in any longer....the tears and frustration just came bursting forth. I told God I wanted to know Him as "Father" and that I was tired of feeling alone.

"Each time when I thought there was nothing left within me to hand over to Jesus, Sister would play one song after another that referred to God as "Father"....our Father....my "Father" and I would break down again and again. That day, God revealed Himself to me as my Father. I know with confidence that I have a Father who cares for me and that I am His child, His son," David shared with deep emotion. The silence in the room was so profound as David spoke, it would have been possible to hear a pin drop on the carpeted floor.

The retreat concluded and all the young men were picked-up by their parents. Later that afternoon, I sat on a stone bench under the protective shade of a large old tree listening to the birds as they cheerfully serenaded me. I was waiting for my religious sisters to pick me up from the retreat house and I suddenly realized how thoroughly exhausted I was – exhausted but elated! As always, God once again stepped up and did His work. God had taken things in hand by transforming pain and feelings of rejection and abandonment into the beauty of a healed heart in this young man, David. I thought back to the days before I assumed my position as Campus Minister and my feelings of being unqualified and then to that day in Adoration, when in the role of campus minister one has to be all things to all students.

Yes, I had to lead students in prayer and help the squirming ones focus; I had to keep my eye on David as he bared his wounded heart in prayer; I had to pick the music; I had to keep an eye on the clock in order to not go over the class period, all while trying to pray myself. Then realization dawned!

"Lord, I wasn't the one who picked that music, YOU did!" I exclaimed aloud. "David thought it was me, but no….honestly, Jesus, you are the best contemporary Christian DJ there is! You really do qualify the unqualified called! Thanks, Lord!"

* = denotes names have been changed to protect privacy

The Miracle in Room 207

by Sister Maria Elia, O.C.D.

A s Carmelite Sisters of the Most Sacred Heart of Los Angeles, we have a deep devotion to the Heart of Christ and as such, we had a long-standing interest in the cause for canonization of Blessed Claude de la Colombiere. Blessed Claude, a Jesuit priest who promoted the devotion to the Sacred Heart of Jesus, required a second and final miracle attributed to his intercession in order to be approved for canonization. To this day, I am overwhelmed by the loving graciousness God has shown our community by permitting that miracle, the healing of Father John Houle, SJ, to occur at Santa Teresita, our then hospital in Duarte, California.

As a missionary in China, Father John Houle underwent tremendous sufferings during his five-year imprisonment and developed severe health issues in addition to the chronic back problems that had plagued him since childhood.

Father Houle came to Santa Teresita in late December 1989, in the days when it still served as an acute-care hospital. Father already had a long history of serious coronary issues, as well as emphysema by then; however, he was still able to walk and every day I would accompany him to the main chapel so he could celebrate Mass. However, as he gradually became weaker, walking became more difficult and even a few steps would leave him very short of breath. It was apparent that his condition was worsening by the day. In February 1990, the doctor ordered a fiber optic bronchoscope, a test by which Father Houle was diagnosed as having pulmonary fibrosis, which is a terminal condition.

Father Houle's condition deteriorated dramatically and rapidly and he was put on very high dosages of 100% pure oxygen. Just after the bronchoscope test was done, I recall that one of the doctors remarked, "I very much doubt if Father will be alive by the weekend." It was Thursday.

Father Houle's superior, Father Francis Parrish, SJ, had a great devotion to the Sacred Heart of Jesus and was in charge of the Sacred Heart devotional programs in Los Angeles. As a result, Father Parrish established many prayer groups in the U.S. and Canada. Father Parrish was also very interested in Blessed Claude's cause. Now, Father Parrish enlisted the aid of the many Sacred Heart prayer groups he had formed in praying for Father Houle's cure through the intercession of Blessed Claude de la Colombiere.

It was now Friday. I was scheduled to attend a two-day conference, but I would visit Father Houle upon my return in the late afternoon to see how he was doing. His condition had worsened and it was apparent that Father Houle was beginning to succumb to his disease. On Friday, Father Parrish came to visit the mostly unconscious priest, prayed for him and blessed him with a relic of Blessed Claude de la Colombiere. Father Parrish was absolutely certain that a miracle would happen.

By Saturday, a male nurse was stationed by his side. Father was almost totally unresponsive. I helped the nurse to rub his back and adjust his position. His entire body was cyanotic, (a condition in which the skin and mucous membranes take on a bluish color because there is not enough oxygen in the blood), and he was cold and clammy. I had seen many gravely ill patients in the hospital die and I knew that the doctor's prognosis was correct; in Father Houle's case, in all likelihood, it was probably just a matter of time. Still, I was aware that many people were praying for a miracle and that when one prays with trust and confidence, leaving things in God's hands, miracles do happen – and He worked a miracle now!

On Sunday morning, I was surprised to find Father Houle doing much better. I wondered if he had been given any medication aside from the oxygen, but his chart confirmed that no medications had been given.

Three days later, Wednesday, Father Houle was sitting up in bed reading the newspaper and asking for his favorite food – pizza! Just days before, Father Houle was at death's door, now his lungs had been miraculously restored and there was no sign of illness!

Father Houle's cardiologist confirmed the miraculous healing.

"There's no doubt in my mind that Father John Houle was dying in February 1990," the doctor said. "He'd been on oxygen for a month and was in an increasingly weakened state. While, as a physician, I can't affirm or deny miracles as such," he said, "I'd have to say, and I have attested, that there's simply no medical explanation for the sudden turn-around in his condition. He was too far gone for that."

"This is a miracle! Father Parrish exclaimed to me some days later. "Sister, will you help me get all the information together so we can send it the Vatican's Congregation for the Cause of Saints?"

I said to Father Parrish, "Yes, we will help you get everything together. We'll even testify and go to Rome with you!" Later on, we did do just that.

We were convinced that God had worked a miracle through the intercession of Blessed Claude de la Colombiere. With the assistance of Father Houle's doctors, we set about gathering together all the medical reports of the doctors, the x-rays of his lungs and the statements of people who were praying for the cure of Father Houle through the intercession of Blessed Claude la Colombiere. Father Parrish forwarded all the information and documentation to the Congregation for the Cause of Saints.

In October 1990, Father Paul Molineri, postulator for the cause of Jesuit saints and martyrs, and Sister Anne Haysen, a sister of Orange, came from Rome to open a deposition with Bishop John J. Ward on the reported miracle. They interviewed all the doctors and nurses who had taken care of Father Houle. I was also interviewed as I was his respiratory therapist. Everything was scrupulously recorded and documented and eventually a report over 200 pages in length concerning Father Houle's unexplainable healing made its way to Rome for a final, extensive examination.

The committee of cardinals, priests and doctors reviewed all the documentation and unanimously ruled that there was no medical explanation for Father Houle's remarkable recovery. Their verdict was then forwarded to the Pope.

The Holy Father approved the recommendation and on May 31, 1992, Blessed Claude de la Colombiere was canonized and is now Saint Claude de la Colombiere!

Sister Vincent Marie, Sister Mary Colombiere, Sister Noella and I were in Rome for the canonization. We stayed at the North American College with all the seminarians. It was such a beautiful experience. We even had the chance to meet some of Saint Claude's descendants. Amazingly, one particular young woman looked exactly like him, with the same profile, the same eyes and nose as Saint Claude who had died in 1682, some 300 years before this young woman was born!

When asked why this miracle occurred, Father Parrish gave a two-fold response: "First of all, because I believe God wanted it, because He willed to have Blessed Claude de la Colombiere declared a saint. But, most especially, to give an impetus to the devotion to the Sacred Heart."

Our community is especially blessed in that God willed for this miracle to take place in our hospital. How beautiful is God's love and mercy in our lives!

1 Think 1 Know 1t Now

by Sister Timothy Marie, O.C.D.

*I*T IS GOOD FRIDAY. Within our convent, all is silent. My Carmelite Sisters walk a little more slowly than usual, more prayerfully, along the polished corridors. With their measured pace, lowered eyes, and hands tucked softly under their brown scapular, a tangible silence envelops them. The whole scene speaks of prayer that once uttered wafts into the very atmosphere of the place and whispers, "Holy ground. This is holy ground." Grand Silence, a prayerful period of time without speaking at all, begins.

It is Holy Week. A total observance of the Holy Week Triduum takes place in Carmel each year. Life keeps pace with liturgy. We move within, we meditate on the themes of Holy Week. We pray; we remember; we prayerfully accompany Christ as we remember His Passion, Death, and Resurrection. These are, indeed, Holy Days.

Our Sisters know many people because we teach their children, nurse their sick ones, care for their beloved elders, or lead their retreats. Yes, we are teachers, nurses, and retreat leaders, who give these and a myriad of other services to God's people. We plow daily the field given us by the Church. This is what people see. Yes, like the apostles, we go where we are sent. Wherever we are assigned, we carry within our very being our Carmelite heritage – our times of prayer, Carmel's special celebrations of the Church's seasons, our treasured customs, our passionate mission to foster the spiritual lives of God's people.

There exists a part of us that people don't usually see. Every morning, evening, and night, we chant the Liturgy of the Hours together in community. Each afternoon we pray the rosary and meditate during our daily Holy Hour before the Blessed Sacrament. We live lives interwoven with threads of prayer, silence, and apostolic works. Before dawn, when all is silent and the morning star begins its rising in the sky, all of us begin our day praying together in community. It is during this hallowed time that we intercede for the needs of the world and savor our quality prayer time before Our Lord in the Blessed Sacrament. During Holy Week our prayer intensifies for, indeed, it is HOLY week.

This, then, is the setting of the true story which happened on a Good Friday not too long ago. Sister Carmelina and I were on our way to the chapel for the 3:00 p.m. Good Friday Liturgy. We walked along in silence, enjoying the beauty of the verdant spring day. Because we resided at our hospital convent during that school year – we are high school teachers – we passed by the hospital on our way to the chapel. That's when it happened. One of the nurses from the intensive care unit walked quickly out of the building and beckoned to us. She stopped us and said, "Sisters, would you please do us a favor? A young teenage boy has just come to us from the emergency room. We don't think he is going to make it. There was gang-related violence at his high school, and he got banged in the head many times with a baseball bat. The doctor says he won't last the night. Would you come in for a minute and say a prayer with the family? Everyone else is at the church services, and I don't want to bother them on Good Friday. Would the two of you come with me for a few moments? The parents state they have no religion and no minister."

Well, she was talking to two high school teachers who had seen the effects of gang violence. We both knew alumni who had died from it. We had students who participated in it. Quietly, we accompanied the nurse to ICU.

Our lives as Carmelite Sisters are a blend of contemplation and apostolate, of prayer and active ministry. The Divine Weaver weaves the tapestry of our vocation with two threads -- intermingled, mixed. Just as the needle goes in and out, forming the design of each tapestry, so the pattern of our lives as Carmelite Sisters is formed. From the Grand Silence of the cloister, to the halls of the largest high school in our archdiocese – we are used to it. This time, however, the Divine Weaver took us from the Grand Silence of Holy Week to the ICU of our hospital. It was a short walk. We arrived within two minutes.

His parents were there in the waiting room. We saw at a glance that both of James'* parents were in shock. No, they had no special religion. No, they did not attend church. No, they had no special prayers they would like us to say. Yes, we are welcome to go in and pray with him. His name? Oh, yes, his name is James.

The doctor's diagnosis and prognosis were, indeed, grim. I looked at Sister Carmelina, and she looked back at me. This could be one of our students. We could so easily imagine what had happened. Not wanting to intrude, but remembering that the nurse had asked us to come and pray with James, I asked the parents if they were Christian. Well, sort of, was their reply. Did they know a minister or would they like us to call one? They shrugged their shoulders. Not really, they said. We buzzed the button that alerted the nurses we wanted to enter the ICU. The door clicked. A voice over the inter-com whispered, "Come in." His parents followed us as we crossed the threshold.

Sister Carmelina and I took long, deep breaths. We were teachers, not nurses, and we prayed for the stamina to withstand the sight that would soon be in front of us. We pulled the curtains and walked in with the nurse. James had blood oozing from his ears, eyes, mouth, and nose. His face was swollen up like a balloon. It is hard to describe. It was hills and valleys of black and blue. We knew he was in very bad shape. He appeared to us to be dying.

Although James was in a coma (induced by the doctor), we hoped he could hear us. We decided to pray the Lord's Prayer, because it is a common universal prayer and most people know it by heart. Sister Carmelina has a beautiful singing voice, and I asked her if she would sing the Lord's Prayer. We thought that would make our prayer special for both James and his parents. While I placed my hand onto the boy's shoulder, Sister Carmelina placed her hand into James' hand. We invited the parents to join us. All of us joined hands. Sister Carmelina sang the Lord's Prayer slowly and reverently. The parents closed their eyes. I watched James. When the hymn was finished, we all recited the Lord's Prayer one more time – together – with the parents repeating the words after us – phrase by phrase. We added the ending phrase "for Thine is the Kingdom, the Power, and the Glory forever. Amen."

Stillness filled the room. So, here we were. It was Good Friday, just a little after 3:00 p.m.

At the conclusion of the Lord's Prayer, Sister Carmelina and I prayed aloud intensely. From our hearts, we begged God for James' complete recovery. The parents stood nearby on the other side of James' hospital bed listening as we prayed. We asked for a miracle. We asked God, in his great mercy, to restore James, to heal both his body and his soul. This appeared to give the parents some comfort. Shortly afterward, the two of us said goodbye to the parents and quietly left. The nurse followed us out. "Thank you," she whispered.

Police and security guards surrounded the ICU, as well as the doors leading into the hospital because the school authorities feared gang retaliation.

We arrived at the Good Friday services about twenty minutes late. Following the services, we returned to the convent. On Saturday evening, when both the Easter Vigil Liturgy and Grand Silence were over, Sister Carmelina looked at me. I nodded. We asked permission to go visit James. We both wanted to know how things turned out for him.

We entered the ICU. James was still there, and even from a distance he looked better. Although still in the coma induced by the doctors, his vital signs and breathing were normal. The same nurse walked over to us. She smiled and told us that the doctor came in Good Friday afternoon shortly after we had left. He told her, "This does not appear to be the same case that the ambulance brought in earlier. I made a wrong diagnosis. This boy is going to make it. I don't understand."

On Easter Sunday we visited again and saw even more improvement. Each day when we visited James, Sister Carmelina sang the Our Father and if the parents were there, we prayed it together with them.

A few days later, James woke up. Sister Carmelina and I were the only ones present in the room when it happened. He focused his eyes on us and grinned slowly and said, "Which one of you is the singer? I heard you every time you sang to me, and I heard your prayers. Please pray with me again. I think I know it now."

James recovered with no intellectual impairment. He needed to use a cane for a while, but in time he maneuvered again on his own. Some months later, he returned to ICU and brought some candy to the nurses. He asked for us, but we were back in the classroom.

We did see James on his following visit. After talking for a while, James had a request. "Sister Carmelina, will you please sing the Our Father for me one last time?"

There we stood, the three of us, in the lobby of the hospital. Sister Carmelina nodded and began singing the Lord's Prayer. This time, we saw him move his lips. He was praying with us.

With eyes closed, James absorbed each note like a flower absorbing sunlight.

* = *denotes names have been changed to protect privacy*

Inherent Value

by Sister Margaret Ann, O.C.D.

*M*ANY YEARS AGO, A WOMAN – A MOTHER – walked into the front office of our elementary school with a little girl of about eight or nine years of age in tow. It was apparent that they were homeless and living on the streets.

I happened to be standing near the front desk. "Can I help you?" I asked with a smile for both the mother and the child.

The woman regarded me for a long moment before speaking. Then she asked, "Can my daughter come to school here?"

I looked at the child, who appeared to be about 3rd or 4th grade. "Yes, she can." So we set this little girl up, Kathy*, with all that she would need – a uniform and school supplies – and she was now ready to begin attending class.

Her mother would come and do odd chores for us, such as cleaning the lunch tables. Occasionally, she would bring a can of soda and say, "This is for my daughter's tuition."

We kept an eye on Kathy and her mother over the years and would try to help them as best we could. Sometime later, we heard that one of the parishioners had a garage that was set up to provide living accommodations and eventually, Kathy and her mom moved in.

A couple of years later, when Kathy was in 5th grade, she was having trouble with math and one of the Sisters brought her into the kitchen of our convent, where another Sister happened to be baking cookies. The enticing aroma of warm, freshly-baked cookies beckoned to me, calling to mind fond memories of the times my own mother spent baking goodies, so I made my way to the kitchen. As I walked through the door, I stopped in my tracks in astonishment at what I heard Kathy, who was by now 10 years old, telling the two Sisters.

"It smells so good in here," Kathy said, her voice filled with hushed awe. "I've never been in a kitchen before and I don't even know how to turn on a stove."

None of us knew quite what to say.

Kathy eventually ended up graduating from our school and we helped her get a scholarship to attend one of the local Catholic high schools. Shortly before graduating from elementary school, Kathy stopped by the front office for a visit.

"Kathy, in a few years you'll be ready to get a job and earn a paycheck," I said to her. "Have you thought about what you are going to do with your first paycheck?" I asked.

Without hesitation she said decidedly, "I'm going to buy my mom a pair of shoes." After a moment's thought, she added, "….and a dress."

Quite a sobering thought…...realizing that a 13-year old child's first goal in life is to buy her mother a pair of shoes and a dress. This is not the usual dream of the typical 13-year old. It certainly makes one stop and think. I find it interesting to think about the significant impact our decision had in allowing this child to attend our school. Beyond receiving a good basic education, the lessons she learned were invaluable, beyond anything money could buy. She learned of her inherent value, worth and dignity as a person and that she was loved and accepted, regardless of the difficult circumstances of her life. Those lessons, gifts really, that she learned from our Sisters in all probability made a positive, life-long impact on this child.

* = denotes that names have been changed to protect privacy

Jesus' Healing Love

by Sister Isabelle, O.C.D.

MARY* WAS ONE OF THE MOST FORTHRIGHT WOMEN I have ever met. She was not shy about expressing what she didn't like about certain situations and beating around the bush was not something Mary was wont to do. During the course of her life, Mary had experienced a number of hurtful relationships and there had been some rough periods that hadn't quite healed. She carried the resultant hurts and pains of the past with her and she was definitely angry with God about these many painful things from years past. Fortunately, because of her forthright nature, Mary was not one to wallow in self-pity and by the time she came to live at the Manor (our skilled nursing facility), Mary was learning to let go of the hurts and was slowly but steadily coming back to God. We would often talk about it and pray together.

Mary was unique among our residents in that she was still able to get around independently. She made good use of this blessing and would frequently attend different events, activities and social occasion with her friends. Mary was also an amazing and gifted pianist, who had a virtually unlimited repertoire at her command which she played by ear – "oldies but goodies" – and she would share her talents with our own residents twice a week for an hour. I fondly called her "Twinkle Fingers" and she called me "Twinkle Toes" because I found tapping my toes irresistible when she played all her great tunes.

In time, health issues caught up with Mary, including a heart problem that took her to the hospital ER a number of times. One of the other sisters and I always made sure to visit Mary during her hospital stays.

"Twinkle Toes, I knew you'd come!" she would joyfully greet us as we walked into her room.

During these visits, Mary always was her usual self, speaking in her typical straightforward manner. She especially enjoyed sharing with us the goings-on in the hospital.

On one visit, however, Mary seemed a bit more circumspect.

"Sister, she began quietly, "do you see anything in the window?" She pointed toward the large window that looked out upon the San Gabriel Mountains.

I turned toward the window. "No, Mary, I don't see anything out of the ordinary," I replied.

"Well, I saw something yesterday," she told me, "I saw what to me looked to be an angel."

"How do you feel about it, Mary?" I asked.

"It made me feel very comforted and I feel very peaceful about it," she said with conviction.

A few days later, we again visited Mary and she was her gregarious self and we had a wonderful visit.

She suddenly fell silent. We waited for her to speak as we could see she was trying to find the words for what she wanted to tell us. Finally, she spoke.

"You know that picture in the Manor of the Divine Mercy? I saw that picture here..... I saw that image of Jesus here at the foot of my bed," she said very matter-of-factly. From the look on her face, it was apparent that Mary was deeply moved by what she had experienced.

Well, we were floored! Mary was not the kind of lady given to flights of fancy. She was not one to make up such stories, least of all about religious or pious things. In all the times we talked, she never once brought up such topics, so we innately knew that something was happening with Mary.

The next morning, Mary was scheduled for heart surgery. We encouraged her and prayed with her and we gave her a rosary. Mary wasn't Catholic, but she made it very clear she wanted that rosary and she kept it right by her bedside. It was apparent that Mary was at peace and we thanked God for restoring the peace to her soul that had eluded her for so many years. As it turned out, Mary died during surgery the next morning.

Upon learning of Mary's death, we knew without a doubt that the Lord had come and prepared her to come home to Him. To this day, when I reflect on the manner in which He worked, the way He healed the hurts and scars of Mary's heart, I am amazed. Through talking and praying with the sisters, she gradually learned to hand over to Him all the pains of the past so that when He came for her, she was ready.

We have a CD recording of Mary playing the piano and to this day, we play it often in the Manor. Her musical gift still delights our residents to this day. Mary was a special lady... she really was something else.

= denotes that names have been changed to protect privacy

The Depth of His Mercy

by Sister Gaudencia, O.C.D.

*T*HROUGHOUT THE CENTURIES, God has been leading His children to a deeper understanding of His love and mercy. In the 20th century, one of the people God chose to deliver this message of Divine Mercy was a simple nun in Poland. She lived and died in relative obscurity but she is now known around the world as Saint Faustina. Her diary, written in obedience to her spiritual director, records the words of our Lord to the world. He called her His Secretary of Divine Mercy and directed her to write about the depths of His mercy for all mankind, especially for sinners. All we need to do is trust Him.

Not too long ago, we witnessed His Divine Mercy in action.

One of our residents at the Manor, Marilyn* a non-Catholic, had been in declining health for some time and she eventually fell into a coma. One afternoon, around 3:00 p.m., I stopped by her room intending to say a prayer for her. When I entered the room, I found that Marilyn's daughters happened to be there visiting her.

"Would you mind if I pray for your mother?" I asked them.

"No, of course not," one of the daughters replied.

"Yes, please say a prayer for our mom," the other daughter agreed, "we would appreciate it very much."

Since it was just about three o'clock in the afternoon, I began the Divine Mercy prayer, focusing specifically on Our Lord's Passion and death on the cross, just as Jesus had asked in His revelations to St. Faustina.

Imagine the astonishment the three of us felt when no sooner had I finished the prayer, than Marilyn's eyes fluttered open and she peered up at us!

Then focusing back on her daughters she asked, "What are you two doing here?"

The two daughters were stunned speechless! Here their mother had been in a deep coma for some length of time and from which she had not been expected to emerge and then suddenly, she was back as if nothing out of the ordinary had occurred!

We gave thanks to the Divine Mercy of Jesus for bringing Marilyn out of her deep coma. There is no depth too deep for His mercy. All we have to do is trust Him.

* = denotes that names have been changed to protect privacy

And the Angels Danced:
A Story of Healing

by Sister Timothy Marie, O.C.D.

*T*HERE I WAS . . . STRANDED, SURROUNDED by the big oil refinery. . . with its oil derricks and wells. . .

It was a magnificent winter evening. The air was crisp and cold as the distant sun began to descend behind the oil derricks in Carson, California. Our convent car gave a shudder as I turned the key in the ignition and carefully backed out of the driveway. Yes, I would be there on time. This time I wouldn't be late. Driving carefully through the school playground surrounding our convent, I made my usual left turn onto Main Street and began driving south. Prayers at our nearby convent began promptly at 5:00 p.m. and I was looking forward to joining my other Carmelite Sisters in singing God's praises. Little did I know, as I made my left turn onto Sepulveda Boulevard, that this would be no ordinary journey.

How long did I drive before it happened? I can't precisely remember, but it might have taken eight minutes or so since pulling out of our driveway. I do remember, however, exactly where it happened. While motoring on Sepulveda Boulevard just past Wilmington Avenue, the convent car wheezed and coughed as if catching an enormous cold from the onslaught of icy wind slapping its windshield. With one last gasp, the convent car sputtered to a graceful stop as I instinctively eased it nearer the curb. A long exhale emitted from the engine and there I was, stranded, surrounded by the big oil company's refinery, oil derricks and wells. It took me a full minute to assess the situation. Not able to make up my mind what course to follow—to stand on the side of the road as a hitchhiker would and wave down a passing car or to start walking back home; but it was so cold and I wasn't sure what would be best. So, I closed my eyes and said a quick prayer, asking my guardian angel to help me decide what to do. Now, it wasn't as if I were really stranded on a high mountain or in the middle of some desert landscape. No, I was near Wilmington, California, and cars were whizzing by, eager to get home for the supper hour. Finishing my prayer, I thought, "Well, at least, they will see me; wearing my long Carmelite tunic and scapular and flowing black veil, I will stand out," and began to plan my emergence from the car onto Sepulveda Blvd. That is when I saw her; a beautiful, young Hispanic girl, possibly in her twenties, standing there on the street meridian, selling bouquets of beautiful flowers.

"This is the answer," I thought to myself. "I can trust her. She will understand and I will feel safer standing by someone else," I figured out within myself. About a minute later, there were two people standing on the street meridian of Sepulveda Boulevard, both facing south – a young Hispanic girl and next to her, a Carmelite Sister watching the cars speed by. I introduced myself and my situation in my broken Spanish and she replied *"Dios se le bendiga,"* which means "God bless you."

Standing there on that street for about five minutes gave me a new view of life. I had never sold flowers on a street corner and here I was stranded, sharing in the exquisite hospitality of my new-found friend. She accepted me and I accepted her. I believe that is when I had the first inkling God was at work at the heart of this situation; there were lessons to be learned, and growth, both human and spiritual, to be accomplished. Sunset came. My new friend began to pack up her unsold flowers. It was at then that I suddenly saw Spires Restaurant. In retrospect, I wonder now why I hadn't seen it sooner. It was right there-- set back a short distance from the street corner.

A lot of big trucks were parked nearby. Truckers! My answer had come. Saying good-bye to my new-found friend, I went to the crosswalk and feeling like Julie Andrews in "The Sound of Music" scene where she is toting that suitcase down the street singing, "I have confidence," I lifted my head and walked steadfastly and confidently into Spires Restaurant.

Warmth enveloped me as I stood in the entrance. "Excuse me, can anyone help me, please? My car just died outside." Yes, that's what I did, and about twenty sets of eyes turned toward this shuddering Carmelite, who remained hopeful that chivalry was not yet dead and that charity still resides in the human heart. It seemed as if time stood still.

Slowly, someone seated at the counter, purposefully got up and walked over to me. "Roosevelt's my name," he offered. Roosevelt appeared to me to be in his sixties. "Take me to that car and we'll see what we can do." So I led him out onto the nearby street. He said, "Can't fix it here. Have to bring it in." He told me, "I'll get my truck and push you into the parking lot. You just steer." So that is what we did and the convent car was soon in the Spires Restaurant parking lot. Prayers at our nearby convent had already started. I was going to be late – again!

Roosevelt tinkered with the car's innards. "Yup, that's it. Battery's dead." He proceeded to take jumper cables out of his truck and attached them to our convent car. "May I buy you a cup of coffee? This will take fifteen minutes." Looking at Roosevelt, I replied, "Thank you very much, Roosevelt. It would be much appreciated." Now that the sun had totally set, it was getting colder. The beautiful flower girl was gone and Roosevelt and I disappeared into Spires Restaurant.

I remember Roosevelt and I talked for a period of time. He told me about his work and his family and his dreams. After a while, we returned to the parking lot. The convent car was fixed. Its battery had been recharged. I turned to thank Roosevelt. It was only then that I saw the tears in his eyes. "What's the matter, Roosevelt," I asked. "Why are you crying?"

"May I tell you why I fixed your car?"

"Yes," I answered, not knowing quite what to expect.

"I was born a long time ago in Mississippi. We were very poor. Every winter I contracted pneumonia as a child – our house was so poor. One year, I must have been about ten or so, I was rushed to the hospital. With no antibiotics (recall this is in the 1930's, so antibiotics had not yet been discovered,) pneumonia caused the death of many children. The doctors had just told my mother that I would not last the night. That evening two Catholic Sisters, dressed just like you, entered my hospital room. I had a high, high fever and I remember one of the sisters came by my bed, put her cool hand on my forehead and prayed for me. I didn't know what to do, or how to respond. I had been well taught that no black could dare get near a white woman. And now here was this white Catholic nun,

not only placing her hand on my head, but praying to God with all her heart for me. I had never heard nor seen anything like it. That's just how it was in those days. That's just how it was. Well, the next day my fever was gone.
The doctor said I had passed the crisis – he didn't know why or how. But I knew. I never saw the Catholic sisters again. Throughout all these following years, I have wished I could find them and thank them. Today, just now, when you came into the restaurant and said, "Can someone help me?" I said to myself, "Roosevelt, your time has come to thank the sisters. That's why I got up and offered my help. It was finally my time to return the favor."

By now tears were glistening on both our faces. It was a sacred moment. The parking lot of Spires Restaurant became a sacred place. We were standing on holy ground. Yes, times have changed. Thank God! I looked up at Roosevelt as he stood at least a foot taller than I , and I said with immeasurable respect and reflection, "Roosevelt, may I hug you?" A big smile spread across his face as he turned to me and answered, "Yes, ma'am." At that moment in time, right there, a cold and frigid night, just off Sepulveda Boulevard, two of God's children embraced, shattering centuries of ignorance and prejudice.

More than a battery was made right that evening....

. . . and the angels danced.

Please Pass the Salt

by Sister Gaudencia, O.C.D.

A WHILE AGO, A PARTICULARLY NASTY STRAIN OF A VIRAL FLU swept through one of our skilled nursing facilities. It seemed like no one was immune – residents and staff alike suffered from it. Relapses were common. Frustrated by the staying power of this virus, I decided it was time to appeal to a higher Authority, so I pulled out our blessed salt.

"Salt? Why salt?" some people ask. If you investigate a little, you can learn some very interesting things about the importance of salt in the ancient world and to the Jews. For one thing, it was expensive so it was seen as a fitting offering to God. It also had meaning in relation to the people's covenant with God. In Numbers 18:19, the Lord makes a "covenant of salt" with Aaron, a covenant that is to last forever. This could refer to the fact that salt is a preservative but it also refers to the ancient custom of eating salt together to render a contract unbreakable. In the New Testament, Jesus calls each of us the "salt of the earth" reminding us that salt that loses its flavor is useless.

The Church blesses salt, just as it blesses water, and uses it as a sacramental, an object which does not confer grace but helps prepare us or dispose us to receive God. Other sacramentals include blessed rosaries, holy cards, a crucifix, etc. We are body and soul, and visible reminders, tangible signs of His power and grace can greatly aid us in our relationship with God. The use of sacramentals united with prayer and faith in God's power to heal and save can have tremendous effects in the minds, hearts and even bodies of people.

So one Sunday morning, first thing, I took some blessed salt with me as I walked through our facility and I put a few grains on every resident and staff member. No one suffered a relapse that day. The next day, Monday, I was very busy and did not make my rounds with the blessed salt. Sure enough, relapses resumed. People were getting sick again right and left.

"This must be the last remnants of this flu," I thought to myself, "we should see the end of it in a day or so."

Was I ever wrong! After a few days, with still no end in sight to this virus, I pulled out the blessed salt again with the determination to sprinkle a few grains on every resident and staff member until the epidemic was finally wiped out. I would make my rounds daily if I had to.

I started immediately, walking through each room, sprinkling a few grains of salt on each resident. In the fifth room, the resident was sound asleep, but I knew sprinkling the salt on her would not disturb her sleep. I stood right next to her bed and pinched a tiny amount, four or five grains of salt, between my fingers and sprinkled it on her hair.

The lady suddenly sat bolt upright in her bed and started trembling violently. Her shaking was so bad that it frightened both of us. I just froze, not quite certain what to do. After what seemed a very long several minutes, her shaking subsided and then stopped altogether.

"I was shaking so badly!" she exclaimed a bit breathlessly, eyes wide.

"Yes, I know you were," I agreed, still feeling a little shaky myself.

I remained with this resident until we both calmed down.

This was a powerful experience for me as it was a visible reminder of the spiritual realities we are dealing with every day. Our prayers really do have a profound effect on the soul and in this case, our Lord let me see it.

Later, that same day, one of the nurses approached me.

"Sister, what was it you sprinkled on my shoulder this morning?" she asked.

"Oh, it was blessed salt," I replied. "Why?"

She furrowed her brow as she tried to articulate her feeling. "I don't know if I can explain it, but I felt different when you put the salt on me," she replied. "It was a beautiful kind of different," she added.

Shortly after we started the blessed salt campaign, the epidemic was finally halted and the experience of using this powerful sacramental impressed all of us. We experienced renewed health in body and a renewed gratitude for the graces God gives us when we turn to Him in faith with the help of sacramentals like blessed salt. So the next time you are facing a challenging situation and could use a visible reminder of His power to save, simply say, "Please pass the salt."

To Everything there is a Season

by Sister Faustina, O.C.D.

*A*LTHOUGH IT IS AN ARBITRARY PROCESS, when children are brought together in first grade, they eventually bond as a "class", and sometimes they might even form a particular group consciousness or group identity that attaches itself to them over the course of their elementary school years. This was the case with an eighth grade class I taught one year at our school in Colorado.

Collectively, this class got off to a rough start, and the course never quite righted for them. By the time they reached eighth grade, they had logged a number of very difficult years behind them, to the extent that they bestowed upon themselves the epithet, "the bad class". This group had earned a reputation early on; they knew it and they seemed to take a perverse pleasure in living up to that reputation. This reputation seemed to reach its zenith during seventh grade – an especially rough year. Most unfortunate were the comments and impressions they heard from their teachers, which did nothing to assuage this very negative and unhealthy group self-image. The fact of the matter was not all the children contributed to "the bad class" mentality, but it certainly was a group dynamic into which all the students were pulled.

However, the beautiful words of Ecclesiastes 3:1 came to mind: *"To everything there is a season, and a time to every purpose under heaven."* It seemed that the start of their eighth grade year signaled that the season had come for these children to redefine their "purpose".

At the start of the school year, we took them to our retreat center for the annual overnight class retreat. In order to get the children comfortable and loosened up, and this group needed considerable help in accomplishing that, among the first activities we held with them were a number of ice breaker games. They slowly began to respond, but what really changed the whole mood of the retreat was an ice breaker that calls for two people to sit back-to-back on the floor, linking elbows with their feet in front of them. They are then instructed to stand. The only way to accomplish this is for each person to push against the back of the other person.

Now, eighth graders in general, and this class in particular, being as divided and self-centered as they were, are not wont to touch each other.

The teacher leading the ice breaker called on two girls, who happened to be close friends and therefore were not averse to touching each other, to try this exercise. The girls did, and working together succeeded in standing. A surge of interest rippled through the group. So the teacher called on two boys to give it a try. Having observed what the girls did, the boys did the same and they were successful too. By now, the rest of the group was eager to give it a try, but the teacher challenged them by upping the degree of difficulty.

"How about the *four* of you try it together?" the teacher challenged, as exclamations of "no way" and "that's too hard" sounded from the audience.

The four, however, were up to the challenge. They sat on the floor, linked arms and tried to stand. It definitely was considerably harder, but their determination to succeed was written on their faces and that determination paid off – they were able to stand! So a fifth, then a sixth, then a seventh student was added to the circle, until every member of the class sat back-to-back, arms linked, ready to try standing.

What happened next, was truly extraordinary. I had never seen so much as a hint of compassion in any way, shape or form in these children, but as they wrestled as a group to stand, a unity heretofore unseen began to emerge. They attempted to stand as a group over and over again – seven, perhaps eight times but they just couldn't seem to do it. Some would fall trying to stand, others became frustrated, but the majority of the group encouraged the rest, "No, we have to try. We can do this! We're in this together – **TOGETHER!**"

So they gave it one more shot with the teachers standing around offering encouragement and cheering them on, "Come on, you can do it! You can do it!"

Finally, on the ninth try their perseverance was rewarded. The students pushed and pulled against each other until they were all standing with linked arms. An amazed silence descended on the room, as all the students just gazed at each in wide-eyed wonderment. Slowly realization dawned on them that this exercise was probably the first time in all the years they had been together as a class that they had ever attempted and accomplished anything as a cohesive unit. They were so proud of themselves as cheers and exuberant laughter erupted in the room from students and teachers alike. Needless to say, the tone for the entire school year was dramatically altered for this class.

"To everything there is a season, and a time to every purpose under heaven." The season had finally come for these wounded children to discover that their purpose under heaven was perhaps not so "bad" after all.

Later that year, the class chose as the theme for their yearbook – *"One"*. To illustrate this, they melted all colors of crayons together to form one multi-hued crayon. They finally came to understand that despite their differences, despite adversity it is still very much possible for them to be strong if they stand united as one.

Wild and Tame

"All you beasts, wild and tame, bless the Lord;
praise and exalt him above all forever."

- Daniel 3:81

The Dove in the Dome

by Sister Miriam Amata, O.C.D.

O NE RECENT MONDAY, AS WE WERE DOING EXAMEN after lunch in the Sisters' Choir, I heard the call of a mourning dove. This was not unusual in that we have several pairs of mourning doves in our garden. However, this call echoed quite loudly, sounding as if it was actually coming from somewhere inside the chapel. We also heard the answering half-call of the bird's pair, and we then definitely suspected that the dove was indeed inside the chapel. Sure enough, we finally saw him high above in the dome perched on a ledge. For three days this poor dove was in the dome trying to find a comfortable perch, and unable to find one kept flapping its wings and flying around hitting the walls. The poor creature had to be exhausted and we wondered if it was going to survive.

Four days later, on Thursday, during the 9 o'clock Mass, the most extraordinary thing happened. At the moment of the consecration of the Precious Blood, the dove gently floated down from on high, crossed above the altar and landed right in front of it. For a few moments, he kept still, then, started walking back and forth in front of the altar for the duration of the Eucharistic prayer, as if he was a little sentinel keeping watch over the proceedings of Mass.

Once the Eucharistic Prayer concluded, the little dove walked over to the side of the sanctuary close to Father, then, after a few moments he moved over toward the statue of Our Lady that we had for the May Crowning. He seemed to be hiding behind the statue because we couldn't see him for several moments. As we began the Agnus Dei, the little dove came out from behind the statue, hopped down the steps, turned to the left and walked right in front of the residents toward the open doors and proceeded to walk right out the doors as if nothing had happened! The little mourning dove at last seemed to have found divinely inspired directions on how to exit the chapel!

Later, I found him over by the medical building. He must have become disoriented stuck in the chapel's dome, but now he is happily back with his mate in our garden.

Scooter

by Sister Faustina, O.C.D.

*S*COOTER WAS ONE OF TWO DOGS who belonged to our community at our convent in Long Beach. Over the years, we would keep a dog or two for the sake of protection. Scooter, however, defied description as a "guard dog", yet he remained a convent fixture for many years. Scooter was an extraordinarily old dog who was into his 20's. He was blind, deaf, and had difficulty walking because of an arthritic bent to his spine, but somehow he managed to get around. By the time I got to live with him, it was the final years of his life.

One day, a very unfortunate thing occurred. One of the sisters had left the gate open and the two dogs escaped. The younger dog was able to find her way back, but no such luck with Scooter. He was gone. The poor Sister who had left the gate open was getting a bit panicky, so she and I got in the car and drove around the area looking for the runaway Scooter. Frustration began to set in as we continued driving up and down surrounding streets looking for him, all to no avail. We pulled over and tried to think which way we should try searching next. Since we are located on two very busy roads, we thought it was impossible that he would have crossed the street, so we continued to look for him closer to our immediate area.

We finally ended up across several highly trafficked streets and as we were driving down the street, we suddenly saw a dog, away from the road, lying on the grass next to a palm tree. We slammed on the brakes, parked and jumped out of the car to investigate. He was laying so still we thought perhaps he was dead.... but no, Scooter was very much alive. As soon as he sensed we were there, he cheerfully wagged his tail. As we approached him, we noticed that not only did he have food and water laid out in front of him, he had also acquired a new leash and collar and even a toy! Obviously, someone had already begun to take care of him and we figured we couldn't just take the dog without finding out who this person was.

In driving around looking for Scooter, we had wandered a bit far afield from our convent and the neighborhood in which we now found ourselves was a bit on the rough side. We just happened to be in front of a transient hotel. We knocked on the door and out came a man, in shabby clothes who apparently lived on the streets much of the time.

Sister said to him, "You found our dog."

"That's your dog?" the man replied.

"Yes," I answered, "He's our dog; he ran away earlier this afternoon."

"We all thought he was homeless … he's so skinny and gnarled." This homeless man thought Scooter was unloved.

As it turns out, Scooter managed to cross a very busy street and back again. This man saw him having difficulty and came out and rescued him. Even though this man himself was homeless with no money, he bought Scooter the leash, collar, toy, and food and was ready to take care of him.

We felt rather bad and Sister said, "You can keep him."

"No, no, this is your dog, you can have him back," he said. He sadly told us his own dog had recently died.

So we scooped up Scooter and took him home where he continued to "guard" us and our convent while basking and napping in the warmth of the sunshine in the backyard.

Somewhere In Santa Barbara

by Sister Mary Colombiere, O.C.D.

A NOTHER SISTER AND I HAD SOME FUN when we were looking for the "yellow billed magpie" near Santa Barbara. The bird's habitat is located on a very small strip of land. We were anxious to get a good look at this beautiful, rather large bird. We had driven onto a kind of dirt road that led through overgrown trees and streams on each side. It was hard getting the car through, so we decided to get out of the car and go on by foot. Lo and behold, two men approached us.

I'm very focused when I'm looking for birds and I don't notice what otherwise would be obvious to me. These men were wearing suits and a ties, dark sunglasses and had binoculars. All I saw was their binoculars, so I stopped them.

I asked them, "We're looking for the yellow billed magpie. Have you seen it?"

The men seemed rather stunned to find us walking along the dirt trail. They appeared at a loss for words as they glanced at each other, when finally one of them said, "Well, not recently."

"What are you doing here?" they asked.

I assumed they probably didn't know the yellow billed magpie.

They continued looking us over and noted our binoculars and bird book.

"Where are you going to continue to?" the second man asked.

I replied, "Well, we're just going to continue following the road and then we'll leave."

The men left us after that and a bit later we did find the yellow billed magpie. However, the other Sister, who had paid more attention to the men than did I, said as sudden realization dawned, "Do you realize where we are?"

"Well somewhere in Santa Barbara." I replied.

"We are on Ronald Reagan's ranch and those are his Secret Service body guards!"

Twilight Time

by Sister Timothy Marie, O.C.D.

ONCE A YEAR, WE SISTERS MAKE AN EIGHT-DAY silent retreat. It is wonderful. To me it is such a special opportunity when I can take quality time to meditate, pray, and read some good spiritual books in a spirit of renewal and spiritual restoration. I LOVE my summer retreats and so very much look forward to them each year.

The following story happened during one of my summer retreats. It is true.

Dusk has always been a special prayer time for me. There is just something so special about the quiet of the sunset. The world hushes. Stillness descends. A panorama of beauty explodes as the sunset splendor spreads across the sky.

So, it is very natural for me to go outside after supper, just before the sunset and enjoy the twilight time. I have a twilight time special place where I read and pray in the early evening each year during my retreat on the lush green lawn by Our Lady of Lourdes' grotto. Facing the grotto in a lawn chair, rosary in hand, I pray my rosary as the sun goes down. As I am facing west, I pray and just take in the glory of God's goodnight sunset.

A few summers ago, there I was on my lawn chair, eyes closed, rosary in hand, drinking in the beauty. As I prayed, I dropped my left hand to the side of the chair. Within a few minutes, I felt warm, cuddly, fur brushing up against my hand. I gently whispered, "Here kitty, kitty, kitty." I felt doubly blessed. This evening I would have one of my favorites as a guest with me as I prayed. I love cats. I grew up with those purring, self-willed, independent darlings. I know them and they know me. So, with eyes closed, one hand holding the rosary, and the other hand stroking my furry friend, I prayed until my rosary was finished, maybe ten minutes or so.

Then I opened my eyes and looked down.

For over ten minutes I had been stroking a skunk! A real, live skunk! I couldn't believe it. Having heard somewhere, that animals can smell fear through some instinct they have, I whispered, "Just stay calm, just stay calm. . . . Nice kitty. Pretty kitty. Skunky kitty." I didn't take my hand away, I just remained still whispering endearments. Not too long after, the mother skunk came into view and saw her baby, still under my left hand. The little guy got up and slowly waddled away.

You may ask, do you still sit there on summer evenings and pray the rosary as the sun sets? Yes, I do, and if it happens to be dusk, when the setting sun is fading softly into the night sky, I always glance around to see if my furry friend will stroll by on his way at twilight time.

Caught On the Roof

by Sister Vincent Marie, O.C.D.

A NUMBER OF YEARS AGO I WAS ASSIGNED as Directress of our sisters in Temporary Vows. Back then, we called them Juniors, and we all slept in the same wing of the convent dubbed the Juniorate. One night, we were kept awake by a cat who cried piteously the whole blessed night. Nobody could get any sleep, and of course, as a result, everyone was just a bit cranky the next day. The next night, just as I was about to change out of the white habit – I was serving in the hospital during the day so I wore white – I heard the cat start in again with his meowing.

I thought, "Oh, no, not again you don't!" I peeked through the venetian blinds but couldn't see anything, so I tried listening out the window.

"This cat's on the roof!" I thought out loud to myself.

So I went down the hall of the Juniorate, out the back door, jumped from the stairwell onto the roof and investigated the length of the roof in an attempt to find this cat. I finally located him over by the air conditioning unit. It appeared that a cat had her litter up there and one of the little kittens got his ear cut, which is why he was crying.

"Well, this isn't going to do," I said to myself. I couldn't leave the kitten, especially as he was crying and it seemed that mom had taken off. So I picked the kitten up and walked back across the top of the roof to take him down. Before I made my leap back across from the roof to the stairs, something made me look down. Much to my chagrin, there was Mother Margarita Maria, our provincial superior, standing down below looking intently up at me.

"Sister!" Mother called up to me crisply.

"Yes, Mother?" I replied, trying to adapt a tone of nonchalance.

"What are you doing on the roof?" she asked.

"Well, uh, catching a cat," I stammered. I unfortunately didn't know that Mother was downstairs having dinner with Mrs. Walters* and Mrs. Blackman*. Hearing my footsteps, she thought there was a prowler on the roof and she was about to call the police. But as she could see, there was no prowler, only me – with a cat in my arms.

"Sister, get down at once!" Mother said sternly.

"Uh, yes, Mother, at once," I answered. Although I said "at once", I wasn't going to let her see me jump, in case I went down mid-leap between the roof and the stairwell. But she still stood there waiting.

"Sister, I said get down at once," Mother repeated.

"Yes, Mother, I will," I replied all the while thinking, *pleeeaaassse* go back inside to your dinner!

Finally, Mother turned to go back inside and as soon as she got out of my sight, I jumped back over. I then took the kitten all the way back down the hall, out the other door where we got a nice box and some nice rags to make the little fellow comfortable. We also gave him a generous serving of milk. In the meantime, the kitten had stopped crying.

I thought with some satisfaction, "Good, now I'm going to sleep."

I returned to my cell and shut the door, when suddenly I thought of the kitten's mother. I looked out the venetian blinds again and sure enough, there was the mother cat sitting on the edge of the roof right above my window, obviously looking for her kitten. She patiently waited until no one was walking back and forth down by the kitchen and then she made her way down, picked up her kitten by the nape of the neck, went down the stairs and took off with the kitten in her mouth. We never saw them again … she must have decided that our roof was no place to have kittens!

= names have been changed to protect privacy

Whatever You Do, Don't Run!

by Sister Mary Colombiere, O.C.D.

*T*HE DATE WAS JULY 30, 2001.
After visiting our sisters in California, another Sister and I were returning to Arizona, and on the way, we stopped at Grand Peak Canyon because it is always a very good place to discover new species of birds. Having gone birding so often in California, I was always aware of and had seen signs telling what to do if you encounter a mountain lion. While I was very familiar with what to do when encountering the big cats, I would never go into a nature park with knowledge of their presence.

It was late afternoon by the time we went into Grand Peak Canyon, so we didn't have much time to bird watch. We asked the docent if anything unusual had been sighted in the canyon and she told us, "No."

However, as it turned out, there was something unusual for us to see. At the mouth of the nature center, there is a spotting scope set up and there at the top of the pine tree was a nesting bird. It was a tiny little Beryline Humming bird, which is an unusual find for Arizona. Unfortunately, I couldn't see it even when it flew from the nest. It was so tiny, it looked like a little dot and I couldn't say I actually saw it, because it was so high up.

As Sister and I were standing there, the docent asked, "Would you like to look through our binoculars?"

She had some really good ones, so I happily borrowed them, but at that moment, the little bird flew all the way down from the nest to my feet – hovering about a tree right there by my feet, so I got a perfect look at it. Well, that was all the enticement I needed to really want to go into the canyon area. The docent was so thrilled to see this little bird up so close, without binoculars, she let us in for free.

Even though it was quite late, Sister and I went in and we passed an elderly gentleman, walking with a cane, just leaving the area. I was very happy he was not in the canyon at the same time we were because of the adventure about to unfold.

Sister and I continued walking into the nature center and were almost to the end of the grassy area where visitors would actually go down into the canyon. Due in part to the lateness of the hour, I had no intention of going down. At one point, Sister and I separated; she was looking at one thing and I was looking at another. After some time, I called to Sister and mentioned to her that it would be best for us to start getting back because it was getting rather late.

We had wandered pretty far from the nature center and as we were retracing our steps, I heard a gobbling sound. Looking toward the source of the sound, I saw a flock of turkeys take off, just exploding into the air. Then, as I watched the last bird take off into the air, I couldn't believe my eyes! I thought I was surely watching a wide screen version of the television program, "Wild Kingdom." There was a mountain lion running at full speed trying to get that very last turkey and he was so close to us! I was so stunned, I froze in my tracks and realizing the danger we were in, all proper steps to take in such instances all but flew from my head.

I said to Sister, "Whatever you do, don't run!"

The mountain lion came to a skidding halt when he missed the last turkey. He was obviously hungry and must have sensed us because he turned and faced us. We could see every muscle of his body and how beautiful this animal actually was. Unfortunately, I wasn't appreciating the beauty at that moment!

I quietly repeated to Sister, "Don't run, whatever you do, don't run."

So we stood facing him…he looking at us and we looking at him. I didn't know what the next step should be because I didn't know what his next step would be. He seemed rather fascinated by us and just kept staring as we stared right back. After a while he actually sat, it was as if an invisible someone (St. Francis, perhaps?) put an invisible hand on his shoulder from behind and pushed him down. The big cat calmly sat down in the grass just looking at us.

At that point, I knew we had to try and do something, we couldn't stand there all night.

"We're going to start back, but we're going to walk very slowly. He knows the terrain and we don't. He can cut us off at any point because the road curves around and even if we were to scream, they couldn't hear us at the nature center at this distance," I told Sister.

So we began walking back. Sister kept a watchful eye on the big cat as she was taller, and I watched the road. We stayed very close together. After we got out of sight of him, I cautioned Sister that that didn't mean we were safe.

Finally, after what seemed an interminably long time, the porch of the nature center came into sight. By that time my knees were rubbery! As we stepped up onto the porch, the docent came out and asked "Well, did you see anything unusual?"

I replied, "Yes, we came face-to-face with a mountain lion!"

The docent was quite shocked. There were no signs posted, so they obviously didn't know they had a danger of mountain lions so close to the nature center.

Finally, as we were leaving the nature center along a narrow dirt road with barely room for only one car to pass, a truck pulled up beside us and the driver rolled down his window and asked, "Are you the ladies who saw the mountain lion?"

I said, "Yes, we certainly are."

I don't know if he went back to go look for the mountain lion, but I would certainly never go back without proper safety precautions!

The Indignant Cow

by Sister Faustina, O.C.D.

IT IS QUITE COMMON FOR MANY ARDENT ANIMAL LOVERS to indulge in bestowing anthropomorphic traits to their beloved pet. Well, this is the story of one bovine that needed no such assistance in displaying a very human-like bit of attitude!

A number of years ago, Sister Mary Jeanne and I drove north to a town on the central California coast to visit a good friend of our community. By all accounts, it was a typical road trip, although it did take us a bit of time driving around and backtracking in order to find the dirt road off the main highway that led to our friend's property. There was really only one remarkable thing about this trip – we were greeted by a welcoming committee comprised of a small herd of about 10 cows.

For the most part, the cows kept to their grazing, although a few did lift their heads in mild interest as we drove past. However, we did pique the curiosity of one particular cow which seemed determined to escort us all the way to the front door of the house, as she fell in step with us, trotting alongside our car. Needless to say, this made me just a bit apprehensive. The cow seemed awfully big and our car suddenly seemed rather small, and living in southern California, I was not accustomed to freely mingling with these large creatures. Fortunately, as we made our way up the road, the cow eventually lost interest in us and rejoined the rest of the herd. I heaved a big sigh of relief!

We had a lovely visit, and the time passed all too quickly. We had a long drive ahead of us, and the approaching dusk signaled that we should be on our way. As we made our way back down the narrow dirt road leading to the main highway, our cow friends seemed to be dutifully waiting for us to see us off. As we slowly drove down the dirt road, we had to come to a sudden stop. A big black, furry cow was taking a leisurely stroll right down the middle of the road! Unfortunately, the "road" was little more than a one-lane drive and definitely not wide enough for our car to pass the cow on either side.

The cow nonchalantly ambled along the middle of the road in seemingly ultra-slow motion, throwing the occasional backward glance over her shoulder at us, as if we were a member of the herd just moseying along, following her lead.

"This is taking forever," I remarked to Sister, "we really have to start on the trek home."

"Well, perhaps if you tap the horn gently, she'll know to move out of the way," Sister Mary Jeanne suggested.

I raised a dubious eyebrow at this suggestion, but not having a better idea of how to let the cow know that we wanted her to move out of the way, I ever so gently tapped the horn. The car emitted a rather dainty little beep.

I've never seen anything the likes of what happened next. At the horn's beep, the cow stopped dead in her tracks, paused momentarily, then turning only her head back toward our direction, indignantly shot us a look of complete and utter disdain! She actually seemed quite offended and annoyed by the "off-putting" little beep that came from the car! The cow just stood glaring at us and the "expression" on her face said it all: "Are you seriously making this insulting noise at **me?!?**"

Our "standoff" continued for several minutes and I think it would be a fair assessment that Sister and I were quite intimidated by the cow and considered ducking for cover under the dashboard! After an interminable several minutes, the cow apparently decided that this "strange" looking new cow (our car) was benign enough and dismissed us with an imperious shake of her head and moved off the road into the grass. I half expected to hear an irritated "Harrumf!" accompany the head shake!

Finally, we were on our way home to the city, but not before a good long laugh that had tears streaming down both our faces!

The Real Thing

by Sister Emma Luz, O.C.D.

ONE DAY AS I TOOK A SHORT WALK DOWN THE ROSE PATH at our Motherhouse in Alhambra, California, I noticed a Scrub Jay watching me from afar. I knew what he was looking for – a peanut. After all these years, the birds still remember their friend, Sister Mary Colombiere, who, until the day she was assigned to another convent, used to place peanuts for her birds on tree limbs, on fences, and even on her hand where they would perch for a moment to get their treat.

I took a flower bud from a nearby bush and placed it in the middle of the palm of my hand, like she used to. I thought to myself, "Maybe I can fake the bird into thinking this is something he can eat. "My feathered friend cocked one eye to the left, looked at the flower bud, then turned his head and cocked his other eye toward my hand.

Suddenly, he flew into a nearby bush and began digging deeply into the ground. After some labor, he pulled out a large shelled peanut almost as big as himself and flew back on the branch close to me. He stared at me with his large peanut in his small beak as if to parade the peanut before me. With a look close to reproach, he seemed to being saying, "This is what you are supposed to give to me." His message was clear.

I smiled to myself. I understood, no one wants second best given to them. We all want the real thing. And God wants the real thing from each of us!

Pepé Le Pew and the Priests

by Sister Mary Scholastica, O.C.D.

*F*ATHER ADRIAN TOMLINSON HAS BEEN A DEAR FRIEND of our community for many years. He lives in England, but takes his vacations here at Sacred Heart Retreat House during the summer months. Father Adrian is also an avid practical joker, who very much relishes playing jokes and pranks on us all the time. He is not above throwing a rubber spider from behind a bush at unsuspecting sisters who happen to be walking by, chuckling merrily at the resulting shrieks. We certainly have had much fun and laughter with Father Adrian and his practical jokes throughout the years. We've also learned to defend ourselves accordingly.

I do not recall how the conversation came about. Somehow, it came to our attention that Father Adrian is quite fearful of skunks. So, of course, we taught him how to "protect" himself against these creatures that happen to believe our retreat house was built for them. Though I imagine they inhabited the land before we arrived. Father learned to jingle his keys whenever he was walking around the property. He learned to turn on nightlights and to avoid all dark corners in the latter part of the evenings.

Sometime later, Father Adrian was again spending his vacation at the Retreat House and as was his custom, would take his strolls to the rhythmic accompaniment of jingling keys. During one of his strolls, Sister Gloria Therese and I happened to see Father Adrian from a distance. We looked at each other and the light bulbs went on simultaneously.

"Are you thinking what I'm thinking?" Sister Gloria Therese asked, her eyes twinkling.

"You bet I am," I replied with a big smile.

So off we went to find our superior to request permission to play a prank on Father Adrian. We wanted to be sure to obtain God's blessing upon our endeavors. To our delight, we were given FULL green lights.

Father Adrian was staying in one of the priest cottages, the entry to which just happens to be a bit more secluded than the others. One day, Father Adrian and his dear friend, Father Dan Wathen, who was also staying with us at our retreat house planned to go out that evening. How wonderful for us!

We waited until the two priests left the Retreat House grounds and then quickly got out our plush toy skunk (that was actually quite life-like) along with some fish wire and headed toward the cottage, which Father Adrian occupied. Now each cottage has a screen door in addition to the regular wood entry door and when an occupant leaves, the screen door is closed but remains unlocked.

Our plan was simple: we tied a length of the fish wire around our fake Pepé Le Pew's neck, then tied the other end of the fish wire onto the inside knob of the screen door. We then tucked Pepé between the wood door and screen door, making sure that the screen door latched properly to stay closed, thereby keeping Pepé in place. The idea was that when the screen door was opened, it would pull the fish wire attached to Pepé's neck making it appear that a skunk was walking out from behind the screen door. We knew the two priests would be returning later that evening after dark. Some large trees block direct illumination of the entry to Father Adrian's cottage, and as a result, Father wouldn't be able to clearly distinguish that a fake skunk was waiting to welcome him!

Shortly after 9:00 p.m. that evening, we went to the convent to wait for the festivities to begin. The convent is on the 2nd floor of the main building which overlooks the front lawn and the driveway into our retreat house. Looking out from this vantage point, the priest cottages are immediately to our right. We all dutifully turned off all lights on the second floor, opened our windows and quietly waited.

Our patience was rewarded. We heard the two priests come in through the main gate. It was only later we learned of their conversation, which was about, believe it or not, skunks! Father Dan was telling Father Adrian that he thought Father had an over-active imagination. He pointed out that during all his stays at our retreat house, he had yet to encounter a skunk. Good for you, Father Dan!

The two priests reached the door of the cottage and we heard one of them open the screen door.

Well, the next thing we knew, pandemonium broke out. With startled shouts and practically tripping over themselves, they wildly scrambled to get away from the skunk that had just trotted out from behind the screen door and across their shoes! I have to admit, the yelling was quite something and there was one particularly unholy shriek (which we learned later, kindness of Father Adrian, was Father Dan).

We're not exactly sure what transpired in the very unnatural quiet that followed. How they mustered up their courage to approach our little black and white friend to learn that it was FAKE.

After the quiet, the storm hit. They then walked up the steps to the front porch of our Administration building and we heard Father Adrian, who has a resonating voice, yell out, *"WHERE ARE THEY?!? WHERE ARE THE SISTERS?!? This means payback!!!"*

Well, we sisters were up on the second floor of the convent laughing so hard tears were running down our cheeks as we thoroughly enjoyed the fruits of our prank on Father Adrian and the very good sport, Father Dan!

The Javelina

by Sister Mary Colombiere, O.C.D.

W HENEVER YOU GO LOOKING for different species of birds, you're almost certain to encounter other types of wildlife, as well. That was the experience we had when another Sister and I went to Portal, Arizona. Portal is a very small town, with a main street about a half mile long and the bank, the post office and small grocery store are all contained therein. On the side roads, you'll find private homes, but they are very far apart from each other. One famous home in Portal was that of Sally Spofford, who went by the nickname "The Bird Lady." She had a degree in ornithology; a very unassuming, extremely intelligent woman who would never flaunt her knowledge. She always remained very simple and would only share what she knew if you asked.

In the yard of her home, (I believe she owned approximately 15 acres of land,) there was only enough room for parking for perhaps three cars. Inside the yard, next to her house, it was all set up for birding. She had a clothes line that contained many different kinds of feeders – hummingbird feeders, seed feeders, and others. The clothes line had a pulley so you could bring it over to the window in order to refill them. The huge old trees also held multiple feeders, and they also had sizeable holes in them in which she would put peanut butter for the animals to find. Everything throughout her yard was set up to feed the wildlife, and she fed any kind of wildlife that came in, whether it was bears or any other creature. She fed anything that came in besides the birds.

When we visited there, we didn't actually see her. She was somewhere inside her house; however, we did encounter a young couple sitting on the bench watching the feeders. I don't know if they were connected with each other in any way. One was a young woman who wore a pair of leather boots that went up to about her knees. The other was a gentleman standing behind her. As the four of us were standing behind the bench and looking at all the feeders, suddenly, a lone javelina came into the yard and we all froze right where we were. Javelinas can be dangerous animals. If you look at it from the side, it looks flat, but the front legs are higher than the back legs and they do have a hook on their back leg that can easily slice your foot or leg. The javelin resembles a large rodent or perhaps a pig, but it's not a wild boar.

The javelina somehow spotted the boots the woman was wearing and was attracted to them. So he inched his way over toward her. The man did nothing, I think he was too scared to do anything. She couldn't move because she didn't want to be chased and the javelina came all the way over and began sniffing the toes of the boots all the way up to her knees and we just stood there with baited breath waiting to see what he would do next. Finally, he turned around and left. Well that was the green light for the couple to get out of there.

Sister and I, however, stayed and I walked all about the yard looking to see what interesting creatures I might find. When I circled back near the bench again, I happened to turn around so that my back was to her house and I was looking toward the back of her property, which was up against a hilly ridge.

For anyone who has watched any of the old westerns or cowboy movies, these usually feature scenes where the covered wagons are down in sort of a valley that is enclosed by a fairly high ridge. Then suddenly there appears up on the ridge a whole line of Indians on horseback ready to converge on the covered wagons down below. Well, that's sort of what I thought I saw. As I turned around, there on the ridge of the hill was an entire herd of javelinas looking down at us.

That day I happened to be in sandals with open toes. The leader, who had been the one who had already come into the yard, was in the center of the herd. I saw him eyeing my sandals and I thought "No way!"

Again, you don't want to run, you just have to wait it out. So as he kept his eyes on my sandals, he broke rank and came down into the yard again. He moved toward me and when he got close enough, I stomped my foot into the dust as hard as I could. It scared him so much he turned around and ran back to the herd. Suddenly, as if realizing that he shouldn't be the one to be frightened, he turned around and looked back at me with a look on his face that said, "I'll get you for this!" There didn't seem to be any fight in him though, and he led his herd out of the yard. That was our cue to depart, too!

A footnote about Sally Spofford: she was the only woman permitted and given a special invitation to attend the releasing of the captive California condors, when these large, almost extinct birds were released back into the wild. She has since died and her relatives did not want to keep up the house as a nature center, so they sold it. As I understand it, a nearby neighbor was so disturbed by that that he turned his house into a birding area.

Hobbes

by Sister Faustina, O.C.D.

D URING THE TIME I WAS ASSIGNED TO TEACH in Colorado, one year there was a profusion of class pets. One class had just gotten a legless lizard, which looked suspiciously like a snake. The children named him "Pepe". Even though Pepe resembled a snake, we were informed by the students that calling Pepe a snake would be quite the insult – he's a legless lizard, after all. Another class, the 4th graders, got a cute, furry, whiskery gerbil, named "Chloe". Virtually each class in the school had some sort of class pet; every class, that is, except for my class. Needless to say, they were feeling very left out. I had very little enthusiasm about adopting a class pet because of the required maintenance and costs. However, not only were my students very serious, they were also very persistent. Finally, I relented.

"Alright," I told them resignedly one day, "do your research and type something up and tell me how much it will cost us to have a class pet."

In the end, the class settled on a frog.

"Hmm," I thought to myself, "this is do-able; I can handle a frog. Frogs don't require much exercise and are pretty low maintenance" or so I thought. "This should work out fine."

I spoke with the principal and my superior and let them know about my class' desire to have a frog as a class pet and that each child would bring in $5, which would cover the supplies and costs of food for the frog for the rest of the school year. The science teacher generously donated the aquarium. So it was that with the blessings of the principal and our superior, Sister Julianna and I set out to the pet store to buy the frog.

The frog we settled on was about the size of a silver dollar and he was actually kind of cute…well, cute as far as frogs go. I didn't go so far as to hold him in my hand, but Sister Julianna did. The little fellow sat in her palm peering up at us with his little red beady eyes. We also purchased the moss and other necessary items for his aquarium, including a supply of crickets for his meals and off we went, frog in hand.

The next day, my students were bursting with excitement and anticipation in meeting the newest member of the class and it was with great solemnity they named him "Hobbes" inspired by the toy tiger in the cartoon strip "Calvin and Hobbes".

The weeks and months passed and all was well. Hobbes received his due attention and care and I occasionally lent a hand to help clean his aquarium. Hobbes seemed to be growing into a happy, contented frog – although I failed to realize that he would grow from the size of a silver dollar to about that of a cell phone!

As the end of the school year approached, I realized I was going to transfer and I suddenly had to worry about what to do with Hobbes. I found myself wondering what was the life span of a frog? In the end, the science teacher informed me that frogs can live up to *eight years* and he also again kindly came to the rescue by adopting Hobbes. And thus Hobbes became the permanent science class pet for years to come!

Grace in Action

"May your life in that little corner of the earth be as a bonfire of love, consuming itself in the love of God and zeal for souls. Yes, win many souls for Him by your prayers, good example and teaching."

- Venerable Mother Luisita

"They's All My Brothers"

by Sister Marie-Aimée, O.C.D.

A FEW YEARS AGO, I WAS TEACHING 7TH GRADE in one of our elementary schools. One night at recreation, a sister shared about the time one of her first graders declared to his classmates that Kobe Bryant was his dad. The other children laughed at him but he insisted through his tears that it was really true. She looked down into his bright blue eyes, taking in his pale skin and blond hair, and wondered how to explain to a first grader the impossibility of such a claim. She wisely called home. His mom answered the phone and sister shared the reason for the call. The young woman started to laugh and quickly explained that she had given her husband a Kobe Bryant jersey for his birthday and he had been wearing it often; Hence the little boy's belief that it was his dad's name. As sister shared this story at the table, we all chuckled and I thanked God that I taught the older students who don't present so many "how to explain this" moments. I love young children but the thought of thirty-five six year olds, all day, in one room leaves me feeling very grateful to be teaching junior high.

A few days after sister shared that story I was supervising my 7th graders at the benches during lunch. Other classes were also eating as the teachers took turns supervising them. I was chatting with my girls while they ate their food when I felt a tug on the sleeve of my habit. I looked down to see a first grader standing next to me. He held up his orange and said, "Sister, will you please open this for me?" We walked down to the other end of the lunch area where the first graders were sitting. I stood by their table and peeled his orange conscious that all the other first graders were watching my every move. As soon as I handed the peeled orange to him and turned to go, a dozen hands flew up in the air. Each hand held an orange. "Mine too, Sister." "Me too." "Can you open mine?" I sighed and turned around again. Whoever included a whole orange with the hot lunch has never eaten with first graders, I thought to myself.

As I started to peel orange number two, I asked the children to tell me their names. We went around the table and when we got to the last boy who was on the end of the bench next to me, he looked up at me and grinned, saying, "My name's Samuel.*" Then with a sweeping gesture of his arm that took in all the little boys at the table, he said to me, "theys all my brothers." I slowly looked around the table, seeing blue eyes and brown ones, sandy hair and jet black hair, and a wide variety of skin tones represented. I also saw every small head at the table nodding in agreement. My heart sank as I looked back into Samuel's earnest dark brown eyes and remembering the Kobe Bryant incident, thought, "now why didn't I stay at the junior high table?" He must have seen the question in my eyes because before I could open my mouth he said happily, "sister, theys all my brothers cause of Jesus." I smiled, partly from relief, as the other boys agreed. Just then one of the first grade girls ran past the table. "Yeah," piped up another pint sized evangelizer, "and she's our sister!"

As adults we can make things so complicated. We look at other human beings and see their skin color or the clothes they are wearing or any number of external characteristics, and we categorize and label and mentally judge based on all the things we "know" about them because of what we see. That day at the lunch table, a six year old reminded me that relationships really don't have to be all that complicated, after all: "They's all our brothers and sisters." Maybe I should visit the first grade table more often!

* = *denotes names have been changed to protect privacy*

The Day the Light Dawned

by Sister Timothy Marie, O.C.D.

I AM A CARMELITE SISTER WHO TEACHES 200 high school students daily during five class periods beginning at 8:00 a.m. and ending about 2:30 p.m. Each of my classes has 40 students. Each student is a cherished, never-to-be-repeated, unique human person. Each one of them has an immortal soul, so I can truly say that there are 400 souls in my care during a school year, because my religion class is only a semester. That makes 200 souls the first semester and 200 new souls the second semester.

Now, we are all composed of body and soul. We can see the body, but we can't see our soul. So as people progress through their lives, it is easy to forget about the spiritual component which makes them who they are. Words are only words until they penetrate into the very soul.

That's why it is sometimes very difficult to teach teens. Why? Their minds and hearts are filled with so much – friends, activities, sports, clubs, schoolwork, and often a part-time job besides. It is hard for them to calm down enough to learn. For example, they come from a P.E. class into mine and then off to one of their favorite elective classes. Their bodies may be present, but their minds are most of the time very far away.

I suppose each teacher deals with this "bringing them in" to the present moment in the classroom. Each tries to find a way. Some have just given up. Others become extraordinarily animated as they teach, but who can keep that up all day long, every day, year after year? Like I said, each teacher deals with it in their own way.

I would like to share with you my way and I think families can also do this within their homes.

Upon arriving in the classroom (a little early) I take some holy water and sprinkle it lightly on each desk and chair. I find some beautiful music –usually praise and worship music – and have it playing softy when they come in. Then I begin class with the sign of the cross and play the music for the day with printed words if possible. This introduces the lesson of the day.

The name of my class is "Sacraments and Worship" and I teach juniors at a Catholic High School in southern California. Twice in my high school teaching career, I used a teaching strategy that was extremely different and at first I wasn't sure whether to use it or not. But the nudging to use it remained strong, so I changed my lesson and did something very new.

You see, it was a very important lesson. Both times I used this new approach, it was for very important lessons. This is what happened. I was scheduled to teach that Jesus Christ is the son of God, not symbolically or figuratively, but really and truly. And that is a mighty awesome concept to teach to someone who comes in thinking about their date that very evening.

I had already prayed in the classroom that morning and sprinkled some holy water. Praise and worship music was playing as they students entered. Our classes are fifty minutes in length, so I told them to clear off their desks of everything and wait.

Then I told them that I wasn't going to talk at all that class period. One of them muttered, "Well that's a first-class miracle!" Others laughed. Then I put on a recording of the outtakes of testimonies of some people. This took about five minutes.

Then I said, "And you aren't going to talk either. We are going to meditate."

I didn't define what meditation is.

Next, the praise and worship music began playing and I began writing on the board a sentence from the Mass of Our Lady. It is also found in the Little Office of the Blessed Virgin Mary.

Slowly, I wrote the words slowly, deliberately, respectfully, and in large letters.

" *Blessed is the womb of the Blessed Virgin Mary which bore the Son of the Eternal Father.*"

For the next 35 minutes, we listened to the music and looked at the board. The bell rang. We finished the class with a prayer. One student lingered behind and asked me, "Do you really believe that?" I replied, "Yes, I do. It defines who Jesus Christ is –the son of God, born of the Virgin Mary. Both." He just shook his head and said, "I never knew. This changes everything."

The second time I did this, I followed the same format, but with a different quote. It was the day I was scheduled to teach about the True Presence of Jesus in the Blessed Sacrament. I wrote,

" *Jesus Christ is truly present in the Blessed Sacrament. That is why we call it the Real Presence. This is not a symbolic presence. He is really and truly present in each consecrated host and in each particle of the consecrated host.*"

Again, no one talked. Praise and workship music played softly in the background. After class ended, a young man came up to me. He was one of our top football players. He said, "Excuse me, Sister, but is what you wrote on the board true?" I said, "Absolutely, 100% true." He looked up until we were face-to-face. With tears in His eyes, he said very quietly, "Thank you. I didn't realize."

There are so many days when after you teach, you come home tired and a little down, asking yourself, "Is it worth it?" Little positive feedback finds its way back to the teacher trying his or her best.

Yet, once in a while it happens. The light dawns in such a powerfully tangible way that you can see it and almost touch it.

Thank you, Lord, that I am a teacher.

Awesome Promptness

by Sister Isabelle, O.C.D.

A T Santa Teresita, our assisted and skilled nursing facility, we offer an extensive pastoral care program for our residents, including: Holy Mass, daily rosary, adoration and Bible study. We also make pastoral visits to our residents who are hospitalized. Some time ago, we had two seminarians staying with us here at Santa Teresita and they were assigned to assist us in pastoral care.

We thought it would be beneficial for the seminarians to experience what it is like to visit residents who are in the hospital. At the time, we happened to have several hospitalized residents, so one day I made plans with another sister to visit them with the seminarians in tow.

Our first stop was with a resident, Margaret*, who was in critical condition. She was no longer able to take anything by mouth, neither solids nor liquids, and she was suffering terribly from an extreme sensation of thirst and repeatedly kept asking for water. Although she was longing for something to drink, had she actually consumed water, it would have been harmful due to her physical condition.

On the day we visited Margaret, both her daughters, Anne* and Christine*, happened to be there. Because Margaret was under "contact isolation", only the two seminarians and I went into the room. The other sister accompanying us chose to remain outside the door. We stood around her bed, talking with her and she repeatedly told us how thirsty she was.

"Could somebody give me some water? I am very thirsty," Margaret lamented.

The seminarians and I exchanged glances with Anne and Christine. Even water was forbidden under doctor's orders, so we were not quite sure how to respond to Margaret.

"Mom, you know the doctor specifically said you are not allowed any liquids," Christine tried to soothe her mother.

"How can they not give me water? " Margaret persisted.

In an effort to distract her, one of the seminarians asked, "Margaret, how about we pray with you?"

Margaret readily agreed.

We all laid our hands on her and started praying to the Holy Spirit asking Him to come upon her and heal her, strengthen her and comfort her.

As we paused in our prayer, one of the seminarians asked, "Margaret, do you want us to pray for something in particular?"

Now, all her life, Margaret had been a very matter-of-fact woman. If she felt the need to say something, she would do so without sugar-coating it, just saying it like it is.

So in response to the seminarian's question, Margaret, ever true to form blurted out, "*WATER!*"

All of us kept right on praying, asking the Holy Spirit to help quench Margaret's physical thirst.

Less than five minutes after concluding our prayers, a nurse came into the room with an incredible announcement.

"I just spoke with the doctor," the nurse stated, "and he said it will be all right if we give Margaret a little bit of water every so often. It won't do any harm."

We were all floored and stood gaping at each other.

"Is something wrong," the nurse asked startled by the incredulous expressions on our faces.

"No, nothing is wrong, in fact, everything is right!" I exclaimed.

Thanks be to God! Not only had the Holy Spirit heard our prayers for Margaret, He had answered her prayer with awesome promptness!

* = denotes names have been changed to protect privacy

"*The Treatment*"

by Sister Regina Marie, O.C.D.

WHEN I WAS TEACHING
at Sts. Felicitas and Perpetua School, there were many incredibly beautiful families. This story is about the Drellishak family. The parents, Ken and Peggy were the PTA presidents when we took responsibility for the school. I taught their eldest son, Steven, a wonderful student. The following year, their second son , Scott, entered 8th grade. I knew this boy had a high IQ and needed to be challenged.

Just as school started, I spoke with his mother and said, "Peggy, I'm not going to be able to meet this child's needs."

"Oh, yes, you are, Sister!" she emphatically replied. "He is 13 years old and we need to give him character formation. We can take care of the IQ later.... character formation is what we need to focus on."

At one point Scott's welcome began to wear thin at home because he was not helping out with chores, and he wasn't helping his little sister, Stacy, with her homework ... he was basically living at home and eating their food while the extent of his contribution was burying his nose in his personal favorite reading. I'm not sure if Scott was even aware of the thin ice he was skating on.

Sister Mary Elizabeth taught language arts and one day she gave the class the assignment to write a fable. Scott thought that this was truly beneath his dignity. So the effort he put into the assignment was next to zero and as a result his grade was a D-. He was very definitely flirting with trouble. This occurred on a Monday and his mother found out about it on Wednesday, and that was when the fur began to fly.

It was during the middle of art class on Friday that one of the boys, Andrew, was fooling around and not doing what he was supposed to be doing. Andrew had a mass of curly hair and he was cute and he knew it. He continued messing around and I walked over to him, leaned over the desk, put both my hands on top of the desk and let out a long, exasperated breath.

With extremely clear enunciation, I whispered, *"Draw neat!"*

Scott, who sat right next to Andrew, overheard my comment and chuckling said, "Draw neat**ly"**.

I had just taught a lesson on adverbs that very morning! I knew better!! I totally ignored Scott, didn't even acknowledge that I heard him and with my attention still on Andrew, rewording the sentence correctly, I said, "You have artistic talent, Andrew. You can do so much better. I want to see you give it your best. Draw neatly."

I continued circulating through the class, dismissing the incident as "one among many" in the daily life in an Eighth Grade classroom. I thought the incident was over. Not so.

At home that evening, Scott exercised unfortunate judgment in sharing his mirth by relating this story at the dinner table.

Appalled, his mother said, "No, no, no…let me explain it to you, Scottie. When Sister says 'jump', you don't ask her how high, you her ask *permission* to come down. This is not the way our family conducts itself and do you know why you are sitting at this table eating from these dishes? Because you are part of this family but you are not acting like part of this family. Therefore you're not going to eat at the table anymore."

Eyes wide and slack-jawed, he asked in shocked surprise, "Well, what does that mean?"

His mother said, "It means you are going to fix your own food and you're going to eat privately because you're not acting like part of the family and we're going to stop pretending your behaviour is acceptable."

Completely stunned, Scott stammered, "Well how long does this last?"

His mother replied, "Until I get a phone call from Sister Regina Marie and she says 'I don't know what's happened to Scott, but he's involved in school, he's volunteering for service projects and he's helping younger students.'"

Resigned to his fate, Scott entreated, "Well, Mom, can we at least call her and tell her so she knows what to look for?"

The "treatment" lasted for a long time. He had to make his own food, couldn't eat at the table with the family, his mother no longer picked up after him. This went on for several weeks. I knew what was going on as Peggy told me about it on Day #1 of the Treatment. She was simply fit to be tied.

Finally, it was Open House, just before Thanksgiving time. As I walked with parents around the classroom, I deliberately made a point of saying, "Oh, Mrs. Drellishak, look at this science project Scott worked on with ….. " and I named the two girls who struggled with science. "He signed up to be on their team and they really did a wonderful job!"

I also pointed out, "And look Mrs. Drellishak, Scott helped the 2nd graders with the Good Manners Poster Contest."

Looking at Scott she said, "Well, I think we've achieved our goal."

He replied, "Can we tell Sister Regina Marie about it now?" It came out somewhat mumbled.

"Scott, this was your medicine so it's really your decision," his mom replied.

So he turns to me, his eyes and voice very sincere, "Well, you see Sister, I have a character defect and my mother is trying to help me overcome it."

"Scott, your growth has really been remarkable and consistent. You have every reason to be proud of yourself." It was one of those moments that *every* teacher relishes.

One of the hallmarks of the Eighth Grade year is the process of identifying the high school of choice. Many of the schools are highly competitive so most of the students tested at two or three different schools. At that time, the schools all had different evaluations, some as long as six to eight pages. Do the math: thirty students, a minimum of two applications, average seven pages per application. It was a lot of time-consuming work.

This particular class had a large number of students who were still very immature for their age. They weren't taking their education seriously. Their fooling around was becoming habitual and one day I had had enough. You can say that I calculatingly lost it that day. Sister Mary Colombiere calls it my "gummy bear fit" because she was there and saw the whole episode unfold. It was after lunch recess on a particularly hot afternoon. Sweaty Scott Drellishak brought in a fist full of gummy bears. The kids had been throwing gummy bears at each other on the basketball court. Now remember, in those days gummy bears were new. They were only sold in gourmet sections of stores; quite expensive to use as playground "ammunition." Anyway, Scott knew better than to leave them on the basketball court for the younger students to see. He picked them all up, brought them in and slammed the big wad, asphalt, dirt and all, square in the middle of my desk. Now it was my turn to be completely stunned. The boy was angry and I shared his sentiments.

I turned to the class. They went silent. They scurried to their seats. I made eye contact with every single one of them. I breathed so deeply I knew they could all hear it. They didn't move a muscle. I paced the floor in front of the room. Their eyes followed me back and forth. I pulled my veil down on my forehead so far that the white band of my veil distorted my eyes and cheeks. The students really didn't know what to do. Had their teacher really completely stepped over the bridge to insanity? I continued to pace. I picked up the glob of gummy bears from my desk and walked as if in a solemn procession to the trash can. I dramatically let the mess fall through my fingers. I turned to the class again and with every ounce of drama I could muster I finally spoke.

"There are children STARVING in Africa….and what are **_MY_** students doing?!?" I said in a low, deliberately ennunciated question.

"THEY ARE THROWING GUMMY BEARS AT EACH OTHER!!!" Crescendoing as I answered my own rhetorical question.

The kids didn't know what hit them ... .it really was quite funny... .they were so stunned!

"This is how it is," I continued on, "your parents are paying tuition for me to be your educator. However, it is consummately apparent that you have a different goal in mind. You think I'm your baby sitter. So, until we can all get it straight and we are on the same page in our purpose here, I am no longer going to teach you." I began the pacing again, partly for dramatic effect and partly to give them time to absorb the impact of this message. "When you walk into the classroom in the morning, all of your written assignments will be on the board. Do not worry. There will be enough to keep you occupied throughout the day. I will spend my day writing out your evaluations telling the high school administrators what I really think about your readiness to enter their high schools. Are there any questions?!?"

Silence.

"Good. Then we will begin now. Get out your assignment notebooks." I turned to the board and began writing. The next morning, their assignments were written on the board. As they entered the room the next morning, I smiled (to let them know they were in safe hands for the day) but I did not speak (to let them know that the coast was still not clear and I really did mean what I said the day before). All went well that day. We proceeded into another day. On the third day one of the girls, a genuine soul for whom studies did not come easily but who consistently worked hard, walked up to my desk and hesitantly asked, "Sister, I forget with this algebra, if the "x" goes in front of the "y", then do you divide or do you multiply?"

I whispered, "Don't forget that the order of operations is important if you want to find the correct answer. First work through grouping symbols, then you will know when to divide or multiply."

Later that afternoon, when Scott got home ... .he really was such an innocent ... .. he exclaimed to his mother, "Mom, Mom! You've got to get down there to school right away! You've got to support Sister. She just put us on *"The Treatment"* and now she's letting up too early! It's not going to be effective, Mom! Get down there and encourage her!"

Scott and his classmates have grown up to be amazing spouses and parents.

Many of them continue to keep contact with each other. One of their favorite stories that still circulates among them is the story of "The Treatment."

God bless them . . .
God bless us, Everyone!

Taught By a Child

by Sister Francis Marie, O.C.D.

S EVERAL YEARS AGO I HAD THE JOY OF SERVING at Holy Innocents School in Long Beach, California. Little did I know that it would be the youngest children who would be teaching me valuable life lessons.

In the schoolyard stands a place of sheer delight for the students – a playground. It has circular slides, tubes to crawl through, an assortment of climbing objects and the MONKEY BARS. These monkey bars are a favorite place of the littlest ones. Some children fly across the bars as if they were running on the ground, and some slowly savor the moment as they move across. In the first grade, the "smallest" child in the class was a young girl with "large" enthusiasm and heroic determination. She was ready to take on the monkey bars.

Generally, I stood close by to assist any of the students who were swinging on the monkey bars. The platform where they stepped off was at the height of my shoulders (I'm 5'9"). I heard a soft voice call out, "Sister, I want to do the monkey bars." I looked up and peering down at me with a smiling face and bright, excited eyes was Megan. I nodded and moved toward her. She said, "I'm afraid though." I told her it was all right to be afraid, but that I would hold her as she moved her hands across the bars. She was so happy, and I was eager to do this with her. Our journey together began.

Megan's arms were too short to reach the first bar, so I held her as she reached out and began moving her hands across the bars. She was so afraid that I heard her whimpering all the way across. As she set her feet down on the opposite platform and looked back, she literally jumped with excitement and said, "I did it … I'm just practicing … but I did it." I encouraged her for making it all the way across. She ran around and got in line to do it again.

This continued on for some weeks. Megan was determined to learn this and she kept going on the monkey bars over and over. The first ten times or so she was still afraid and whimpered all the way across, but slowly she began improving and her fears diminished. Over time, her little arms got stronger, and she learned how to swing with her legs and hips and she enjoyed the journey more and more. Now, I did not have to hold her, but followed closely behind her and encouraged her. Occasionally, her hand slipped. She would look at me, and I would help her. She would take a deep breath, and then reach up and continue on her journey.

I spent these weeks marveling at Megan's determination and enthusiasm to accomplish her goal. Her constant, joyful demeanor throughout her ups and downs inspired me deeply. I found myself thinking often of this and questioning, "Am I living my own Christian life with such determination AND enthusiasm?" It occurred to me that Megan's journey of learning the monkey bars was a great analogy for the spiritual life.

First of all, the journey of the spiritual life takes faith. You have to reach out and trust that there is a journey to be taken and that a Person is journeying with you. This first step of faith is like Megan reaching out to the first bar that was so far away. She could possibly fall, but she took a leap of faith and reached out. All we have to do, too, is reach out in faith to God and not worry about the risks involved. She had a person who promised to help her across. On our spiritual journey so, too, do we.

There is also the fear factor. Megan's very real fear was to fall on the ground and get hurt. On our spiritual journey, the fears are as diverse and complex as each individual human, but God gives us the strength to overcome our fears.

On our journey, we have the freedom to continue with enthusiasm, determination, and love. We find ourselves both fulfilled and enjoying the journey. We also have the freedom to choose to walk in doubt, anger or cowardice. Megan's example was simply beautiful. Ours, too, can be.

Each time after going across the bars, Megan was not disappointed. She did not do it perfectly or a with certain speed or with the proper form. She was just practicing. She was fulfilled and happy in the journey itself. Often in our own journeys, we set unrealistic expectations that no one – especially God – expects from us. The Lord wants us to delight in, and enjoy the journey with Him.

When Megan's hand slipped occasionally from the bar, I was not disappointed or angry with her. All I did was hold her, let her get her bearings, take a deep breath, and then she continued. It is the same with the Lord. In fact, He acts with infinite tenderness and mercy. He does not get mad at us or want to punish us when we fall either by weakness or sinfulness. He just holds us until we get our bearings by coming back to Him, and when we are ready, He lets us go in greater freedom to continue our journey.

As Megan was developing her monkey bar skills, I no longer had to hold onto her tightly as she crossed. I just walked closely behind her. She could not see me, but she trusted me and knew I was there. There are times in our spiritual journey where we do not "see" the Lord or experience Him in our prayer, but He is always walking close to us. All we need to do is trust Him and know He is there and will never leave our side.

During the course of these weeks and months, Megan and I developed a special relationship of love and trust. I had not been around children for a number of years and I was amazed to look at her trusting gaze. I found myself very humbled by this gift of trust. When she saw me, her eyes would light up. If she could greet me, she would run over and grab me around the knees. Of course, I was always so happy to see her and enjoyed her presence. A wonderful relationship developed, and I thanked God for such a blessing.

As we make our way in our own journey, we discover with amazement and joy that we have this incredible relationship of love with the Lord. Our own trust in Him grows, and He treats this trust as if we are giving Him an amazing gift. We look up to Him with abundant, childlike simplicity and we experience His boundless love for us.

Yes, our journey is like learning how to play on the monkey bars – with the difference that you do not ever master the journey in this life and the reward is eternal.

Yes, you can learn life's most important lessons in the first grade.

God's Timing

by Sister Faustina, O.C.D.

M Y PARENTS ARE BOTH TEACHERS
and I have a degree in Theology, so I was surprised to find myself working as
a Certified Nursing Assistant (CNA) during my Candidacy rather than in the
classroom. To say that working as a CNA didn't come naturally is a nice way to put it.

After six weeks of intensive training, which included how to take a blood
pressure reading and how to take care of peoples' day-to-day needs, I received
a very good orientation at both the Manor and the Hospital. The other CNAs
were helpful and friendly, but as I began my first day on my own I found myself
feeling overwhelmed.

Upon my arrival, I was given a very quick tour of the patients assigned to me.
Under normal circumstances, a CNA is assigned seven or eight patients. I was
assigned five, three of whom were lucid and could do almost everything for
themselves, so it seemed that I was off to a pretty good start. However, as a brand
new CNA, I wanted to do everything right and as a result was extremely careful
(read "slow"). I also struggled to find the things I needed; all the supplies were
there, I just couldn't seem to locate them that first day. I would be looking for a
hairbrush or toothpaste in this drawer and that one until I would finally find it
buried in the last place I thought to look before giving up. I was trying to maintain
my interior peace but it was becoming increasingly hard to remain calm.

By 11:30 a.m. I still had one more patient to attend to as I noticed the lunch trays
beginning to arrive. Even though I was new, I knew that this meant I was very

late. I tried to move more quickly but my overly cautious and careful "quick" was still not very speedy.

My last patient was a woman who was clearly very sick. She was in a room by herself, unconscious and quite swollen. I found out later she was in heart failure. The duties of a CNA include giving the patient a bed bath by washing down their body and then changing their hospital gown. With the zeal of a brand new nursing assistant, I wanted to give this lady the best bath she had ever had. Before I started I asked the nurse to come in and unhook her IV. I talked to the patient as I began to carefully bath her. Interiorly, I was wrestling with the frustrations of the morning and feeling overwhelmed. The patient was heavy due to the swelling and as I struggled to bathe her, my frustrations mounted.

Realizing that I needed to do something to regain some sense of peace within, I decided to pray the Divine Mercy chaplet. Actually, I decided to sing it. Out loud. I already had a great devotion to Divine Mercy and knew that this would calm me down but it would also be a gift I could offer to this patient.

The promises attached to the chaplet are very significant. One of them is that if the Divine Mercy chaplet is prayed for someone who is dying, Jesus stands before the Father as merciful intercessor. I wasn't sure how far out that promise held … did the person have to die within the hour? Within the month? I didn't know but I figured that since this lady was very sick, I would pray the chaplet for her and let God figure out the details.

I finished tending to her needs with the utmost gentleness and care as I sang the chaplet quietly for her. Once finished, I called the nurse back in to reattach the IV and I hurried out to begin passing out the lunch trays.

The nurse came out of the room immediately and asked, "What happened?"

Confused, I said, "What do you mean? I gave her a bed bath and changed her gown."

"She died," the nurse replied.

The patient had died while I was taking care of her, during the Chaplet! She had most definitely been alive when the nurse unhooked the IV. I found out later that death had been imminent and expected, but in the moment all I knew was that she had died in my care. I didn't have the courage to stay around and face the family to tell them I had been praying for their mother because I felt pretty awful about her death. Looking back, it probably would have given her family consolation to know she hadn't been alone, that she was being cared for and prayed for at the moment of death.

That day I learned a great deal about grace and mercy, about God's timing, about God's providence. My morning of frustration and stress became in His hands a precious gift for this woman as her soul entered eternity. She died in the company of someone who cared and who was praying for her.

That was my first day as a CNA … I'm a teacher now!

The Holy Eucharist

by Sister Isabelle, O.C.D.

*N*OT LONG AGO, ONE OF OUR VOLUNTEERS, JACK*, came to us at the suggestion of the wife of one of the doctors in the medical office building (at Santa Teresita our assisted living and skilled nursing facility). Jack plays the guitar for our residents. Although his wife was Catholic, he was not but he felt a certain pull within him and he would ask many questions about the Catholic faith.

However, the one concept he just couldn't understand is the Catholic belief in the Real Presence in the Holy Eucharist. This belief in the Real Presence means that under the species of bread and wine "...in the most blessed sacrament of the Eucharist the body and blood, together with the soul and divinity, of our Lord Jesus Christ and, therefore, the whole Christ is truly, really, and substantially contained." (CCC 1374).

Later that year, he attended our Corpus Christi feast and procession, during which all the Sisters were praying for him. Later he shared with us his experiences on that special feast day.

"You know, Sister," Jack began, "during one of the blessings for the Holy Eucharist, I felt something come over me, but I just can't find the words to describe just what happened – I couldn't shake this indescribable feeling all day," he continued.

"And can you imagine, the following morning when I woke up, I had one thought and one thought only and that was – the Eucharist is Jesus! Those words just kept ringing loudly in my brain and I couldn't get it out of my head no matter how hard I tried," he explained.

"What do you think about this, Jack?" we asked.

"All my doubts are gone – Jesus is wholly present in the Holy Eucharist," he stated with conviction."

Thanks be to God!

About one year later, almost exactly to the day, Jack and his wife, Marianne*, had their marriage blessed in our chapel. Marianne was again able to receive Holy Communion for the first time in 46 years. During the festivities following the blessing of their marriage, Jack made it known that he would like to enter the Church.

* = *denotes that names have been changed to protect privacy*

God's House

by Sister Faustina, O.C.D.

*T*HE YEAR I WAS TEACHING 8TH GRADE at St. Joseph's in La Puente, was the same year the school added a kindergarten class for the first time. While all the students would attend weekly Mass, the kindergartners initially were not included. Being so young, they tended to squirm and there were safety concerns, as well, such as having to cross the busy street when going from the school to the church. We wanted to first "practice" safely crossing the street with the children.

About a month into the school year, we decided to enlist the help of the 8th graders by having them "buddy up" with a kindergartner. They were to show them how to cross the street when walking over to the church, how to genuflect, how to kneel, show them what the church was like inside – all to help ready them to attend Mass with the rest of the school for the first time. We had these practices or "dry runs" about three times before the kindergartners were brought to Mass on a Friday morning.

Among the kindergartners was a little girl whose name, I believe, was Sarah.* She was a handful and very precocious. We seated her next to me because she tended to be a bit unruly. I was leading the group, (the teacher was new too), and trying to show the children how to be quiet with Jesus for a few minutes. We were all sitting quietly in the pews, and this little girl, who is *never* quiet, was sitting next to me. With great interest she was looking all around her and gazing up at the ceiling. After about thirty seconds, she leaned over and whispered to me, "God's house is really clean."

"That's true, it's very clean," I replied, neglecting to point out the cobwebs up in the corners near the ceiling.

Warming to the subject, she asked, "Who cleans God's house?"

"There are some people who come every once in a while to clean," I told her.

A few minutes passed as she seemed to think about this. I then commented, "God's house is really clean, but did you know that God lives in my house, too?"

With eyes wide as saucers, she breathed an awed, ***"Really?"***

"Yes, really," I replied, "God lives in my house. Across the street, we have Jesus living with us and I can visit him anytime. Isn't that beautiful?"

She mulled this over with a look of wonder on her little face.

A few more minutes passed and we continued to quietly sit in the pew. I glanced at Sarah and she seemed to still be turning over in her head the thought of Jesus living in our house.

So with an eye toward a possible future vocation, I asked Sarah, "Would you like to live in God's house? You could be a sister."

The minute the words left my mouth, I could see by the expression on her face that the spell had been broken. I asked her, "What's your name?"

Refusing to divulge her name, she emphatically stated, "I don't want to tell you my name," and that was the end of the discussion.

All of five years old and she knew very well that she should not give her name to a Sister, lest she might become a sister herself!

* = denotes that names have been changed to protect privacy

"Wait!"

by Sister Marie-Aimée, O.C.D.

*E*VERY SISTER SPENDS THEIR FIRST YEAR OF PROFESSION rotating through each of the various apostolates and the various duties within each apostolate. This year of apostolic internship helps broaden and deepen our young sisters' understanding of how our mission is lived and expressed in healthcare, education, and retreat work before she is assigned for a year to one specific assignment.

During her first year of profession, one of our sisters spent three months teaching 8th grade religion at one of our elementary schools. Delighted with the junior high students' ability to grasp the content and enter into discussion, she had just finished a unit on the Eucharist when she moved on to her next three month assignment.   She found herself at Little Flower Educational Child Care in the classroom with the four year olds doing "Jesus Time," the preschool variation of religion class.

She quickly realized that preschool was a different world than junior high. "How am I going to teach them about the Eucharist? About the Creed?" Her little students did not seem able to sit still for a picture book much less for a religion lesson. Seeing how much the children enjoyed moving, she put their energy and enthusiasm to good use by acting out songs and stories with them. As Christmas drew near, she knew the children were going to really enjoy the story of Jesus' birth.

During Jesus Time that day, she chose a Joseph and a Mary, two innkeepers, shepherds, angels, and wise men. Everyone had something to do. Even Sister. She was the donkey. The whole class watched in interest as Joseph and Mary and the donkey traveled around the classroom to Bethlehem. Joseph knocked hopefully at the first innkeeper's door but his request for lodging was met with an emphatic, "NO! I don't have room for you." The rapt class sighed in sympathy. Joseph turned to the next door and was met with another resounding, "NO!" Another groan from the four year old onlookers.

Both innkeepers were now watching with growing concern as Joseph trudged sadly back to Mary. Before Joseph could tell Mary the bad news, the first innkeeper called out to the second innkeeper, "WAIT! I can take Joseph if you can take Mary."

The Power of Divine Mercy

by Sister Isabelle, O.C.D.

PRAYERFULLY APPROACHING GOD, in a spirit of true contrition, and asking Him to pour forth His Divine Mercy can result in great blessings and graces.

By the time Rose* came to live in the Manor, (our skilled nursing facility), she was in her mid-70s and was dying of cancer. Although she had been away from the Church for a while, she had come back into the fold and was able to receive all the Sacraments. Rose was a staunch proponent of *Alcoholics Anonymous* and she had mentored many people through this program over the course of many years. At the time of her coming to live in the Manor, she, herself, had been sober for 46 years. As we got to know Rose and her husband, Dan*, we discovered that he, too, was away from the faith. In fact, we learned he wasn't Catholic, he was Protestant, but he had not been practicing his faith for many years.

Rose's cancer steadily progressed and when we realized that she did not have much time left, we spent more time praying with and for her in her room, singing to her, comforting her and helping her draw consolation in the truth of Jesus' loving and merciful Sacred Heart. Dan was very grateful for the physical and spiritual care Rose received in her final days.

One night, when we knew the end was fast approaching, I had an idea and I enlisted the aid of her husband. We went out to the corridor and lifted a beautiful, large (about three feet tall) picture of Jesus as the Divine Mercy and we brought it into her room. We held it in front of her so that her eyes fell on the image Jesus. We wanted that the very last thing she should see in this life is the image of Jesus as Divine Mercy. Dan and I held the picture for her to gaze upon until she fell into a deep slumber.

It was quite late by the time I was able to go home, around 11 p.m. It seemed to me that I had barely closed my eyes when a call came from the Manor that Rose was dying. I arose, dressed and hurried back to the Manor. I barely arrived in Rose's room when sure enough, she drew her last breath and she returned home to the Lord. Dan arrived shortly thereafter and another sister and I supported him on either side as his legs were close to giving out on him.

After Rose's death, we kept in contact with Dan and he, in turn, would come join us for different events and social occasions. One day, and I specifically remember that it was a Marian feast day – The Annunciation – I received a call from Dan.

"I'm coming by," he said, his voice sounding quite chipper, "can I come see you? I'll be bringing Jean* along. You remember, Rose's friend who spent a lot of time at Rose's bedside in her final days," he added.

"Why, certainly," I told him.

After hanging up the phone, I thought to myself, "Hmm, he happens to call on this day? That's interesting."

Dan and Jean arrived and we all sat down together for a nice visit. We talked about how he was doing and adjusting, when all of a sudden, with a gleam in his eye and he asked me, "What does it take to become a Catholic?"

I was so amazed that I was momentarily speechless. After Dan's call earlier that morning, I had suspected that something was up, that something BIG was going to happen, but this?!? I had no inkling!

We have since connected Dan with a local parish and he is enrolled in their RCIA (Rite of Christian Initiation for Adults) program.

When asked about his decision to embrace the Catholic faith, Dan tells us, "The reason why I want to become a Catholic is because of the great, great love that was shown to my wife, Rose, in her final days, and not only to Rose but also to me by all of you here at Santa Teresita."

In holding the picture of the Divine Mercy before the eyes of his dying wife, Dan, too, was touched by the graces, consolation and mercy that flows so ready from Our Lord's Sacred Heart. So much so, that it drew him home to the Catholic faith.

* = denotes that names have been changed to protect privacy

A Picture of God

by Sister Mary Colombiere, O.C.D.

AT HOLY INNOCENTS, I HAD A STUDENT, a little boy, named Willie, who I believe at that time was in the 6th grade. Willie* was a very delightful little boy with big brown button eyes which would melt you right away.

I had given the children an assignment over Lent to put a booklet together and I had indicated what was to be included on each page. Once the assignment was completed and turned in, I took the booklets home and as I was looking through them, I came upon Willie's. It was very, very well done, cover to cover, as was the inside. However, what puzzled me was that in the middle of the book, where the page indicated to draw a picture of God, it was totally blank. Well, I didn't know whether Willie was going to come back to it later and just forgot….I didn't know what happened and I didn't want to put a grade on the booklet until I had spoken to him.

So the next morning, taking the booklet from among the others, I called Willie aside and showed him the one he made.

I said, "Willie, you did a beautiful job on this booklet, but I don't understand why this page is blank?"

He just looked at me with his big brown eyes that seemingly had grown even bigger with surprise as the expression on his face read that I didn't get it.

He finally said, *"Sister, you said draw a picture of God. I can't do that. God is love!"*

* = *denotes that names have been changed to protect privacy*

A Good Habit

by Sister Faustina, OCD

W E DON'T CELEBRATE HALLOWEEN AT OUR SCHOOLS, but we do celebrate All Saints' Day and every year our students dress up as a particular saint. Very often some of the girls choose to dress up as a Carmelite saint because the Carmelite Sisters are their teachers and we teach them a great deal about our saints.

We have a couple of little costumes in our costume closet that resemble habits and one year a little girl asked to wear one of these miniature habits, to dress as St. Teresa of Avila. After the parade, the carnival and all of the festivities, we had the children take their costumes off for lunch.

This little girl looked up at me with her really big, round eyes and said, "Sister, I don't want to take this off."

"Well, you have to take it off now, but you can wear it for the rest of your life," I replied.

Upon hearing my response, the biggest smile lit up her face and the joy in her eyes was truly radiant.

Now this girl is a senior in high school and she is still close to our community, and I believe she is openly discerning her vocation. We're hoping it will flourish and bring her into our Carmelite family – the Carmelite habit is indeed a very good habit to have!

Leaving the Big Jobs to God

by Sister Emily, O.C.D.

*T*HERE WAS A LADY LIVING WITH US – a truly beautiful resident, who was very witty and clever. She had a knack for making genuinely funny observations or comments at the most appropriate times (or perhaps inappropriate) times.

One day I was leading the Rosary with the residents and I was leading the Creed. When we got to the part *"....from thence He shall come to judge the living and the dead..."*, she suddenly piped up and said "Well, that's an awfully big job, don't you think???"

Pausing (and simultaneously trying to suppress the laugh that bubbled to my lips), I thought to myself, "Well, yes, I guess it is a big job... I've never considered it. So it's a good thing He's God and we can leave the big jobs to Him!"

You Never Know

by Sister Maria Olga, O.C.D.

*L*ATELY, WE'RE BEEN PRAYING FOR VOCATIONS during Jesus Time with the children. We were also praying for the Holy Father because it was said he wasn't feeling that well.

During this time, the mother of one of the little boys, Paul*, came to me and in some amazement said, "We were saying our prayers last night, Sister, and do you know he told me he wants to be pope one day when he grows up?

The mother continued, "I said to Paul, 'Are you sure you want to be pope?'"

"Paul emphatically replied to me, 'Yes!' He really seemed to know what he was saying."

So I told her that Paul must have been inspired by our prayers for vocations and for the Holy Father with the children during Jesus Time. I shared how I had asked how many wanted to be priests, and they raised their hands; and then I asked how many wanted to be sisters, and they raised their hands. I think Paul raised his hand when I asked how many wanted to be priests, but I never thought he'd want to be pope!

But you never know…..anything is possible with God!

* = denotes that names have been changed to protect privacy

Going Home to God

by Sister Isabelle, O.C.D.

"SISTER, STAY AND PRAY WITH HER."

Last night, one of our residents, a lady who had been with us in all levels of care, went home to the Lord, with interesting circumstances. At the end of recreation, I asked the Sisters to all pray for her because I knew she would most likely be going home within the next day or two at latest.

After recreation, I went to her room in the Manor to pray Night Prayer with her. The nurses happened to be checking on her while I was present.

One nurse told me, "Sister, I think she is going to make it through the night as her blood pressure is still good."

After the nurses left the room, I said good night to the lady and sprinkled her with holy water. As I was leaving the room, her roommate, who knew her from Avila Gardens, sat bolt upright in bed and said to me with conviction in her Irish brogue, "Sister, stay and pray with her."

So I did. I went back to the lady's bedside and knelt down beside her. I felt really moved to pray God would take her, as she was really suffering and sure enough, barely two minutes later she died … she went home. It was incredible.

The nurses were quite surprised and shocked, and said to me, "Sister you were praying, weren't you?"

"Yes," I conceded, "but Eileen* is the one who did it! She told me to go back and pray!"

It was really powerful, being by her side at the moment she crossed that threshold into eternal life.

* = denotes that names have been changed to protect privacy

The Ultimate Treasure Hunt

by Sister Mary Joanne, O.C.D.

*I*N THE SECOND GRADE CLASS THAT YEAR there was a young man who was a very religious, very prayerful, smart little boy.

We decided to have a treasure hunt at the last religion class of the year so that the children could hunt for treasure – the real Treasure. Little clues were planted along the way to direct the children along the path leading to where the Treasure was hidden. The first clue took the children to the statue of the Blessed Mother. The next clue took them to Our Lady of Guadalupe. Additional clues led them to the bleachers, then to the library, with the final clue leading them to the Treasure.

We led the children out of the school grounds and over to the parish center. As they approached the chapel, they kept their eyes wide open for more clues. When we arrived in the chapel, the children quickly realized that the Treasure they had been seeking was right there. They genuflected, taking their places in the pews and knelt down to quietly pray.

After a short while, the little boy previously mentioned, turned to his teacher and said, "I see Jesus."

The teacher smiled and replied, "Listen to Him."

A few more minutes went by. He turned once again and said, "Jesus told me to do something."

"Do it," the teacher urged.

With that the little fellow got up and went to the monstrance, bringing it very carefully just a bit closer to the edge, so he could kiss the base of the monstrance. He then gently pushed it back in place and returned to his seat.

A beautiful, innocent act of faith.

The Heart of a Mother

by Sister Juanita, O.C.D.

*I*T IS NOT UNCOMMON FOR TOTAL STRANGERS TO GREET US with stories about the sisters they grew up with in their elementary school. Sometimes they joke about rulers or how strict their teacher was, other times they get a little teary when they share the impact a sister made on them. When sisters serve in the classroom, they have a profound opportunity to touch the hearts of their students for a lifetime.

Our sisters know this, and approach the task of teaching with much prayer and love for the students in their care. Sister Maureen exemplified this. Serving in education for most of her religious life, Sister's experience with children and families had deepened her already compassionate heart and given her a vast supply of wisdom to draw on when dealing with the many challenges children can face at school. She had a mother's heart for her students and their families, whether she was their teacher or their principal.

Jimmy was in the pre-Kinder class at Saint Theresa School in Florida. Four years old and full of energy, Jimmy was not interested in nap time with the rest of the class. Being still long enough to fall asleep was beyond him with so many exciting things to see and do all around. The teachers tried many different tactics with no success.

His mom was concerned and made an appointment with Sister Maureen, the principal at the time.

"Sister, Jimmy just can't seem to keep still in order to take a nap with the rest of the class. What can we do about this?"

Sister Maureen thought for a moment and then said, "Well, Jimmy needs to move, to get some of his energy out of his system. And I need to exercise. So here's what we'll do. During nap time, I'll go pick him up and we'll help each other out. He'll use up some energy and I'll get some exercise.

Jimmy's mom gratefully agreed that the plan was worth a try. Some days later, she was curious to see if it was working so she drove over to the school during the scheduled nap time. As she pulled up to the curb scanning the playground, her heart was warmed by the sight that met her eyes.

There was Jimmy walking hand-in-hand with Sister Maureen around the track field, each relishing the other's company, talking together as they enjoyed the quiet peacefulness of their early afternoon stroll.

Sister Maureen saw the person, not the problem, and found a way to help the person which solved the problem. Isn't that what the heart of a mother does?

* = *denotes names have been changed to protect privacy*

"I Do Believe in God"

by Sister Faustina, O.C.D.

A NUMBER OF YEARS AGO, I HAD THE PRIVILEGE of teaching 4th grade. I quickly discovered that 4th graders are absolutely beautiful because they are so open to all we try to teach them and it is quite easy to get them excited just about any topic. I also quickly realized that developmentally they think their parents are right about everything because, well they are their parents! However, during the journey through the school year, the children begin to realize that their parents have certain areas where perhaps they aren't quite so perfect. I watched this happen one year during our religion class, which we had every day.

In this particular case, we were talking about the sacrament of Baptism and in the class was a little girl who had not been baptized. She was a beautiful girl, from a lovely Catholic family, but sadly, Baptism had not been a priority. I suspect that her family's faith might have died completely. And although they had all been brought up Catholic, there were real questions as to whether God even existed.

During religion class, I would take special note of this girl when we talked about Baptism and original sin and the life of God in our souls; about the Trinity and being a child of God – a daughter of the Church….. her eyes would just light up with such passionate joy.

One day, later in the school year, she approached me and said, "I want to be baptized."

"Well, why aren't you?" I asked her in reply.

With slightly downcast eyes she softly replied, "My mom and dad don't believe in God anymore."

It was a very sad statement, but she had gained a certain amount of maturity and had come to understand that maybe this was something about which her parents were not right. So, I believe at that point, she began to ask her parents for Baptism.

Soon it was time for the parent-teacher conferences and part of my job as a teacher is to ask about the spiritual growth and the opportunities the children have to practice their faith at home. So the question about how they are receiving their Sacraments and the ways their family prays together are relatively routine questions during these parent conferences, in addition to discussing the students' grades and behavior and such.

It was in preparation for these conferences that an inspiration came to me. I thought that some parents might be reluctant to really listen to a teacher, even though as a Sister, they do nod affirmatively when asked if they attend Mass. However, parents do listen to their children. But because these children are so young, they might not have the courage to say "I want to go to church" because they don't want to upset the apple cart with their parents. This is how my idea of having the children write a letter to their parents came to be. I thought that such a letter, included in their report card, might help smoothly pave the way for the children to communicate to their parents their desires in practicing their faith at home more fully.

The next day in class, I made my suggestion to the children, adding that those who came to the parent conference would have a chance to share their letter with their parents. The children were excited and very eager to begin writing down their desires to practice their faith more perfectly at home. They all enthusiastically wrote down everything that was in their heart about actively living out their faith.

Some of them wrote courageous things that I knew would be hard for them to say out loud to their parents. The young lady who desired Baptism ardently wrote several pages, which for a 4th grader is quite a lot. While I did skim the letters prior to including them in the report cards, I can't say I scrutinized them very closely.

The day for the parent-teacher conferences arrived and the little 4th grade girl was sitting there with her mom and me as we discussed her report card. Her mom was proud of her hard work and we talked about some areas of growth and improvement. Then we pulled out the letter she had written in class and read it aloud.

I was taken aback by what she had written and the courage and conviction with which she wrote about her desires to grow in the faith. She started by addressing her parents saying that during family dinnertime, when talk revolved around how they didn't believe in God, she boldly stated that she was lying. She wrote, *"I do believe in God and I want so much to be baptized because I want to be a child of God and be able to receive Jesus in the Holy Eucharist."*

At the time, I didn't realize she had been telling her parents that she, too, didn't believe in God, but here was this 4th grade girl mustering all the courage she possessed to tell her parents that she was taking back those words about not believing in God.

Her mother was silent for several minutes. She clearly saw that her child was very sincere and that what she was asking was coming from her and not from me. The mother took the letter home promising to share it with her dad and the rest of the family. I just prayed for her that her mother would indeed help her get closer to Our Lord.

At the end of that school year, this student and her family had to move, but the little girl and I were so happy because the situation that she was moving into was going to definitely allow her to be baptized and also attend daily Mass. From what I understand, the following year this did in fact happen – she was baptized, she was able to go to a Catholic school and attend daily Mass. As a result, this little girl was so full of joy and so full of peace finally being able to live her faith.

Today, she should be a senior in high school but I haven't been in contact with her since. One day I hope to find out how her faith blossomed.

The Wisdom of Innocence

by Sister Maria Corazon, O.C.D.

I WAS TEACHING 2ND GRADE MANY YEARS AGO and as the new year was approaching, I reminded my 2nd graders, "Make sure that you have a plan for your new year's resolution."

One little girl came to me later and proudly announced, "Sister, I made my new year's revolution."

Even as I corrected her, I thought to myself that, in a sense, her words are true. When we need to change and have to do something about it, it is kind of like a revolution. The little girl's mistake became food for thought for me. Conversion does, in fact, mean a 'revolution' within!

The Italian Love of Life

by Sister Isabelle, O.C.D.

S OME PEOPLE ARE BORN WITH A DEEP SENSE OF "JOIE DE VIVRE"
– those exultant souls, who are possessed of a cheerful enjoyment of life.
Giovanna* was just such a lady, a vivacious woman of Italian descent and a real
fighter, too – one who fought 'til the very end.

Giovanna and her husband, Joe* were professional musicians. She was a singer
and he was a jazz pianist who also enjoyed playing "old time" rock and roll.
They had spent their entire married life performing together; she singing to his
piano accompaniment. Together as a team, they performed at the Manor (our
24-hour skilled nursing facility) several times, much to the delight of all the
residents. This couple's music and singing always enveloped the Manor in the
most infectious of festive moods and many residents couldn't resist getting up
and dancing to all those great "oldies, but goodies" tunes!

Time went on and Giovanna was eventually diagnosed with cancer, which as
the disease progressed, significantly decreased not only her stamina for singing,
but also her mobility and energy in general. However, being the fighter that
she was, Giovanna battled her disease with steely resolve. When her illness had
progressed to the stage that she needed round-the-clock skilled nursing care, she
became a resident at the Manor.

As the months passed, Giovanna's decline became more and more apparent and
eventually she had to be transferred to an acute care hospital. During her hospital
stay, one of the other sisters and I went to visit her. It was apparent that she was

tired and she wasn't talking much, but that old, unmistakable twinkle in her eye shone forth when she caught sight of us as we walked in the door of her room.

"Why don't you sisters sing something to her? She would surely enjoy that," Joe encouraged us.

After a moment's thought, we started to sing the song *My God* from the movie *Sister Act* to her and suddenly, by sheer force of will of that indomitable spirit of hers, Giovanna's voice joined in singing with us! Although unbeknownst to us at the time, this would be the last song we would ever sing together. It made for a beautiful and poignant moment.

Giovanna did end up coming back to the Manor, where she would spend her final days. However, she flat out simply refused to accept the fact that she was dying. Cancer might have ravaged her body, but it had certainly proved powerless in extinguishing that undaunted, fighting spirit within her. She intended to press on and on.

Every night I would go visit her and bless her with holy water, and during one such visit, I noticed that Giovanna was not wearing a scapular. So the next evening, I brought a brown scapular for her. As a devotional, sacramental item, I knew the brown scapular can bring special graces to those who wear it, especially at their hour of death.

This particular evening, her family happened to be there visiting, gathered around Giovanna's bed. I showed them all what I had brought for her and explained the graces to be found in using a sacramental, such as the brown scapular. Unfortunately, I made a mistake in my explanation.

"When this scapular is given to those preparing for their death, great graces and consolation can be gained," I said. No sooner had the words left my mouth when I realize my mistake.

I chanced a glance at Giovanna. Well, the expression on her face told me in no uncertain terms that she didn't like that last statement one bit! The rather disgruntled *"tsk-ing"* sounds coming in my direction from the lady occupying the bed only served to punctuate her displeasure. What a very fierce scowl she wore and I realized that she was quite angry with me! That fighter within refused to surrender.

So I gently, but quickly, excused myself. Some of her family members followed me out into the hallway and graciously said, "Sister, please don't feel bad. We understand and we don't want you to worry about it."

As it turned out, Our Lord decided to call Giovanna home that same night. She died peacefully several hours later.

The next day, Joe was coming to pick up her things and I hoped to catch up with him before he left. As I walked toward the Manor, I prayed for Giovanna and spoke to her.

I said, "Giovanna, are you okay? I know you're angry with me but I still want to know if you're okay."

By the time I was able to make it to the Manor, I was disappointed to find that Joe had already come and gone. A nurse approached me to tell me that Joe had collected Giovanna's things and had left, when suddenly, right at that moment, a song came on through the piped-in music in the overhead speakers and the lyrics went straight to my heart:

> *"No more tears, no more pain;*
> *No more fear; no more shame.*
> *I will be yours, You will be mine*
> *Forever in eternity."*

At that moment, without a doubt, I knew Giovanna was just fine. I knew that indomitable, fighting Italian spirit was right. She never wanted to die and she never did. She lives eternally in heaven with all those who have gone before believing in Jesus Christ.

I had genuinely been worried about Giovanna, which is why in prayer I asked her if she was all right and she answered me. I am convinced she answered me through the lyrics of that song that played through the speakers in the Manor!

As for her husband Joe, to this day he still comes and plays jazz piano for our residents. He carries on, generously sharing his musical gifts with others just like in days past when he and Giovanna performed as a team. We're certain Giovanna would be pleased.

* = denotes that names have been changed to protect privacy

"If You Can't Beat 'Em, Join 'Em"

by Sister Faustina, O.C.D.

A FEW YEARS AGO, I WAS TEACHING A READING CLASS EVERY DAY immediately following lunch to a class of 30-plus rambunctious eighth graders. And to be perfectly candid, they liked recess far more than they liked my class! I tried to make it fun and interesting for them, but they had a finely-honed, subtle way of rebelling and they always rebelled en masse with a united front! They were basically good children, possessed great charm, which sometimes made it difficult to get angry with them; but the fact remained, it was rather irritating!

Most days, it was during the lunch recess that the students would plot some rebellious prank. Like clockwork, at precisely 1:30 p.m., it could be counted on for the rebellion to commence. We would be in the middle of a reading lesson, when suddenly they'd all stand up, laugh for a moment or two and then sit back down. The class had a whole variety of tricks up their collective sleeve. One of their favorites was "planking". I had no clue what that was. It turns out planking is when you get on top of a desk or cabinet and lay flat like a board. This group made it more interesting by making noises like a whale.

I soon learned that I had to start going with the flow if I wanted to save the wear and tear on my nerves, because there was just no effective way to crack down on these kinds of pranks, I'm afraid. Hence, I adopted the motto – *"If you can't beat 'em, join 'em."* I would join them in the prank of the day, much to the students' delight, and then a few minutes later, we could move on with our reading lesson!

Someday in Heaven

by Sister Faustina, O.C.D.

W HEN I WAS TEACHING, each school year we would talk about the beauty of life and the gift of life. This particular year we devoted an entire week to Respect Life. During this week, we talked about poverty, the homeless, about imprisonment, justice and euthanasia. In science class, we spent the whole week learning about the development of the child in the womb. It was very beautiful to see our students are open to the gift of life and are 100% in accepting the Church's teaching on the sanctity of life in all its stages.

We had a guest speaker come in who works at a shelter for pregnant homeless women where they can have their baby in a safe environment as they find assistance in getting back on their feet. The speaker shared some of her stories and experiences about her ministry and talked about a number of times she prayed at abortion clinics and things of that nature. During her talk, she said something especially striking.

We had a guest speaker come in who worked at a shelter for pregnant homeless women where they can have their baby in a safe environment and where they find assistance in getting back on their feet. The speaker shared with us some of her stories and experiences about her ministry and talked about a number of times she prayed at abortion clinics and things of that nature. During her talk, she said something that was especially striking.

It was about two weeks later when one of my students came running up to me just before school wanting immediate attention. As I wasn't able to talk to him right away, I asked him if he could wait a few minutes, which he did. When we spoke outside the classroom he was obviously very disturbed about something, so I asked him what was on his mind.

He shared that he overheard a conversation between his aunt, who lived with his family, and his mother the night before. His aunt told his mother that she was pregnant and they were discussing abortion. What concerned my student the most was his own mother counseling in favor of an abortion as being the only option. There were lots of good reasons for having an abortion – his aunt was a single mother and already had too many children, poverty.... there were lots of "good" reasons.

At this point, he burst into the conversation and said, "Mom, Mom you can't kill that child! It's a baby!" He then explained that the baby had a heartbeat, and it was his cousin, and he urgently pleaded with them to reconsider the planned abortion.

Very sadly, they refused to listen to him, telling him it was none of his concern, and his mother severely reprimanded him for intruding into their conversation. So he came to school the following day asking for help from me and from the sisters. We gave him a lot of pro-life materials, including phone numbers for resources and adoption services. We knew his mom would not be open to speaking with us about this matter and that it would be a battle our student would have to see through on his own. That afternoon, this young man took home all the resource material we had provided. As for the Sisters, we fasted and prayed that night.

The following morning, our student reported that he had given the material to his mom, but she refused to give it to her sister, his aunt. She told him repeatedly this was not his business; it was an "adult thing," it was not his choice, and it had to be done.

Several days passed and we prayed. And, we prayed and we prayed. As a class, we prayed for a special intention with him.

A few days later this young man came to school and told me his aunt had indeed had the abortion. His sadness was palpable. I, personally, was crushed and very weighed down by the brokenness of humanity. I found that I really didn't have much to say to this young man, but after he shared his news, we stood there silently just looking at each other and we shared a real and unspoken understanding that he had intervened to the extent he could. I told him how proud I was of his courage; how it took courage to speak the truth in love. Within his home he was a voice of truth and I assured him Our Lord would reward his courage and his valor. I really felt his courage was on the level of martyrdom, as he so strongly spoke the truth even when no one listened to him in his own home.

I asked the young man what name he wished to give his cousin as he, the sisters and I were aware of the sad outcome and were deeply mourning the loss of this little life together.

Eyes downcast, he quietly said, "I don't know what name to pick."

"Well, do you think it was a boy or a girl?" I asked.

"I think it was a little boy," he said with conviction.

"What do you think about the name 'Matthew'*?" I suggested.

"That sounds good," he agreed, after a moment's thought then looked up to meet my eyes.

 So, from that moment, we named the little boy Matthew, who has a cousin here on earth who is eager to meet him someday in Heaven.

* = *denotes names have been changed to protect privacy*

The Ultimate Event Planner

by Sister Isabelle, O.C.D.

*D*URING THE WEEK OF SEPTEMBER 30 - OCTOBER 6, 2013 Santa Teresita held its first ever *Spirit Week* – replete with a candlelight dinner, parades and rose petal hunts, moonlight movies, ice cream socials and more. *Spirit Week* was a campus-wide event and included the Manor, assisted living and Hayden Child Care Center.

I was the event planner for *Spirit Week,* and as we worked our way through the planning phase, it occurred to me just what a big project this had grown to be and I have to admit to a case of the jitters. We had so many activities planned for each day of the week … had we, perhaps, bitten off more than we could chew? What about the logistics and supplies? Would we be able to procure all the "things" and "items" needed to pull off this week-long event? Would all the planned activities go smoothly? So many worries, so I decided to take all my cares and concerns to the Lord in prayer.

"This isn't an average spirit week, Lord," I prayed. Suddenly, inspiration struck. "This is a *Holy Spirit Week!*" I added. I immediately asked the Holy Spirit to be in charge of the week and placed all the planning and details into His care. The results were beyond incredible!

So many people came through for us! In passing, I mentioned our planned *Spirit Week* to some friends of Santa Teresita, who happen to be the proprietors of *Stonefire Grill.*

"Well, what can we do? We want to help you make this a great week!" they responded enthusiastically and completely out of the blue, *Stonefire Grill* donated a huge platter of brownies and carrot cake. Many other people generously pitched in too! It was amazing.

When the first day of the big week arrived, I again had a case of butterflies. Suddenly, one of the nurses came up to me with a big poster in her hand. Pictured on the poster was a little cartoon knight in armor and on each part of the armor was a scripture passage from Saint Paul referring to putting on the armor of God, referring to the Spirit and such. I knew without a doubt this lady was a God-send. Another comforting sign came a little later than morning during the kick-off celebration – a white dove was seen in the overhead branches of one of the large trees.

Each successive day of *Spirit Week* turned out seemingly more beautiful than the previous. On October 1st, the patronal feast of Saint Thérèse, the children from Hayden held a grand parade, processing throughout the entire campus, singing a song about Saint Thérèse and handing out a special gift for all they met along the "parade route."

One evening, residents and their families enjoyed an elegant dinner by candlelight, complete with after-dinner entertainment provided by two of our residents, Joanna Williams* and Carolyn Baker*. Another evening, the Sisters joined the residents of *Good Shepherd Cottage* for a hilarious game of Charades. Undoubtedly, the highlight of the week was the chance for all the seniors and children to gather together to be blessed with a relic of Saint Thérèse.

What a phenomenal week it was – a truly grace-filled week with many blessed events! So many people worked together beautifully and the fruits of their labors brought much joy to our children, residents, staff and sisters alike. Based on these results, I'm convinced we've begun a new annual tradition here at Santa Teresita.

Seeing the wonders of the Holy Spirit, I have decided that henceforth, I will always pray to the Him asking Him to be the one to guide all our activities at Santa Teresita. He is the ultimate event organizer!

---

* = *denotes names have been changed to protect privacy*

Santa Teresita Sanatorium:
The seed is planted . . .

Excerpts taken from <u>To Love Me In Truth</u> *and The Early Chronicles*

*I*N MAY 1929 A MEETING WAS ARRANGED at the Chancery office in Los Angeles at which Bishop John Cantwell, Father Leroy Callahan, Mother Mary of the Eucharist, and Mother Margarita Maria were present. Father Callahan laid their plans before the Bishop and told him that Mother Luisita was willing to have the Sisters take over the work of establishing a tuberculosis sanatorium for Spanish-speaking girls afflicted with tuberculosis. The Bishop listened attentively, but he was reluctant to give his approval. He spoke very candidly of the financial risk involved, of the lack of experience, of the youth of Father Callahan and of the Sisters who were present. All were under thirty years of age. "Alright. You have my approval, but you must start on a small scale."

A few months after the decision to begin Santa Teresita, the Great Depression occurred. The Wall Street Crash of October, 1929 spread rapidly worldwide. The market crash marked the beginning of a decade of high unemployment, poverty, low profits, deflation, plunging farm incomes, and lost opportunities for economic growth and personal advancement. The Sisters, relying on God's grace and contributing their own hard work, continued to plan for the new sanatorium.

The foothills of the San Gabriel Mountains seemed ideal for the sanatorium they intended to open .... there was an old farmhouse, a dilapidated garage, and several small old frame single rooms, all of which were being offered for $17,500.00. A loan was arranged and a first and second mortgage placed on the property. The Sisters, who were without funds of their own, were assuming a large debt. Sister Margarita Maria sat down and wrote two hundred letters of appeal, all in longhand. She received ten replies. But it was a beginning.

The property, having been long neglected, was badly run down. The old farmhouse could be used by the Sisters temporarily. The other buildings were so badly run down that any other purchaser would have demolished them. There was no way the Sisters could undertake a building program at once, but they felt the building could be fixed up and used until they could provide something better. It was a start. They converted the old garage into a recreation room for the girls who could be out of bed. They lined the walls with seats from an abandoned bus. They fashioned bedside tables out of orange crates.

A small ad placed in the Los Angeles Examiner asking for a donation of used furniture for the sanatorium brought a tremendous response. The Sisters rented sewing machines to make the linens themselves. To get as much as possible finished before the rental period was up, the Sisters arranged shifts among themselves around the clock, putting the sewing machine to use twenty-four hours a day, two days a week.

Hot water was not yet piped into the buildings. TB was a communicable disease, and it was absolutely necessary to sterilize all of the dishes used by the patients by boiling them for 20 minutes in a strong solution. The neglect of the property prior to its purchase by the Sisters turned to their advantage, because the trees had much dead wood. The Sisters used it to enkindle fires under huge rocks where they boiled water three times a day to sterilize the dishes after each meal. No sooner was one load of dishes thus scalded, that it was time to prepare for the next meal. Day after day, the same routine, the same hard work, yet the Sisters laughed and sang as they worked.

Santa Teresita Sanatorium:
The seed takes root ...

Excerpts taken from <u>*To Love Me In Truth*</u> *and The Early Chronicles*

*T*HE FEAST OF OUR LADY OF THE ANGELS, August 2nd, 1930, was chosen as the day of the formal opening of Santa Teresita. Mid-morning as planned, the Sisters heard the first ambulance from Olive View Sanatorium laboring up the unpaved road. Five young girls were lifted out, frightened, tearful, and very ill. They did not even see the smiles of the Sisters as they waited to greet them and welcome them to Santa Teresita. Life was a tragedy for these victims, stricken, just as they were beginning life, with the dreaded tuberculosis.

A great challenge was being presented to the Carmelites, which they fully recognized as the first patients were transferred to their care. And a great responsibility was also assumed. But they would do all they could to help restore health; they would minister to their little sisters in whom they saw Christ. Life in those early days certainly presented its challenges, but the Sisters remained undaunted as they resolutely entrusted the "hard stuff" to God's care confident He would provide, and went about their daily business of healing and comforting their desperately ill charges.

In their first years at Santa Teresita, the Sisters did not have a chapel. Each morning, six of them walked the one mile each way to assist at Mass at Immaculate Conception Church in Monrovia, while three remained to care for the patients. As they thus alternated, it meant that every third day, three were deprived of Mass and Holy Communion, a sacrifice offered to God with joyful generosity.

Then a friend who had noticed the Sisters walking to the early Mass donated a 1917 Ford to them. Old as it was, this was a veritable luxury for the Sisters. However, they quickly discovered that the automatic starter did not always work properly. As a result, it frequently happened that after all were seated in the car, with Sister Margarita Maria at the wheel – for she was the only one who knew how to drive, the car would not start. To the amusement of the onlookers, the five Sisters would then get out and push while Sister Margarita Maria remained at the wheel. Once started, the great worry was that it would die again, so the moment the engine started, the Sisters who had been pushing quickly scrambled to jump onto the running boards (this old model car was a blessing in that respect) and off they went in their "Model 17."

Santa Teresita Sanatorium:
The first shoots appear . . .

Excerpts taken from <u>To Love Me In Truth</u> and The Early Chronicles

OUR FIRST TUBERCULOSIS PATIENTS

To the Carmelite Sisters, every patient entrusted to their care at Santa Teresita Sanatorium was a unique individual in whom the Sisters saw the sufferings of Christ. The Sisters praised and thanked God for the many patients who fully recovered and were able to leave the sanatorium and go on to lead full, healthy lives. However, it was inevitable, that even with the finest of loving care, some were unable to overcome their tuberculosis, as the disease had simply progressed too far.

Decades later, the Sisters still remembered their first patients from those early days and on occasion had the chance to visit and reminisce with many of them. As for those who did not survive, the Sisters recalled the memory of each years, even decades later.

What follows are remembrances of just three of those young women who did not survive.

ROSARIO ALEGRIA

The last of the first five patients brought to Santa Teresita to be lifted from the ambulance was Rosario Alegria, twenty-three years of age. Her face was filled with fear, with bitterness, with defiance. Only a short time before, she had tried to commit suicide. Not only did she feel she was being cheated out of life, but she had been cheated out of death as well. Little did she know that she would spend the last five and a half years of her life as a patient at Santa Teresita, and that her life would be transformed.

Rosario Alegria, being a little older than the other patients, observed everything and thought deeply about it. She began to respond to the Sisters' kindness as the others did. Although Rosario's transfer records indicated that she had been baptized a Catholic, she knew nothing about her religion. When she arrived at Santa Teresita, religion was the last thing she had any interest in. But as she watched the Sisters, and was herself the recipient of their concern, she understood that it was their Catholic Faith put into practice which made them different, made them happy, made the sanatorium different, and her interest was piqued. She began to pray a little. There was no more thought of suicide. Life and suffering were taking on new meaning. A very real change was taking place in her.

The bitterness and despondency were gone. She asked if she might receive her first Holy Communion. The Sisters arranged everything to make it a memorable and beautiful occasion for her. September 24, 1930 was the date chosen. Then, the following spring when the Sacrament of Confirmation was administered, Rosario was confirmed.

Rosario witnessed the many changes at the sanatorium over the years; the new buildings, the gardens. She knew of some of the great advances in the treatment of tuberculosis, but as the months passed and she became weaker and weaker, she knew she would never recover, even though the doctors were doing all they could.

One morning in January 1935, when the Sister in charge asked how she was feeling, she quietly replied, "Oh, so-so. I am happy with everything. I only pray that Our Lord will let me live until the chapel is completed. I have prayed so long to have a priest with me when I die." Each weekend a priest came to celebrate Sunday Mass for the Sisters and patients and to distribute Holy Communion to those who were not ambulatory. Until Santa Teresita had its own chapel, they had to depend on this week-end supply. Usually it was a Jesuit Father from Loyola High School in Los Angeles who would come. At that time, the "big red cars," as Southern Californians always referred to the electric railway, afforded transportation from Loyola to the sanatorium.

Father Austin Wallace, S.J. arrived one Saturday in February 1935. He told the Sisters he would like to get an early train back to Los Angeles on Sunday morning as he had a great amount of work to do. However, it happened that he was delayed for some reason or other and missed the train. To occupy his time during the two-hour wait for the next train, he decided to visit some of the patients. Santa

Teresita was not a usual assignment for Father Wallace so he did not know any of the patients. He went from room to room. On his way he stopped for a moment to greet Rosario Alegria and then proceeded to the next room. Suddenly, the quiet was broken by Rosario calling out, "Hemorrhage!" Sister came running to assist her, and realizing at once the gravity of Rosario's condition, she called to Father Wallace who was still in the next room, to come at once.

Rosario held tightly to Sister's arm. In her other hand she held her crucifix. The priest gave the last absolution and in just a few minutes, she was gone. Rosario's prayer had been answered; a priest was with her at her death.

Father Wallace walked slowly, thoughtfully from the room. He said almost as if to himself, "Now I know why I missed the early train. Never shall I forget this day."

Mercedes Limon

Twelve year old orphan Mercedes Limon came to Santa Teresita less than three months after it opened. There was no possibility, aside from a miracle, that she could ever recover, for both her lungs were badly infected. She came as a bed patient, for she was too weak to be up and around or permitted out of bed.

Mercedes was a very bright and cheerful child, but could also be very serious. Everyone liked her. She asked many questions of the Sisters. She was curious about the little Carmelite "Santa Teresita" who also had suffered from tuberculosis and who was now a saint. Mercedes was fascinated by the thought that she became a saint by doing just ordinary things, little things. She thought about that for a while. Then she asked the same Sister who had told her about the Saint, "Sister, can I be a saint?" and when assured she could, she inquired simply, "How?" The Sister replied that she should ask a priest. The very next time a priest came to visit, she put her question to him. Although she did not repeat what he had told her, when the Sister came into the room, Mercedes happily announced, "Now I know how I am going to be a saint."

A definite change began to take place in Mercedes from then on. She now had a purpose, a goal in mind, and she was determined to do all she could to reach it. No athlete ever worked harder for a coveted prize than did Mercedes Limon, and it was not easy for her. She began to put into practice the little Carmelite Saint's "ordinary way."

As was the custom each morning, Sister came to greet her with a cheery, "Good morning, Mercedes. How are you today?" But on this particular morning, the child did not say a word. Something had occurred to make her angry and she was sulking. Sister offered her a breakfast tray; she pushed it aside and said, "I don't want any breakfast." Sister continued, "Just your milk then." But Mercedes was adamant. "I don't want any milk. I hate the smell of milk."

"Do you think," Sister reminded her, "that the little Santa Teresita would answer that way?" Mercedes looked at Sister for a moment, then she reached for the glass of milk, while with her other hand, she held her nose so as not to smell it. Only when she finished drinking it, did she return the glass to the tray.

Later on Sister returned to Mercedes' room and again said to her, "Good morning, Mercedes." "Good morning, Sister." Then she continued, "I slept very well last night. I am fine. Thank you for your concern. I didn't answer you before, Sister, and I am sorry."

Even with the best of care Mercedes grew weaker as the disease progressed. The doctors said at most she might live only a few days, perhaps only a few hours.

Sister Margarita Maria told the child that she was very soon going to heaven, but she replied, "Oh, I can't. I have a big debt to pay." "What is this big debt, Mercedes?" Sister inquired, for she knew the child had no money to pay a debt and she could not understand how she could have incurred a big debt.

"Sister," Mercedes said, "the debt is one hundred forty-five rosaries—fifteen decade rosaries."

"Oh, do not be concerned, Mercedes," Sister replied, "I will help you. All the Sisters will help you with your debt, but tell me, how did this 'debt' come about?"

"Well, Sister," the little girl said, "You know many priests come to visit us. And Father Callahan comes most of all. And every time they ask us to pray for them. So I promise to pray my rosary, and now I have this big debt."

However, since the Sisters had promised to take care of her 'debt,' Mercedes had only one thought in mind. She wanted to give her full thought to the journey she would soon make. She did not want anyone, other than the Sisters or a priest around her. The Sisters, seeing how weak the child was, and knowing that she could pass quickly, asked the priest from the local parish to bring the Last Sacraments. After anointing her, he gave her Holy Communion.

While she made her thanksgiving, the priest and the Sisters stood at her bedside praying quietly. Suddenly she opened her eyes, looked about and said, "What happened? Our Lord didn't take me." She thought she was going to heaven immediately.

Mercedes lived through that day and night. The next day was Sunday, May 17, the sixth anniversary of the canonization of the Little Flower. A Jesuit priest, Father Gerald Leahy, S.J. had come from Los Angeles to celebrate Mass and distribute Holy Communion. Again Mercedes was able to receive Our Lord. As this was the first time that Father Leahy had come to Santa Teresita, he did not know any of the patients, but when he was leaving, he remarked to Sister Margarita Maria that he would like to return and talk to that little saint (Mercedes). Only God and he knew what it was all about.

Later in the day Mercedes said to Mother Mary of the Eucharist who was at her bedside, "I cannot see."

"Do not be concerned" Sister replied, "You are soon going to be in heaven." Then the child asked for a crucifix which a friend had given her. She was so weak, she had to grasp it with both hands and then Sister had to help her raise it to her lips to kiss it. Then she whispered softly, "Dear God, I love you with my whole heart. Dear God, I want to die loving you."

The death of the first patient, Mercedes Limon, at Santa Teresita occurred on May 17, 1931.

ROSITA VILLANUEVA

The frail little girl who arrived at Santa Teresita on February 8, 1933, looked up into the face of Mother Margarita Maria and said, "I am Rosita, Rosita Villanueva."

"Welcome, Rosita," Sister replied as she smiled down at the little one. "I am Mother Margarita Maria. You and I are going to be good friends. How old are you?"

"I am eight years old." Rosita indeed had the face of an eight year old, but her body was that of a four year old. Rosita was very ill, almost too weak to move. When one of the Sisters asked her how long she had been in bed, she replied thoughtfully, "As far back as I can remember my name has been Rosita, and as far back as I can remember I have always been in bed."

Even with all the advances made in medicine, the Sisters knew this child would never leave her bed. To console her when she told them how she wished she might play outdoors like other children, the Sisters reminded her that in Heaven she would be able to play with the angels and the Infant Jesus. This promise satisfied her for the moment and it was soon forgotten by the Sisters, but not by Rosita.

Sometime later, when the Sister taking care of Rosita came in with her tray for breakfast, she found the child leaning as far as possible over the edge of the bed trying to look under it.

"Rosita, dear," Sister said, "What is it you are looking for? Let me get it for you. You will fall out of bed."

"I am looking for my shoes," the child replied.

"Your shoes?" Sister was indeed puzzled because Rosita was never permitted out of bed; in fact, she had no shoes, but only some little red slippers.

"I need my shoes, Sister," Rosita continued, "because I will have to wear them when I go to heaven to play with the angels and the Baby Jesus."

Closer To God

by Sister Mary Joanne, O.C.D.

D URING LENT, THE 3ᴿᴰ GRADERS AT ST. THERESA'S traditionally prepare the live Stations of the Cross to perform for the school, which also provides a prayer opportunity. The children do it twice once they've got it prepared – first for the little people in grade 1 and then for grades 2-8.

While the students worked very hard, the teachers did have quite a time getting them to be sober and serious and to try to understand a little bit about what they were doing. It appeared that this class was going to be a little more of a challenge.

On the Wednesday before Holy Week, the 3ʳᵈ graders performed the Stations of the Cross for the other students. After their prayer time, the teachers gave the performers a little extra play time because they had worked very hard in presenting the Stations twice. Let loose outside in the field, most of the children were engaged in very active playing.

However, there was one little boy, who was still. The teachers noticed him kneeling in front of the statue of the Blessed Mother. After five minutes, he was still there; 10 minutes later, he was still there. For a good 20-25 minutes, this little boy was completely engrossed in prayer. This little boy was very active and frequently did not do his homework in religion or any other subject. He was not a strong student but was very good at fooling around and at creating mischief. He was the one kneeling, oblivious to the noisy clamor of his classmates playing. The little guy was just lost in prayer before our Blessed Mother.

On the end-of-the-year evaluations, when asked what helped him most to grow closer to God, this little boy wrote that the Stations of the Cross and the sufferings of Jesus helped him grow closer to God.

Mirroring the Love of Christ

by Sister Faustina, O.C.D.

ONE YEAR, I WAS ASSIGNED TO TEACH 7TH GRADE and in that class was a boy named Kevin*. Kevin had very severe dyslexia, as well as other reading and writing issues. His mother was adamant in keeping Kevin mainstreamed, which required that significant accommodations be made for him. However, it was Kevin's classmates who truly rose to the occasion, mirroring the love of Christ in an incredible collective spirit of generosity. Through the years, not only had they learned to deal with Kevin and his handicaps, but in doing so, learned to truly love him for the person he was – just another child of God. In addition to everything else, Kevin also had some social issues, but none of these things kept him from being first or second pick for team games during outside play. It was heartwarming to see that Kevin's classmates wholly embraced him without regard to any physical limitations.

When I think of Kevin and that group of seventh graders, two memories come to mind.

One time, Kevin volunteered to read the responsorial psalm at the school Mass. The Religion teacher had beautifully agreed when Kevin volunteered and she practiced with him for two weeks in preparation. Kevin worked incredibly hard in order to read the psalm well. Proclaiming a reading at a student Mass is a significant occasion. While it is not a "showoff" thing, the individual students and the class as a whole take great pride in the accomplishment of reading the Word of the Lord well.

Soon the important day arrived. The first reading concluded and it was time to read the responsorial psalm. Kevin walked up to the lectern and began to read. Even after two weeks' practice, Kevin stumbled over several words, halted and hesitated, his small smile offered in apology for the less than smooth reading. When Kevin finished reading, the most extraordinary thing happened – everyone just reverently prayed the responsorial psalm as if nothing out of the ordinary had happened. The priest was wonderful, as well. Sitting in the pew, I could feel the class' pride in Kevin as he came and sat back down among them. Kevin's victory was their victory, too. It was so incredible to see.

The second thing I remember about this class was when both seventh grade classes put on the play, *The Miracle Worker*, the story of Helen Keller. Between the two classes, there were 40 students and there would not be enough speaking parts for everyone. I held auditions for the main parts, but most of the students who didn't have lines worked on the sets and back-drops and such.

In order to increase the number of speaking parts, we added "commercials" between the three acts of the play. The first commercial was set circa late 1800s - early 1900s, the era in which Helen Keller lived and "advertised" the "recent" advances in communications, specifically the speed and efficiency of the telephone in comparison to the telegraph. The commercial for the second act fast-forwarded to the 1950s (the time in which the play *The Miracle Worker* debuted) and finally, the commercial for Act Three was set during the present day.

Kevin and his group were assigned the Act Two commercial, set during the 1950s. They decided they were going to be sunglass models showing off the latest Helen Keller sunglasses, walking out onto the stage and posing as if they were on a runway. The students managed to get hold of many different silly styles of sunglasses, too. When Kevin tried this, it wasn't too convincing, so they thought that perhaps he could be a DJ, but that idea didn't pan out either.

As we were brainstorming about other ideas, someone started to hum the old Johnny Nash tune, *I Can See Clearly Now* from the early '70s. The lyrics were certainly appropriate:

> I can see clearly now, the rain is gone,
> I can see all obstacles in my way.
> Gone are the dark clouds that had me blind
> It's gonna be a bright (bright), bright (bright)
> Sun-shiny day.
> *Lyrics by Johnny Nash, 1972*

We thought it would be funny if this song would somehow be incorporated into their commercial, but we still couldn't quite get it to fit. Finally, the students decided that once all of them had walked out onto the runway, modeling their respective Helen Keller sunglasses, Kevin would enter and lip sync this song while they all did hand motions as if they were a band. The idea worked and they all liked it; as for Kevin, he loved it!

Performance day arrived and soon it was time for the Act Two commercial. Kevin must have had at least 20 family members in the audience to watch and cheer him on in this little grammar school production. The "sunglass models" all walked out and posed on the runway. Then it was Kevin's turn. Well, Kevin strutted out on stage as if he was a major "star"! He was totally uninhibited and led the "models" in lip syncing the song, dancing and motioning with his hands. Kevin proceeded to steal the show! It was hilarious and the entire audience roared with laughter. At the end of the play, during the curtain call, Kevin received a standing ovation with cheers and high-fives all around. You would have thought he'd just won a Tony Award or Oscar! What a great victory for this boy who had so many special needs.

Although several years have passed since I taught Kevin and his class, when I think of them, my heart is still warmed at the beautiful and loving ways in which Kevin's classmates embraced him. Sharing eight formative years of their lives with Kevin taught them compassion, through which they learned to find and appreciate the gifts with which God blesses every single person.

* = *denotes that names have been changed to protect privacy*

ℋeavenly ℋarmonies

by Sister Isabelle, O.C.D.

NOT LONG AGO, A DELIGHTFUL COUPLE CAME to live in our independent living center – Avila Gardens. They eventually moved to our assisted living and ultimately, when the husband's health began to decline, they transferred to the Manor at Santa Teresita, our skilled nursing facility.

This gentleman was truly amazing. Frank* was a veteran, a teacher, and was a very loving and caring soul. One of his favorite past times was singing as part of a barbershop quartet – something he had done with great joy for many years. During the last days of his life, we Sisters decided to try to get a quartet together to sing for him in his last moments. We searched the internet to find local quartets and called the very first group we found on our internet search. I explained our situation and what we hoped to do.

The man on the other end of the line said, "Yes, I think I can get a group together for you."

"Our resident's name is Frank," I just happened to add for the quartet coordinator's information. I was greeted with dead silence on the other end of the line for several seconds.

Finally, the man tentatively asked, "It wouldn't be Frank *Thompson**, would it?"

"Why, yes, it is," I replied with surprise.

"I know him! He taught me how to sing!" the man exclaimed.

A few days later, this gentleman and about 10 other members of the quartet came and sang to Frank and his wife, Jeannie*. It was an incredible moment that brought tears to all our eyes.

The following day, with the harmonious strains of the barbershop melodies still gently sounding in his ears, Frank heard God call his name, calling him home.

* = denotes names have been changed to protect privacy

Mightier Than the Sword

by Sister Juanita, O.C.D.

*I*N 2006, I MADE MY FIRST PROFESSION OF VOWS, and during the 12 months that followed, I worked my way through our different apostolic centers on a rotating schedule, in three month increments. During my three months at Sacred Heart Retreat House, I witnessed a retreat experience that deeply touched my heart.

Two special retreats had been planned that were geared toward at-risk teens – one for high school boys, the other for girls. Both retreats were excellent, but the experience that moved me the most happened during the boys' retreat. The boys were scheduled to arrive at St. Joseph Campus on a Saturday morning and stay until late afternoon. They would go home in the evening and return the next morning for the second part of the retreat.

The retreat leader of the boys' retreat was Jesse Romero, a well-known Catholic apologist. Jesse's assistant was a close friend, a man with experience in youth ministry. Both men had a deep personal love for Our Lord and both happened to be retired Los Angeles Sheriff's Deputies. They were well equipped to deal with and get through to hardened, tough personalities.

Saturday afternoon, Jesse instructed the boys to stand around the perimeter of the hall, keeping about three-to-four feet of space between them. He began to speak about taking up arms – weapons they must take up in order to effectively combat the enemy. At the word weapons, surprise showed on faces around the room. Understanding dawned as they realized that the enemy Jesse was talking about was Satan and the weapons required to fight the devil were not guns or knives which are useless in that battle.

"How are you going to fight the devil?!" Jesse asked the boys in a loud voice. "What weapons do you need to engage in the battle against him?"

He had the boys' undivided attention now.

"I'm telling you there are two primary weapons you arm yourself with in order to fight the devil. The first is <u>Confession</u>!" Jesse shouted – he punctuated the shout by throwing a powerful jab into the air with his right arm.

"Confession!" the two men shouted again in unison as they threw another punch, this time with their left arm.

The boys quickly caught on.

"Confession!" the young men shouted as they threw punches into the air with their right arm.

"Confession!" they shouted again, imitating the men and punching into the air with their left arm.

For several moments they kept repeating "Confession" as they swung and threw punches and jabs into the air against the enemy.

Still punching into the air, Jesse said, "The other weapon you fight the devil with is <u>Communion</u>!"

"Communion!" the boys shouted as they threw jabs and punches into the air.

"What weapons will you arm yourselves with against the devil?!" Jesse shouted.

"Confession!" *left punch, right punch,* "Communion!" *left punch, right punch,* "Confession!" *left punch, right punch,* "Communion!" *left punch, right punch,* "Confession!" *left punch, right punch,* "Communion!" *left punch, right punch.*

The rhythmic chant went on and on as these at risk-youth "beat the devil" with a "right" and a "left," Confession and Communion, the weapons they were going to take up in their fight against the devil.

Since that retreat, I have often wondered about that group of young men and what became of them. Did they remember their experience during that weekend retreat? Did they decide to lay aside guns and knives to arm themselves with Confession and Communion as the only effective weapons against the real enemy, the devil?

I pray for them. That they made the right choice. That they experience in the Sacraments a power mightier than the sword.

To All First Grade Teachers:
You Are God's Gift!

by Sister Timothy Marie, O.C.D.

W ELL, THERE IT WAS IN WRITING –
the note from the doctor stating that the first grade teacher, one of our Carmelite
Sisters, had bronchitis and needed to recover at home in our convent away
from her first grade classroom and her first graders within it. Since no substitute
teacher available that week, I made up my mind to teach the class while she was
away. Putting my administrative duties on hold, I walked out of the office and
into the first grade classroom.

Did I have experience with first grade? Well, not really. I was a junior high and
high school teacher, but wouldn't first grade be about the same with the students
– just smaller? Well, no. There IS a difference as I found out. What happened?

When it came time for reading groups, I asked one group to come up and
sit on the reading rug while I taught. Were they listening to me? Yes and no.
The greater part of their attention was on the woven rug they were sitting on,
especially since one of the little ones had brilliantly discovered all by himself how
to unweave the threads. What happened? I don't have the humility to say.

When time for math class came around, it seemed a good idea to get a little creative
about it, since the class was becoming antsy. So, we had a relay race. With colored
chalk in hand, each person, wrote their answer on the board and relayed the chalk
to the next person. Happily, the class was attentive and enjoyed cheering their
team on while they were drilling their math facts. During recess the bomb hit.
One of the girls came up to me and said, "Sister, why did you give us all crayons

to write on the board, our teacher usually gives us chalk?" Horror of horrors, I walked up to the board and there were the colorful results of the creative relay race indelibly imprinted on the board. How would I explain this one?

The *"pièce de résistance"* came the day I received a second note from the doctor stating that it would take one more week of recuperation before the teacher could return. I noticed later in the afternoon that a strange smell was coming from the first grade classroom. Each day thereafter, the smell got worse. Finally the weekend arrived and I gathered up strength to return on Monday. On Monday morning, after the room had been closed up all day Saturday and Sunday, the aroma was really, really bad. We searched on and off all day for two straight days and couldn't find the origin of the exquisite stench.

I finally made the decision to call the Fire Department, convinced that some poor animal had gotten into a vent or pipe and was dead and rotting away. This was serious. It could be a health hazard. So the following morning, before school started, the fire department arrived in the person of one firefighter, who unfortunately had a bad cold and couldn't smell. Nevertheless, I give him credit for believing me. He made plans to come in the following day and smash down the walls by the vent to release the dead little animal from its first grade prison graveyard.

At the convent that evening, Sister told me she had a clearance from the doctor to return to work half-day. After hearing about the dead animal, she chose to investigate the problem herself before the demolition of the walls of her beloved classroom began. So, we called and asked the fire department to wait one day.

The following day I quietly returned to the office, breathing a sigh of relief at my reprieve from first grade. Before lunch, one of the little first grade girls came up to the office with a note for me, "Sister, can you please come down to the first grade for a minute?" Off I went, interiorly rejoicing the last phrase on the paper – "for a minute." Yes, that I could handle. When I arrived at the classroom door, Sister said, "Cancel the Fire Department. The situation is under control."

"Really," I answered. "What did you do with the animal?"

A slow, knowing grin, spread across her face. "Sister, it wasn't any animal at all. Tell me, did you have the students clean their desks the two weeks I was away?"

"Every afternoon, before they went home," I answered.

"Did you have them sit down on the floor and take EVERYTHING out of their desk before replacing their things tidily?"

"Well, no, not really. They just bent over and straightened their books while bending over."

"Aha! That's the problem. You have to require them to sit down on the floor and take EVERYTHING out."

Quietly, she went to a little lunch bag, sitting demurely on the ground by the door of the classroom. Bending over, she picked it up and held it at an arms distance. "Look," she said, triumphantly. I looked. There was one petrified, green, moldy, unbearably stinky, totally rotten, corroding, decaying hard- boiled egg.

St. Paul wrote, "There are many gifts."

First grade teachers, wherever you are, I SALUTE YOU! You are great. You are the best! You are God's gift!

Walls of Jericho Still Exist
... and Miracles Still DO Happen!

by Sister Regina Marie, O.C.D.

O VER THE COURSE OF ITS 85 YEAR HISTORY, Santa Teresita, our 12-acre healthcare campus, has steadfastly strived to meet the changing healthcare needs of the times – beginning as a tuberculosis sanatorium in 1930, then becoming a fully-accredited, acute-care hospital in the 1950s and ultimately, in 2004, transitioning into the elder care campus that it is today.

This story is about our transition from the acute hospital to an elder care campus. Once the hospital was closed, it became readily apparent just how old, decrepit and ugly the buildings were. The old buildings had to come down in order to begin rebuilding anew for the future....and needless to say, the challenges seemed insurmountable.

We turned to our beloved Foundress, Mother Luisita: "Guide us. Help us to see the way forward. Lead us. We want only to do the Lord's Will. We are listening - *really* listening. Show us what the Lord is asking of us at this moment in our lives. We will obey. We will follow wherever He leads and do whatever it is that He wants, just please show us."

An extraordinary financial gift from an anonymous donor – which makes for another story entirely in its own right – came forth at exactly the time we turned to God as our best, most-faithful Donor Who would never let us down. The Sisters, our advisors and consultants carefully studied and planned meticulously how to best utilize **GOD's** money. Not a penny could be wasted, lost or spent twice.

For the next 18 months, plans of renovation, consolidation and upgrade were systematically implemented at Santa Teresita. There was a hum in the air as new life was blossoming everywhere. Then we stalled.

A government regulatory agency, whose name will be withheld for the sake of charity, became involved and we if we did not know the definition of red tape, we quickly learned it now! We learned the meaning of frustration when encountering delay after delay. We learned how to jump through hoops -- backwards and forwards. And with dismay we very quickly learned just how much money all that red tape, delays and hoops cost – something we had not factored into our carefully calculated plans! The entire Santa Teresita campus had been retrofitted, and now we no longer had sufficient funds to bring down the old boarded up hospital building. To make matters worse, the old building was not off in a corner of the property. It was right smack dab in the middle of everything and it looked awful... kind of like an old shamble of a ghost town sitting in the middle of paradise. Our residents, our guests, our staff and our sisters walked by it day after day after day. It would take a six-digit figure to bring the old building down . . . . and we certainly did not have those six-digit figures. We could only trust … we could pray… .and we could even nag… just a little bit.

Mothers' Day was nearing, which is a very special day for us. On the evening of Mothers' Day every year we gather as a Community to honor our Blessed Mother, our Mother Luisita, our own beloved Mothers, our Superiors and the spiritual motherhood of each of our Sisters. This year, one Sister came up with a very unususal way to celebrate.

"Let's have a Jericho walk!" she enthused.

"A Jericho walk???" several of us asked.

Sister explained, "Yes! You know the story of Jericho! Let's invite all the Sisters to make a procession. We can play our musical instruments and praise God as we circle the old hospital building! We can end up by the statue of Our Lady and ask her to ask her Son to bring down those walls for us!"

Sister's enthusiasm quickly caught on. The Sisters eagerly joined the procession . . . wheelchairs and all! Every instrument was brought out: trumpets, drums, flutes, violins and guitars. With a microphone in hand, one of the Sisters led us in song.

With our whole heart and soul we sang. We probably sang badly - but for certain we sang with well-tuned hearts! We held nothing back. We praised God for His goodness to us. We praised Him for allowing us to share in His mission by caring for His people. We praised Him just because He is God.

The following Wednesday, tucked within the regular stack of daily mail, we found a small white envelope. Two years prior a priest-friend of ours had died and upon receiving the news, we had Masses offered for his precious soul. Shortly afterwards, his close friends carefully packed and shipped his religious artwork to us. You can imagine how profoundly touched and grateful we were.

But can you imagine our sentiments when we opened that small, unexpected envelope that held a check made out to the amount of _exactly_ the six-digit figure we needed?!?

We had no idea that this dear friend of ours, who lived a very simple and devout life, had left us in his will.

In all of our lives there are walls.

In all of our lives there is a God Who is worthy of praise.

And yes, miracles really do still happen!

About our Mother Foundress . . .

WHO IS MOTHER LUISITA?

The life of Mother Maria Luisa Josefa of the Most Blessed Sacrament is no ordinary story. Permeated with complete trust in God, her tale is one of daring adventure. A story where trust in God and obedience to His manifest designs bursts forth into great sanctity.

Maria Luisa was born in Atotonilco el Alto, Jalisco Mexico on June 21, 1866. Although she felt drawn to the religious life, at the age of fifteen in obedience to her parents, she married Doctor Pascual Rojas, a prominent physician. Their life together was happy, a mutual growing in love of God and neighbor. God did not grant them children, so they decided that the poor would be their children. They built a hospital to serve those less fortunate. After fourteen years of married life Maria Luisa was left a widow.

Eight years later Maria Luisa entered the Cloistered Carmelites. She spent seven months immersed in the spirituality of Carmel before the Archbishop implored her to return to her work at the hospital which needed her guidance. Trusting God's manifest designs, she obeyed. Along with the hospital she opened a school and orphanage.

When other young women began to join her, the Archbishop told them to join an existing religious congregation. Leaving all her works behind, she joined the Sister Servants of the Blessed Sacrament. Four years later the Archbishop asked her once again to return, the hospital was failing. She obeyed. More women joined her. This time the Archbishop himself suggested that she found a Religious Congregation and the Carmelite Sisters of the Sacred Heart were established on February 2, 1921. Her charism "to unite the spirit of Carmel to the active apostolate" unfolded.

Six years later, escaping the religious persecution in her beloved Mexico, dressed in disguise, Mother Luisita came to the United States as a homeless refugee. God rewarded her confidence as her work became established in the Archdiocese of Los Angeles.

Returning to Mexico in 1929, she continued the work she had begun there, as well as guiding, visiting and directing the Sisters in California. She spent the remainder of her life in hiding, ill and living in extreme poverty. On February 11, 1937, God called His faithful servant home to Himself – an eternal adventure.

In the Year of the Great Jubilee (2000), after extensive study of her life and writings, the Church declared that she lived a life of heroic virtue. Pope John Paul II declared her Venerable and her cause toward sainthood is in progress.

"Don't feel alone because you're not.
Our Lord in the Blessed Sacrament wants to be your Confidant,
your Friend, your Consoler. He wants to fill your soul with His love.
Perhaps that's why He is making you feel the emptiness of creatures.
How good our God is and by how many different paths He leads souls!
Don't doubt it. You're very dear to Him and
it's only natural that He will be jealous with those souls
He loves so much. He wants you all for Himself."
- Venerable Mother Luisita

"For greater things you were born . . .
Be what you are suppose to be - a saint."

- Venerable Mother Luisita

Join us in praying for her Beatification...

O Jesus in the Holy Eucharist, King and center of all hearts! Look with merciful love on the petitions we present to You through the intercession of Your servant, Mother Maria Luisa Josefa of the Most Blessed Sacrament.

(Pause and request your petition)

We humbly beseech You to glorify her who was always such a fervent lover of Your Sacred Heart by granting us these favors if they are for Your greater honor and glory. Amen.

(Written by Mother Margarita María, O.C.D. and approved by Cardinal Timothy Manning, August 28, 1981.)

Mother Luisita has proven to be a powerful intercessor, especially for women desiring to have children. We invite you to share any favors received through Mother's intercession:

Superior General
Carmelite Sisters of the Most Sacred Heart of Los Angeles
920 East Alhambra Road, Alhambra, California 91801
626-289-1353 | www.carmelitesistersocd.com/favors/

*"May the most adorable and holy will of God
be fulfilled in everything because whatever He orders will be for the best.
You see how good God Our Lord is. We should have more confidence
in Him every day and have recourse to prayer,
not permitting anything to discourage us or make us sad."*
- Venerable Mother Luisita

About the Contributors . . .

WHO ARE THE CARMELITE SISTERS?

The way of life of the Carmelite Sisters of the Most Sacred Heart of Los Angeles is rooted in the Gospel, the Church, and the spirituality of Carmel as lived out through the charism of our foundress, Venerable Mother Maria Luisa Josefa of the Most Blessed Sacrament. In His merciful goodness, God has graced our Institute with the Carmelite charism which has its foundation in a long history and living tradition.

The spirituality of St. Teresa and St. John of the Cross is rooted in this tradition. Carmel means enclosed garden in which God Himself dwells. The divine indwelling in the soul is the foundation of Teresa's doctrine. Thus, our vocation is a grace by which contemplation and action are blended to become an apostolic service of the Church as we promote a deeper spiritual life among God's people through education, healthcare, and spiritual retreats.

We are called by God to be a presence inflamed within our world, witnessing to God's love through prayer, joyful witness and loving service. Our mission is a God-given mission which overflows from each sister's profound life of prayer. It is a mission of the heart, a mission of loving service in the fields of healthcare, education and spiritual retreats. Mother Luisita, our foundress, used this analogy to describe our mission, "the soul of each Carmelite raises herself to Christ, Who is her heaven, while her shadow falls in charity upon earth doing good to all people."

Promoting a Deeper Spiritual LIFE . . .

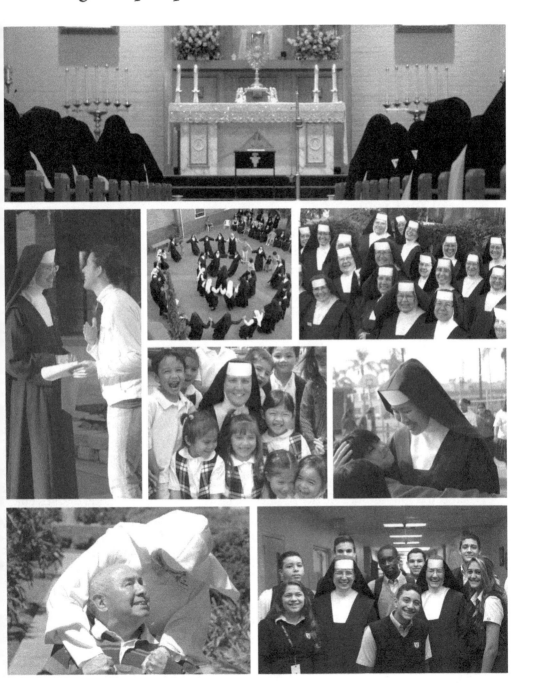

. . . through Education, Healthcare and Retreats

Share our Mission

How can YOU participate in our Mission?

1. Feed Your Soul

The number one way you can share our mission to promote a deeper spiritual life among God's people is to take advantage of the food for your soul we have to offer you on our website and social media and share it with your family and friends.

www.carmelitesistersocd.com | www.facebook.com/CarmeliteSisters
www.twitter.com/CarmelitesOCD | www.vimeo.com/channels/carmelitesocd

2. Share Your Gifts

Volunteer
No matter what skills or talents you have, we can always use volunteers! We also have a special volunteer program for girls ages 13 -17 called Décor Carmeli.

Support Our Mission Financially
Whether it is sponsoring a Novice or an elderly sister or giving a donation towards our apostolic work, we are grateful to all our beautiful friends who support our mission through their financial gifts. If you believe that our Lord is inviting you to support us financially, contact us for more information. We pray daily for all of our financial benefactors and spiritual supporters.

920 East Alhambra Road, Alhambra, California 91801
626-576-4910 | advancement@carmelitesistersocd.com
www.carmelitesistersocd.com/giving-opportunities/

Be a Co-Worker
Join us as a staff member at one of our child cares, schools, health care facilities, or retreat house.

3. Allow Us to Serve You

Come on a retreat! We have retreats for women, men, and married couples, as well as other specialty retreats and many one day conferences on various topics.

Sacred Heart Retreat House and Saint Joseph Campus
920 East Alhambra Road, Alhambra, California 91801
626-289-1353 | www.sacredheartretreathouse.com

"A single word said in the name of God can effect the salvation of a soul."
- Venerable Mother Luisita

Allow us to care for you or your loved ones who are in need of Assisted Living or Skilled Nursing at Santa Teresita or Marycrest or enjoy your senior years with us at Avila Gardens, our residence for independent seniors.

Santa Teresita
819 Buena Vista St., Duarte, CA 91010
626-359-3243 | contact@santa-teresita.org
www.santa-teresita.org

Marycrest Manor
10664 St. James Dr., Culver City, CA 90230
310-838-2778 | www.marycrestculvercity.com

Avila Gardens
1171 Encanto Parkway, Duarte, CA 91010
626-599-2214 | www.avilagardens.com

Consider each patient's room as another Chapel,
the bed as another altar,
and each patient as another Christ.
- Attributed to Venerable Mother Luisita

3. Allow Us to Serve You *(Continued)*

Looking for a good Catholic school for your children or grandchildren? We serve in childcares, elementary schools, and high schools.

Child Care Centers
Sponsored by the Carmelite Sisters

Little Flower Educational Child Care
2434 Gates St., LA, CA 90031
323-221-9248 | www.littleflowerla.com

Hayden Childcare Center
819 Buena Vista St., Duarte, CA 91010
626-932-3489 | www.haydenchildcare.com

Archdiocesan Schools
Staffed by the Carmelite Sisters

St. Joseph School
15650 Temple Ave., La Puente, CA 91744
626-336-2821 | www.st-josephschool-lp.org

St. Philomena School
21832 S. Main St., Carson, CA 90745
310-835-4827 | www.stphilomenaschool.org

Holy Innocents School
2500 Pacific Ave., Long Beach, CA 90806
562-424-1018 | www.holyinnocentsschlb.org

Loretto School
1200 14th St., Douglas, AZ 85607
520-364-5754 | www.lorettoschool.org

St. Theresa School
2701 Indian Mound Trail
Coral Gables, FL 33134
305-446-1738 | www.cotlf.org/School/index

Sts. Peter and Paul School
3920 Pierce St., Wheat Ridge, CO 80033
303-424-0402 | www.peterandpaulcatholic.org

Archbishop Coleman F. Carroll H.S.
10300 SW 167 Ave., Miami, FL 33196
305-388-6700 | www.colemancarroll.org

J. Serra High School
26351 Junipero Serra Road,
San Juan Capistrano, CA 92675
949-493-9307 | http://jserra.org

"Do not simply be good teachers.
Be souls of prayer or you will have nothing to offer the children."
- Venerable Mother Luisita